What Learning Looks Like

Mediated Learning
in Theory and Practice, K–6

What Learning Looks Like

Mediated Learning in Theory and Practice, K–6

Reuven Feuerstein
Ann Lewin-Benham

Foreword by James Bellanca

TEACHERS
COLLEGE
PRESS

Teachers College, Columbia University
New York and London

Published by Teachers College Press, 1234 Amsterdam Avenue, New York, NY 10027

Illustrations were created by Daniel Feuerstein

Figure 12.2 is reprinted by permission of Pei Cobb Freed & Partners

Library of Congress Cataloging-in-Publication Data
  Feuerstein, Reuven.
    What learning looks like : mediated learning in theory and practice, K–6 / Reuven
    Feuerstein, Ann Lewin-Benham ; foreword by James Bellanca.
        p. cm.
    Includes bibliographical references and index.
    ISBN 978-0-8077-5326-2 (pbk. : alk. paper)
      1. Thought and thinking—Study and teaching (Elementary) 2. Mediated learning
    experience. 3. Cognitive learning. 4. Cognition in children. I. Lewin-Benham, Ann. II.
    Title.
    LB1590.3.F48   2012
    370.15'2—dc23   2011046225

ISBN 978-0-8077-5326-2 (paperback)

Printed on acid-free paper
Manufactured in the United States of America

19   18   17   16   15   14   13   12   8   7   6   5   4   3   2   1

The authors dedicate this book to their children, whose devotion and inspiration have turned the book into a reality:

Noa Feuerstein Schwarz
Raphael S. Feuerstein
Daniel Shepard Lewin

While receiving the contract for publication of the book, Reuven Feuerstein was in a surgery that, with G-d's help, was successful. The surgery was for the replacement of an auric valve using a highly complex and innovative procedure. The author has a strong need to express his gratitude by dedicating this book to the Hadassah medical staff who performed this innovative procedure:

Dr. Jerry Lafair
Prof. Chaim Lotan
Prof. Amir Elami
Prof. Teddy Weiss
Dr. Haim Danenberg
Dr. Giora Landesberg

The highly pioneering work was done at the Ein Karem Hadassah University Hospital in Jerusalem.

Contents

Foreword *by James Bellanca*   xi

Acknowledgments   xv

Introduction   1

    Mediation: A Brief Description and Examples   1

    A Word About Deficient Cognitive Functions   2

    Reading This Book   3

    Chapter Summaries   4

    Knowing Your Authors   5

1. **Learning Through Mediation**   9

    Museums' Potential to Stimulate Learning   11

    At a Museum: What Didn't Happen, Why, and Changing It   14

    Recognizing Myths About Learning   21

2. **The Mediated Learning Experience Defined**   26

    Feuerstein: Mediator and Theorist   26

    Theory of Mediation   30

    The Three Partners of Mediation   33

    Essential Aspects of Mediation   38

    Summary: A Picture of Mediation   42

3. **Mediated Learning in Action**   44

    The FIE Programs: An Overview   44

    FIE Lessons by Mediators   53

    Summary: Imaginative, Authoritative, and Responsive Teaching   58

4. **Expert Mediators**   **59**

   Mediation in Two Classrooms   60

   Mediation in an Exhibit   66

   Summary   69

5. **Four Essential Cognitive Acts**   **71**

   Acquiring Basic Competencies   71

   Intersection of Basic Competencies   76

   Summary: Mediation—The Connecting Link to Learning   85

6. **Defining the Effectiveness of Learning Experiences**   **87**

   The Cognitive Map   87

   The Thinking Deficiencies Tool   97

   Two Techniques to Enhance Learning   98

   The Case for Mediation: Demetria's Story   101

   Summary: Analytic Observation Tools   102

7. **Creative Use of Effective Exhibits**   **103**

   Learning from Rich Experiences   103

   Providing Conflict-Producing Ideas   111

   Appealing to Multiple Intelligences   114

   Summary: Mediating Exhibits   117

8. **More Essential Cognitive Acts**   **118**

   Empathy   118

   Acquiring New Skills   121

   Mastering Varied Modalities   122

   Collaborating   126

   Complex Thinking Acts   129

   Museums' Abundant Experiences   131

   Summary: Mediating for Complexity   132

9. **Blue Sky Partnerships**   **133**

   Beliefs About Learning   133

   Adult Interventions   138

Museums as Partners 140

"What If" Ideas 143

Emily's Story: Mother as Mediator 147

Summary: Museums as Learning Centers 148

10. Enlarging the Cognitive Repertoire **149**

Incongruence 149

Repetition 153

Transformation 158

Illusion 164

Stereognostic (Hand/Vision) Experiences 166

Summary: Challenging Designs 168

11. Stretching the Brain to Make Learning Happen **170**

Motivation 170

Summary: Four Interrelated Factors in Learning 177

Moving from Concrete to Abstract Thinking 177

The Brain and Learning 182

Summary: When We Think and Learn 185

12. After Words **189**

For Teachers 189

Questions to Ask of Exhibits 194

Summary: Prepare, Question, Discuss 198

Understanding Exhibit Design 198

Summary: Bringing Learning Home 201

Appendix A: List of Deficient Cognitive Functions **203**

**Appendix B: Children with Learning Challenges:
Notes for Parents and Exhibit Designers** **205**

References **207**

Index **213**

About the Authors **219**

Foreword

FEWER THAN 40 years ago, Reuven Feuerstein stood in a reception line during the Association for Supervision and Curriculum Development's (ASCD) national convention. With him were three dozen prominent American educators, all advocates for increasing critical thinking in the classroom. At the invitation of Ron Brandt, editor of ASCD's *Educational Leadership*, Feuerstein was present to address the annual convention. His trademark black beret and white beard made it appear that the Israeli psychologist had stepped from a Rubens painting. Unlike the others, Feuerstein was not at the convention solely to speak about the revival of thinking skills instruction. He was there to unveil his new theory of structural cognitive modifiability by way of mediated learning experiences.

When Feuerstein spoke, many attendees were surprised. Some were shocked: "Intelligence is modifiable?" "No way." "We know that intelligence is fixed at birth." "Change of intelligence is not possible." "What planet is this man coming from?" "What do we have here? Another Don Quixote?" Some walked out.

Today in the United States, such a speech would be less contentious, even readily accepted. Brain researchers, neuroscientists, cognitive psychologists, and neuro-educators have added "meat to the bones" of Feuerstein's theories. Extensive research studies from many fields have shown the validity of Feuerstein's work, which foreshadowed much of today's research on the brain's plasticity.

Even so, with all of the attention given to brain growth, cognitive development, and its connection to student achievement, Feuerstein's name is familiar to a relatively small number of American educators and psychologists. Howard Gardner, Robert Sternberg, John Bransford, Anne Palinscar, David Perkins, David Pearson, and Linda Darling-Hammond celebrate his pioneering contributions to the field of intelligence. Others in this country, such as Art Costa, Betty Garner, Meir Ben Hur, Shannon Almquist, Kate Bellanca, Robin Fogarty, Donna Wilson, and Beau Fly Jones, quote his research and have joined scholars and teacher educators around the world to translate Feuerstein's ideas. Still, when they hear the name Reuven Feuerstein, the vast majority of American school-based educators ask, "Who?"

In this generation, American school districts employing Feuerstein's approaches to teaching and learning are scattered. In spite of successes in Taunton, Massachusetts; Philadelphia; New York; California; and Schaumberg, Illinois, after his initial visit to the United States, active Feuerstein programs are few and far between today. In Chicago and Alaska, his early childhood program is funded in high-poverty schools. In Illinois, the upper grades version has enabled a special education treatment program for seriously challenged adolescents to earn accolades from its state agency accreditation review team. In Texas, a charter school group is introducing his work. Here and there, a few other districts with leaders committed to full implementation of the mediated learning experience have maintained multiyear implementations of his classroom program, Instrumental Enrichment.

The story is far different in other nations. In Singapore, a country considered among the top performers on international tests, Feuerstein is almost a household name among educators. Every middle school teacher in Bahia, Brazil, was prepared by that large state's Education Department to teach Feuerstein's programs. In Italy, Romania, the Netherlands, Belgium, England, India, Japan, and South Korea, universities have established teacher training programs and conduct research on his practices. In South Africa, the government's workforce preparation office provides Instrumental Enrichment as the foundation of its job training programs. Each year, the European Union sponsors an international preparation program for teacher trainers in Feuerstein's programs with full scholarships offered.

Many reasons are hypothesized for the comparatively tepid attention given to Feuerstein's work in the United States. These include at least seven values held by many American educators that run counter to Feuerstein's underlying belief system and the practices that are at the heart of his work. These objections contrast with the practices in those other nations, which have placed the development of thinking and modification of intelligence at the *center* of their curricula and see thinking as an essential *prerequisite* to learning. These contrary American values say that

1. Higher-order thinking is reserved for gifted and talented students.
2. Teachers work best by following a scripted lesson plan that focuses on basic skill instruction.
3. Based on the theory that intelligence is fixed at birth and cannot be modified, the Bell Curve is spotlighted as the best measure of intelligence.
4. Feuerstein's approach takes time away from teachers' coverage of the established content-centered curriculum.
5. There are no valid measures of student thinking in ways that demonstrate gains in thinking skills or content.
6. The amount of teacher development time required to prepare teachers to adopt the program is excessive.
7. Any thinking that is taught is best done *within* rigorous content that challenges students to think hard and not in a supplemental program such as Feuerstein's.

One American educator who has long understood the power of Feuerstein's work and has challenged the contradictory American values is Ann Lewin-Benham, Feuerstein's co-author of this compact and practical exposition of his theories. Ann discovered Feuerstein's ideas when she was executive director of the Capital Children's Museum in Washington, D.C. Ann had begun the museum as a way to stimulate children's cognitive development. Soon after hearing Feuerstein speak, she went to Israel to study at his institute. Returning with a more solid basis for her "learn from doing" approach, Ann and her staff integrated what they had learned into the museum's exhibits. Later, she founded one of Washington's first charter schools in the museum complex. That program for adolescents, who were considered to be those most at risk in the D.C. public school system, featured Feuerstein's Instrumental Enrichment.

After many years discussing the possibility of writing together, Ann and Reuven have collaborated to provide a remarkable, readable, and systematic exposition that joins the theory and practice of mediated learning experiences within the real worlds of children's museums and classrooms. The book provides concrete examples that show museum directors, teachers, and parents the practical "how to" for building children's cognitive structures. While evidence has shown for many years that Feuerstein's approach has significant impact on the quality of students' thinking, new studies illustrate how his theory, methods, and tools literally change the structure of the brain and impact learning of content. Taken from Ann's long and rich experience, dialogues between teachers and students illustrate Feuerstein's best practices. Employing the special questioning and cueing techniques devised by Feuerstein to develop the quality of students' thinking and problem solving, the essence of what Feuerstein labels the "Mediated Learning Experience," adults work creatively *without* gimmicks or tricks to help students learn how to think.

Feuerstein, a prized student of Jean Piaget, spent many years working with children of the Holocaust whom teachers and psychologists had declared "unteachable." From his success, especially in the development of reading skills, he developed his "content free" mediated learning techniques. In later years, he continued his studies, transferring what he had discovered with culturally deprived children to special needs students, brain traumatized adults, and others struggling to learn, and helping prevent learning disorders and disabilities in regular students and dementia in seniors. As shown with many of Lewin-Benham's noteworthy examples from classrooms and museums, the children are guided through one problem after another as they build their own repertoire of metacognitive strategies.

This book is a welcome addition to the growing number of writings about the powerful applications of Feuerstein's more than 50 years of direct work with children, which has been his top daily priority. Ann has carefully selected examples of best practice to spotlight how the creative application of Feuerstein's criteria make eminent good sense, especially at a time when "teacher proofers" hoist script after script onto the regular school curriculum. Her examples show how well this creative guidance of thinking works, especially with the most difficult to teach children in the school or museum setting.

What shines through this book is the love of both authors for what they do. Just experiencing their commitment makes the book stand out as a treasure for any who share a passion for teaching thinking explicitly. Thus, the book cannot help but draw rightfully deserved attention to what Feuerstein has to teach all educators, including those in the United States. As a rich and practical contribution to the field, veteran practitioners will welcome this latest addition to a celebration of his work. More important, others who are unfamiliar with his name and legacy may have the opportunity to discover the brilliance of the Feuerstein theory and practice for the first time in a book that makes especially clear what well-given mediation looks like and sounds like in any teaching situation.

—James Bellanca

Acknowledgments

MANY PEOPLE HELPED in the development of this book, foremost among them Dr. Louis Falik, a distinguished psychologist. Since retiring as professor of Counseling at San Francisco State University, Dr. Falik has dedicated his time to furthering Reuven Feuerstein's work in his formal capacity as training and research associate at Feuerstein's institute and informally as the professor's right-hand man. Falik generously read early and later drafts and sat through numerous sessions with Feuerstein and Lewin-Benham. Feuerstein's trust in Falik's interpretations eased the process as Falik and Feuerstein debated aspects of the theories that Falik understood were too detailed for this book. Both authors gratefully acknowledge Falik's thoughtful, caring attention.

Feuerstein thanks psychologist L. J. Cronbach (1916–2001) whom Richard Shavelson, former Dean, School of Education, Stanford, said "made major contributions in the fields of educational psychology, psychological testing, and program evaluation throughout a career that spanned more than five decades" (2003, p. 380). Cronbach, who met Feuerstein in the early 1960s, immediately grasped the impact of Feuerstein's ideas, which he stated would change the face of modern psychology. To the end of Cronbach's life, his advocacy gave impetus to Feuerstein's development of mediation theory and practice. Feuerstein also acknowledges many museums that graciously welcomed him as lecturer and visitor, especially those that roused his interest in interactive exhibits, including the Exploratorium and the Capital Children's Museum.

Lewin-Benham thanks many whose work has shaped her beliefs about learning and whose theories ground her practices. In addition to Feuerstein, they include Mihaly Csikszentmihalyi, Antonio Damasio, Howard Gardner, Erik Kandel, Maria Montessori, Seymour Papert, David Perkins, Steven Pinker, educators in Reggio Emilia, Frank Wilson, and numerous educators in whose classrooms or museums she has found examples of effective mediation.

Lewin-Benham also thanks her former, longtime colleague Eddie Goldstein, senior educator at the Denver Museum of Nature and Science. Goldstein is a mathematician and science educator. He read many drafts of many chapters, reviewed all the science references, corrected facts, and added insightful stories and comments from his own observations of visitors to museums. The authors deeply appreciate his effort and they take full responsibility for any errors. Lewin-Benham also thanks her husband, Robert, who suffers her hours at the keyboard with great humor, lends his passion for history to historical examples, reads with an eye for detail, and fixes the printer.

Illustrations were created by Daniel Feuerstein. He painstakingly matched image to text, capturing details in his art that resonate with the written descriptions. His pencil greatly enlivens the ideas in the book and both authors deeply appreciate his work.

We thank Chip Lindsey, executive director of ScienceWorks in Ashland, Oregon, and former associate director of the Don Harrington Discovery Center, for the photograph of the center. We appreciate Edward H. Abelson's generosity in placing the illusion he created, called Checkerboard, in the public domain, where we found it for Chapter 10. We appreciate the generosity of Benjah-bmm27 for drawing and releasing *Tetrahedron* into the public domain, where we found it for Chapter 11. Alexandra Cruickshank made Tetrahedron into Figure 11.1; thank you, Alex. And we thank Emma Cobb at Pei Cobb Freed & Partners for her patience in finding and making print-ready the drawing of the East Wing of the National Gallery of Art.

The editors at Teachers College Press have, as always, gone beyond all expectations to make this book a reality. It would not exist without Marie Ellen Larcada's belief in it. She is a perceptive editor, on top of the field of publishing, always available, and supports authors in every way imaginable. Wendy Schwartz edited the manuscript and made many excellent suggestions large and small. Shannon Waite and Tara Tomczyk attended to every detail, no matter how small. And, no production editor could surpass Karl Nyberg's ability to turn a manuscript into a book.

Lastly, we acknowledge our readers, in whose hands the fate of this book lies. The book will live on in whatever ways you use its material to increase the power of your teaching so that children grow in their capacity to learn how to learn.

What Learning Looks Like

Mediated Learning in Theory and Practice, K–6

Introduction

THIS BOOK CONTAINS a multitude of ways to interact with students in order to increase their learning capacity. The book opens new doors for teachers and children by demonstrating proven teaching techniques to help children learn based on the work of Reuven Feuerstein, a theoretically oriented cognitive and clinical psychologist. Shown in scenarios from museum exhibits and classrooms, Feuerstein's techniques help educators to structure experiences that stretch children's abilities to think along many dimensions. These scenarios show that learning is joyful and that children can master hard content and remote ideas through mediation, the theory and practices that are the meat of Feuerstein's work. Two ideas that are important in reading this book are mediation and cognitive deficiency.

MEDIATION: A BRIEF DESCRIPTION AND EXAMPLES

Mediation means any interaction in which an adult *intends* to convey a particular *meaning* or skill *and* encourages the child to *transcend*, that is, to relate the meaning to some other thought or experience. Mediation means interacting with *intention*, *meaning*, and *transcendence* with the intent of helping children expand their cognitive capacity, especially when ideas are new or challenging.

Watch mediation happen in the following lesson where a teacher uses an overhead projector for the first time. Notice how the teacher, with a class of 30 students, picks up on what a student says and gradually sharpens the student's thinking.

> Student, looking for the first time at a projected image: "Wow! That's like that helium balloon."
>
> The student has made an analogy: Something small becomes large virtually instantaneously.
>
> Teacher, affirming the student's observation, naming the thinking skill he uses, and with the *intent* of encouraging him to be precise: "Good analogy! What is similar about the image and the balloon?"
>
> Student, with great assurance: "They both get big quick!"
>
> Teacher, questioning to determine what the student is focusing on and with the intent of guiding the student to change his expression from the fuzzy "they" to an exact description of the content: "Can you tell me exactly what *they* is?"
>
> Student: "The picture and the balloon."

Teacher, naming what the student did well: "Good! You used precise names." Then, with the intent of urging the student to compare: "What is *different* in how the picture and the balloon become large?"

Student, with some hesitancy: "That projector done it here and, uh . . . that thing done it there."

Teacher, with the intent of seeking more precision: "Does anyone know the precise name . . . ?"

Chorus of four voices: "Helium tank."

Teacher, glad the students know the name, but with the intent of stimulating them to analyze the effect of the helium tank on the balloon: "What is the relationship between the helium tank and the balloon?"

New student voice: "It blows up balloons."

Another new student voice: "Helium *inflates* balloons."

Teacher, addressing the initial student with the intent of having him gather data: "Now! Notice carefully! Take your time. Then, enumerate what differences you see between a projector and a helium tank."

Gradually, the teacher encourages the students to flesh out the analogy with evidence, each time stating the intention of her question and naming what thinking skills students use in their answers. In this way, the teacher builds the students' capacity to observe carefully and to name, compare, and identify. Simultaneously, the teacher makes them aware that the thinking skills they are using include: increasing vocabulary, observing, identifying cause and effect, and building relationships.

At the end of the discussion, the teacher bridges from the example at hand to something different by asking the students: "To what else can you apply the analogy of something small instantly becoming big?" This is *transcendence,* one of the most important parts of mediation—encouraging students to link what is currently being considered to something that they experienced in the past or could experience—or imagine—in the future, and to form relationships.

This interchange is an example of mediation because the teacher makes her *intention* clear to the students, maintains focus on the *meaning* of particular stimuli, and challenges the students to *"transcend"*—to apply the same analogy to different examples. In the process, the teacher learns about different students' command of vocabulary, facts, and thinking processes.

Mediation can be used with students of any age, with any subject matter, and with as many as 30 or as few as 1 student. Mediation can be as simple as an adult's excited comment, "Look!" followed by questions such as: "What do you see here?" "What does it remind you of?" "How do you think this happened?" "Could you make something like this happen?" The attitude of the adult is a critical factor in stretching children's interest.

A WORD ABOUT DEFICIENT COGNITIVE FUNCTIONS

Many conditions are defined by the words *cognitive deficiency.* A current article in the French journal *Acta Paediatrica* states: "A mild cognitive deficiency was defined as a Mental Processing Composite score on the Kaufman Assessment Battery for Children test of between 70 and 84" (Beaino et al., 2011, p. 370). The authors, who are from the Epiage Study Group, say that the term *cognitive deficiency* is "a complicated multi-factorial issue" that depends on both biological and environmental factors. A lot of conditions fall under "cognitive deficiency" and they are varied in their severity.

In his work as a cognitive, developmental, and clinical psychologist, Feuerstein pinpoints problems (ADHD, Down syndrome, autism) through various accepted means of evaluation and remedies them via therapeutic means such as dynamic assessment, a step-by-step approach in which an assessor tests to see what a child can do on a given task, immediately teaches any skill seen as missing, and immediately tests again on a similar task to determine the child's potential to learn. Feuerstein's lifelong commitment to working with children on whom other therapeutic treatments were unsuccessful is testament to his belief in human potential even when other approaches have failed. Feuerstein has been an iconoclast in arguing against labeling children and uses the words *deficient cognitive functions* as an overall phrase to cover many very specific behaviors— for examples blurred and sweeping perception or inability to select relevant cues in defining a problem. Cognitive functions that Feuerstein considers deficient are fully delineated in Appendix A.

READING THIS BOOK

This book was born from the authors' shared belief that museums are fertile laboratories for trying new ways to help children learn. Feuerstein sees more stimulation per square foot in hands-on museums than anywhere. Both authors believe in museums' potential as showcases for fostering children's cognitive processes through mediation. The book makes Feuerstein's theories accessible through a multitude of examples so that educators can easily understand how to employ his mediation techniques. Previously, his ideas were mainly described in thick textbooks for teachers and teacher educators, journal articles and Ph.D. theses, or news articles.

The book has, in effect, two first chapters. Chapter 1 shows by examples what mediation means; Chapter 2 lays out the theory of mediation. If you prefer to begin with examples, read Chapter 1 first; if you prefer a theoretical perspective, begin with Chapter 2.

Examples in this book show students from about age 5 to 11 at various levels of achievement, including some whose thinking is not well developed because of life circumstances such as economic poverty, war, immigration, or genetic makeup. We use many museum examples because exhibits are readily available, diverse in content, and expressed in varied modalities—three dimensions, moving images, text, photos and drawings, live presentations, original art, elaborate dioramas, and hands-on props. Because they are so diverse, exhibits are unusually effective at arousing interest. Once interest is aroused, mediation can help children increase their capacity to focus, observe, analyze, and express themselves.

In using museum exhibits, we generalize the techniques of mediation by:

- translating mediation into numerous, varied teacher/student interactions;
- highlighting the three-way relationship between the person mediating, the child being mediated, and the stimulus that is used as the content of the mediation;
- explaining the three essential acts of a mediator:
    - ✓ intention to help children grasp certain content, concepts, and thinking processes,
    - ✓ selection of specific meaning to convey,
    - ✓ transcending, that is, relating the meaning at hand to something remote.

CHAPTER SUMMARIES

In this book you will see how learning to use exhibits effectively can impact how we help children learn in *any* environment. The following summaries show what readers can expect.

Chapter 1: Readers learn how to turn children's responses into thinking responses. Many scenarios show why children fail to learn and how to change experiences so children do learn. Common myths about learning are debunked.

Chapter 2: Readers gain understanding of the theory of mediation as they learn about its genesis and definition; explore the relationship between teacher, student, and lesson; and think about what it means to mediate with meaning, intention, and transcendence—what Feuerstein calls the three essential acts of a mediated exchange.

Chapter 3: Feuerstein Instrumental Enrichment (FIE) is the title of the series of diagnostic and classroom exercises that feature prominently in Feuerstein's work. Here, readers see FIE in action in classrooms.

Chapter 4: Readers see the techniques of meaning, intention, and transcendence at work in two different classroom lessons and in a museum exhibit. All three scenarios show exemplary mediation.

Chapter 5: Through scenarios, readers see the meaning of four acts that are basic to all thinking: attention, imitation, spatial orientation, and movement. They learn why these acts are foundational thinking skills.

Chapter 6: Readers learn how to use two of Feuerstein's tools. One, the Cognitive Map, is a means of analyzing the cognitive and motivational aspects of an experience. The other, Thinking Deficiencies, is a means of analyzing what children's responses to an experience show about their thinking capacity.

Chapter 7: This chapter shows how to use rich exhibits to best advantage in learning. Watching many scenarios, the reader sees the importance of such techniques as repetition, variety, modalities, detail, redundancy, aesthetics, and conflict-producing material. We explain the impact of these techniques, which are applicable outside museums in classroom lessons and other learning experiences.

Chapter 8: Through scenarios, readers see a second set of brain functions that support strong thinking and the techniques that enable students to acquire them. The brain functions are learning to feel empathy, using many varied modalities, collaborating, and engaging in complex thinking acts.

Chapter 9: Readers' imagination is stimulated by thinking outside the box about collaboration between schools and museums. For example, "blue sky ideas" suggest various museum-generated teacher guides, a youth service corps, student-made exhibits, and diverse apprenticeships.

Chapter 10: Readers learn how to build strong thinking in a context that explains each of five different kinds of experiences and how each boosts the brain. The experiences are incongruence, repetition, transformation, illusion, and tactile/visual stimulation.

Chapter 11: Readers see the role of motivation in thinking and read suggestions for changing a child's negative affect. They examine examples of the progression from concrete to abstract thinking and, in the context of some recent research on the brain, watch two experiences designed to challenge thinking.

Chapter 12: Practical advice guides readers in preparing for and following up on museum visits or other field trips—discussions with students and activities to prepare for a visit, what to do on the way, at arrival, during a visit, and after.

KNOWING YOUR AUTHORS

Reuven Feuerstein and Ann Lewin-Benham come to this book with varied but complementary experience. The authors' collaboration maintains each one's voice. Feuerstein's theories, techniques, and instruments are so highly developed and refined that his authorship is apparent in their descriptions. Likewise, the explanation of what and how children learn are Feuerstein's insights.

Ann Lewin-Benham's visits to museums throughout her life, her decades as a museum founder and director, and her varied roles in education are apparent in the numerous examples from classrooms and museums. Her hallmark as an author—making complex ideas accessible—is evident in the clarity with which she describes Feuerstein's voluminous work.

This book was Feuerstein's idea. His numerous visits to Capital Children's Museum (CCM) in Washington, D.C., founded by Lewin-Benham in the 1970s, spurred him to ask her to collaborate with him. Their partnership has extended over decades.

Reuven Feuerstein

It was known in the village of Botosani, Romania, that Reuven Feuerstein, born in 1921, learned to read at age 3. He regularly read both his mother's Bible and a book of stories, *Tseena Ureena (Go Out and Look Oh Girls)*. Based on "The Song of Songs," the book interprets the Bible, embellishing it with legends and fables.

These rich dramatic commentaries are typical of oral transmission and prominent in Jewish study. The story of Jacob begging Joseph, his son, not to let him be buried in Egypt had a profound impact on Feuerstein as a youngster—a father confessing and asking his son's forgiveness, a mother rising from the grave and weeping, voices coming from the heavens. From age 3 to 7, Feuerstein was immersed in these stories, the images and sounds permeating his mind, echoing in his dreams, and attuning him to the power of the written word.

When Feuerstein was 5, the father of a 15-year-old approached him: "Please teach my son, 'Chayim-the-Simple,' to read; let me die peacefully knowing that my oldest son will be able to say kaddish over my grave." (Kaddish, called the prayer for the dead, is as old as Judaism itself.) The father's fervent plea was Feuerstein's first indication that he was destined to be a teacher. As his success with Chayim-the-Simple became known in the village, other parents, desperate about their children's reading, approached Feuerstein.

Even as a child, Feuerstein felt powerful in his teaching ability. He had studied the Bible in long days at the Heder (Hebrew school), and at night, in the tradition of orthodox Jews, his father had quizzed him on what he learned. At Heder, Jewish males search for layers of meaning in every word of the Bible and in commentaries written by great spiritual leaders over Judaism's almost 6,000 years. Feuerstein says this study fostered the cognitive dimension of his thinking. By age 8, Feuerstein was giving lectures and believed he had enough experience to teach the Bible in Hebrew to young adults preparing to live in Israel. By age 12, he was reading the Bible in German.

Feuerstein's clinical work began full force in Israel in 1945 as youth were being resettled after the Holocaust, starting with the Polish children from Teheran. Herded from their homes, these children were exiled to Russia, where they found themselves on the German/Russian war front. There, they literally ran from place to place looking death in the eye, learning how to escape from Buchenwald, Auschwitz, and other living hells. Those who managed to survive were rounded up at the end of the war and sent through Teheran to Israel. Their gripping story is told in the book *The Teheran Operation* (Omer, 1991). Survivors of war and victims of its brutalities, the youth understood that their lives—and the survival of Judaism—depended on the success of the new state of Israel. Feisty as starving dogs pursuing prey, many became heroes in the War of Independence (1947), where many died fighting to make the dream of the Israeli state a reality.

The plight of these youngsters compelled Feuerstein to help them overcome the horrors they had experienced. So began the work that ultimately yielded his theories and applied programs. Many questioned whether the youth could learn at all. Angered by the doubters, Feuerstein countered for his charges: "Don't ask me what I know! Ask me how I can learn!" Over the ensuing decades, Feuerstein, with numerous colleagues, fleshed out the work. The powerful theories and numerous applications have changed the lives of many people.

Initially working closely with the brilliant psychologist Andre Rey, 14 years Feuerstein's senior, the two used existing psychological tests—many devised by Rey—in a new way and pioneered the form of testing now known as dynamic assessment—a measure not of what individuals know but of their potential to change and learn. Dynamic assessment relies on the mediation techniques explained in this book. Feuerstein's contribution changed the paradigm in testing.

Ann Lewin-Benham

Born in 1939, Ann White Lewin-Benham grew up in Manhattan, privileged and shielded from World War II traumas by protective parents. Raised in a liberal Jewish environment, she was enveloped in a belief in human equality and capacity. Just out of college at age 20, Lewin-Benham became a social case worker in the Jacksonville, North Carolina, welfare department, and the work shaped her life. The sleepy southern town, oblivious to impending civil rights struggles, had an enlightened welfare director who desegregated the agency's waiting rooms, bathrooms, and water fountains—unheard of at that time—and provided a private office for each case worker so clients would not have to divulge their privations sitting cheek by jowl. Lewin-Benham's 200-family caseload included a mother with 10 small children living in a shack in the woods; a family of 12 living in an 8-foot-by-20-foot trailer and, after generations of incest, having IQs around 60; and prostitutes in the Black "red light" district, whose shanties had no electricity and were on stilts because, with no plumbing, rain made their dirt road a sewer. The experiences seeded Lewin-Benham's belief that "they"—the economically disadvantaged—are not to blame for not learning and that unfavorable life factors, not lack of innate intelligence, cause learning problems.

A more powerful event at age 21 was the birth of Lewin-Benham's son Danny. Her marvel at the process of early development led to a quest for a good learning environment, which she found in a Montessori school. Subsequently, she became trained in the Montessori method; taught children, trained teachers, then expanded the Montessori school through 6th grade; and, as Danny and his cohorts reached puberty, founded a junior high school. Continually frustrated by schools' inability to change, Lewin-Benham turned her energy to establishing a children's museum in Washington, D.C.

With few models in this new cultural form, Lewin-Benham was free to design innovative ways to stimulate learning. An exhibition about the Holocaust, "Remember the Children," was subsequently renamed "Daniel's Story" and became the permanent children's exhibit at the U.S. Holocaust Memorial Museum in Washington, D.C. This exhibit, like all others at the museum, combined a great range of mediating effects, including human intervention.

Realizing that children spend a vanishingly small amount of time at museums, Lewin-Benham returned to creating schools—three different ones at the museum's 3-acre facility. Lewin-Benham sent staff from the schools for training at Feuerstein's institute in Jerusalem, the International Center for the Enhancement of Learning Potential (ICELP), and incorporated Feuerstein's theories and techniques in the schools' curricula and museums' exhibits. These varied experiences over 30 years put her at the nexus where theory meets practice.

In this book are scores of examples of what learning looks like for students whose teachers use mediation and of how to use museum exhibits as foils for shaping lessons. You will learn mediation techniques from the psychologist who developed them. So, sit in school classrooms as we watch mediation theory come to life in practice, sometimes with children heretofore unmediated. Then, put on walking shoes as we see mediation used in varied museum contexts. By showing how to use mediation in exhibits, we generalize mediation to any situation where teachers want students to grasp new understandings and, ultimately, become their own mediators.

CHAPTER 1

Learning Through Mediation

The range of what we think and do is limited by what we fail to notice.

—Daniel Goleman, 1985

LEARNING! WHAT HUMANS do throughout their lives, what can be a joy, but can cause consternation—if a child doesn't learn! In this book are examples of how to help every child learn in varying situations and with adults who apply the techniques of Feuerstein's theory of mediation. Mediation theory is explained in Chapter 2, and in Chapters 3 through 6 essential aspects of the theory are described with numerous scenarios from classrooms and museums. Chapters 7 through 12 apply the theory to show how effective mediation can build, strengthen, or stretch cognitive structure. Chapters 7 through 12 address diverse, specific cognitive functions. Examples demonstrate the universal applicability of mediation theory. While we acknowledge that children learn independently in many different situations, throughout this book we are talking about:

- learning experiences that build cognitive function and motivate students to go beyond superficial thinking,
- the role of educators in intentionally structuring such experiences, and
- how to use meaning, intention, and transcendence—the keystones of mediation practice—during adult/child interactions.

Psychologists agree that proof of learning is that we *retain, understand, and use knowledge to actively build new relationships*. Psychologist David Perkins repeatedly states in his book *Outsmarting IQ* (1995) that to learn we must have clear information, thoughtful practice, informative feedback, and strong motivation. Watch those principles in the following two scenarios, first in a classroom, then in a museum.

Scenario 1. Educator/philosopher David Hawkins was primarily a physicist. One of the youngest scientists on the Manhattan Project, he was Robert Oppenheimer's assistant and the official project historian. After the Russians launched Sputnik and beat the United States into space, Hawkins was tapped by The Massachusetts Institute of Technology (MIT) to lead top scientists in revamping science education. During those years, Hawkins wrote a seminal paper—"Messing About in Science"—about teaching 5th-graders to use pendula. The students did not discover the principles of a pendulum's behavior merely by pushing the bobs about during one trial-and-error, activity-based morning. It required weeks of "messing about" to think about the effects. It also required:

- other aids such as images, instructions, explanations, books, video (today, computer simulations);
- a knowledgeable adult to engage students' minds as they confronted the pendulum activities; and
- lots of time using pendula in the presence of a knowledgeable adult. (Hawkins, 1965)

Scenario 2. District of Columbia officials brought 200 children to the Capital Children's Museum in Washington, D.C., to commemorate Head Start's 10th anniversary. After the children explored the museum, they were brought to the auditorium. The Head Start director, an amiable emcee, asked: "Who liked the museum?" Two hundred hands waved gleefully. "What do you remember?" he asked. A hundred hands waved. He pointed to one. "The giraffe!" the child exclaimed. Lewin-Benham recalls:

As the head of the museum, I was embarrassed! We did not have a giraffe; clearly, the child had us confused with the zoo. As I racked my brain, I remembered. In the "Metricville" exhibit on a narrow wall, barely 12 inches wide, we had hung a sign, ZOO, and in bright red had painted large silhouettes of a monkey and a giraffe. On each was a question: "Are you as tall as the monkey's tail?" "Can you reach the giraffe's ear?" The intention was to alert visitors to think about height.

Most Head Start children are preliterate, and even a tall 4-year-old could not reach the giraffe's ear. If, from that huge museum with hundreds of activities, a child remembered the sliver of wall with a giraffe's painted profile, an adult must have *mediated* the experience. Lewin-Benham continues:

I wish I had observed the exchange. Since I did not, here is an imaginary mediation:
Teacher, observing child's interest and reading the text: "Would you like to reach the giraffe's ear?"
Child, excited, nodding yes: "Huh, huh."
Teacher, wanting the child to remember, and gesturing: "You have to be *SOO* tall to reach the giraffe's ear."
Child, pleased, imitating the teacher's words: "Reach the giraffe's ear!"

The teacher was a good mediator. He knew how to observe, pick up on a child's interest, and engage the child further by lifting the child up so he *could* "reach the giraffe's ear."

Feuerstein says that most children who move from lower to higher cognitive functioning have been mediated. That is, an adult has intervened many times in the children's experiences and consequently "trained children's brains" (Posner,

Rothbart, Sheese, & Kieras, 2008, p. 2) so they acquire strategies with which to think about new experiences.

Mediation can involve:

- showing children the precise way to use a tool;
- encouraging children to think about the content (meaning) of a lesson or exhibit or its context (transcendent ideas);
- pouncing on a teachable moment when children's questions or body language show they are curious;
- asking children to explain something in their own words;
- offering or asking for an analogy; and
- posing leading questions that guide children to think logically.

In this chapter, we first show examples from actual museum experiences, then examine common beliefs about learning. Remember the examples as you study Feuerstein's theory of mediation (Chapter 2), see mediation in situations that show how the protagonists of learning (adult/child/stimulus) relate to one another (Chapters 3–6), and see a great diversity of ways to hone children's thinking capacities through mediation (Chapters 7–12).

MUSEUMS' POTENTIAL TO STIMULATE LEARNING

The mission of museums is to impart knowledge, to put pinnacles of human achievement—thoughts and objects—on public display. The knowledge may be oddities—the museum as curiosity cabinet; such exhibits tweak the imagination. The knowledge may be how someone represents reality—Claude Monet's landscapes, Vincent van Gogh's interiors, Salvador Dali's clocks. Such exhibits contrast ways of representing reality. The knowledge may showcase scientific or technological achievements, historical forces, or natural processes; such exhibits enable us to stretch what we know about how things work. Whether museums collect and display artifacts or create scenarios to convey ideas, visitors can feel secure in the authenticity of what they see—firsthand sources that cannot be found on television or in textbooks and objects vetted to ensure that they are genuine and original. The connection between museums and children is that a museum's trove can capture attention, startle the mind, arouse curiosity, cause wonder, or trigger thinking—all conditions that make children ready to learn.

Throughout this book, we utilize museum experiences as a paradigm for how Feuerstein's mediation theory and techniques can stimulate effective thinking. Briefly, mediation theory states that adult intervention is essential to children's learning and that specific techniques make interventions "mediated" interventions. In *mediated* interventions, adults:

- intend to raise children's cognitive capacity, not what they think but how they observe, compare, analyze, conclude, or use any of the many capacities of the brain;

- draw children's attention to specific meaning in a stimulus as a way to help children learn to focus, the basis for learning anything; and
- transcend, which means that the adult encourages children to relate the experience at hand to other experiences in the past or to what they can imagine in the future; in other words, to connect ideas so that children build relationships in their mind.

How Museums Support Learning

Museums are "open-ended" and informal, traits that offer children a different kind of stimulation from classrooms. In museums:

- There is no curriculum or testing.
- No one loses their job if children fail.
- Information is presented in ingenious ways.
- Some exhibits are open to varied interpretations and thereby give mediators many handles to probe children's different interests.
- No bells ring or periods end, so children stay with something as long as they want and repeat it as long as interest lasts.

These conditions provide opportunities for teachers (1) to watch children's reactions and observe what kind of learners they are, and (2) to use museum exhibits as props to challenge the brain to think and learn.

Generalizing from Museum Experience

Despite conditions that seem favorable to learning, some children do *not* think or learn in museums. Figuring out why sets the framework for questions we examine throughout this book. Answers to the following questions provide a schema for effective teaching/learning:

- What is learning?
- What fosters learning?
- What is the adult's role in children's learning?
- What is the role of exhibits? textbooks? other stimuli?
- What provides evidence that someone is thinking?
- What is the relation between thinking and learning?

If children's responses to museum experiences are momentary, eclipsed by the next exhibit, and forgotten after the visit, *mediation can play a critical role*. With effective mediation, children's responses can become thinking responses and, with repetition, children can gradually learn.

Learning means to permanently change how you think, and to:

- make new connections between one experience or stimulus and another,
- understand the role of ideas or objects in diverse contexts,

- grasp the meaning of objects' physical behavior, and
- change ideas that are imprecise or incorrect.

A few children do this on their own. Most require mediation.

Cautionary word: Don't just do! Think! Knowing what to do or using exhibits as designers intend does not mean that children *think* about the principles embedded in the exhibit. To help children learn to think, we must guide them through a learning cycle—explore, form concepts, transfer. Let's watch mediation in each part of the cycle:

- *Exploring*. Encourage children to determine the exhibit's intention: Q: Why are there two tubes? Why are there two balls? A: So we can make a comparison! Q: Why do the balls have to be dropped at the same time? A: So they start the race at exactly the same moment.
- *Forming Concepts*. Encourage children to find meaning and think analytically: Q: How are the tubes different? A: One takes a steep path, the other gradual. Q: Why are the balls the same? A: So they have an equal chance of winning the race. Q: What effect will the difference in the tubes cause? When you drop the balls in, will one roll faster? Which one? Why?
- *Transferring Concepts*. Encourage children to transcend from this exhibit to other experiences: Q: What does this remind you of? How can you apply these ideas to something you have seen (at home, in the museum, at the park, elsewhere)?

In the history of science, exploring and forming concepts extended over long periods. Around 1600, Galileo showed that balls of greatly differing weight fell together when dropped from a height—an exploration. Not until 60 years later did Newton provide the mathematics to explain why—a concept formation. Eventually, Newton's ideas bred calculus, a new branch of mathematics—transcendence.

> The art of mediation is to observe and listen to children in order to determine where they are in the learning cycle and then to intervene effectively.

Summary: What Confounds Learning?

Thus far, we have summarized what mediation is. Next we use examples of children in museums to describe what might go awry and explain why. Finally, we will look at how myths about learning prevent using exhibits to bring about learning. By extension, these ideas apply to learning anywhere. Consider museum experiences:

- a framework for the ideas in the book,
- a lens to focus on what you believe about learning,
- a roadmap to show how your beliefs influence how you teach,
- a blueprint for how to use mediation in diverse situations—museums, classrooms, and elsewhere.

AT A MUSEUM: WHAT DIDN'T HAPPEN, WHY, AND CHANGING IT

Factors that confound learning can be readily seen in museums. Children fail to learn when:

1. Content is unfamiliar.
2. Support is ineffective.
3. Beliefs about what learning looks like are misguided.

Adult intervention can change the factors. Here, we watch that happen.

Confronting Unfamiliar Content

The many examples that follow show how subject matter that is tough because it is unfamiliar or complex can keep children from learning.

Comparative Anatomy. Kim, age 9, examined four skulls in a brightly lit case in the enormous natural history museum. The attractive exhibit with easy-to-view labels had short, to-the-point explanations of the relationship between how the jaw works and what an animal eats. Kim agreed to take part in a study to determine whether the exhibit taught what it was designed to teach. Kim did well, but her third answer was wrong—as were all visitors' third answers. What went wrong?

Visitors said exactly what was on the label, but the label contained the wrong information. When children repeat what they see, it means a lesson has succeeded at communicating specific content. But, if what they see is incorrect, only experts would know; those unfamiliar with the content would leave with the wrong information. Museums are responsible. Most provide correct information most of the time. When the venerable old museum realized the content was wrong, it changed the label. Labels, lessons, or information must be accurate for children to learn, especially if the content is unfamiliar.

Momentum. This is another tough subject because it is a physics phenomenon and research has shown that children often approach physics with intuitive—or naïve—thinking that prevents their grasping the physics principle (Gardner, 1991; Gelman, Brenneman, McDonald, & Roman, 2009; Perkins, 1992). We've all experienced the effect of momentum—on steep inclines things roll faster than on gradual inclines. An exhibit made this point with clear plastic tubing wound around two large, identical cylinders (see Figure 1.1). Tubing was wound steeply on one, gradually on the other. Visitors were supposed to drop a ball into the top of each tube at the same instant, see which ball reached bottom first, and explain why.

Lenny, age 8, approached the exhibit but missed the labels (as most children do). He grabbed a ball from the floor and pushed it up a bit into the bottom of one tube. The ball dropped onto the floor. Lenny shrugged and walked off. Staff noticed that this was a common reaction, so they added illustrations. Still, most children reacted as Lenny had. Visitors understood what to do only after staff made a video showing two people, each dropping a ball at the same instant and exclaiming over whose came out first.

Figure 1.1. How to use the momentum exhibit was not clear from words or pictures; only video made it clear. But video only showed what to *do*, not what caused the effect.

Illustration by Daniel Feuerstein

The museum experimented with three modalities: written labels (verbal), drawings (pictorial), and video (kinesthetic/movement). Harvard professor of neurology John Ratey (2002) says that the brain interprets movement more readily than words or pictures. So, visitors learned what to do from the video, which "mediated" in lieu of a human mediator. If a picture is worth 1000 words, a moving example is worth 1000 pictures.

Mechanical Advantage. Here's another physics problem. We've all noticed that it's easier to move something heavy with pulleys. At the Capital Children's Museum (CCM), an exhibit called "Simple Machines" had huge pulleys, each differently rigged to hoist an 18-pound cinderblock (see Figure 1.2).

The first rig used a *single* pulley, the second a *double* pulley, the third *two double* pulleys. The cinderblocks were heavy, the pulleys huge, and ropes to hoist the cinderblocks were easily accessible. It was apparent what to do: Pull a rope until a cinderblock reached the top of a rig. Huge labels on each cinderblock read "18 pounds" to make it apparent that the weight was identical. Visitors invariably raced to see who could make a cinderblock reach the top first.

Ten-year-old Frank and his teacher approached the pulleys. Frank grabbed the single pulley with the shortest rope. Like most other children, Frank assumed that the cinderblock with the shortest rope would reach the top first. His teacher,

Figure 1.2. Almost all children choose the pulley with less rope; their block *does* reach the top first, but they use much more effort.

Illustration by Daniel Feuerstein

knowing it would take less effort, chose the rig with two double pulleys. Frank strained at the single pulley far more than his teacher. Frank's cinderblock reached the top first, but Frank's intuitive assumption that he would win because he had much less rope to pull was only partially correct because work involves *both* time and effort. The two pulleys his teacher used took longer (more rope!) but required less effort. Although most adults know that more pulleys make work easier, few can explain *why*. Most visitors explained who won by saying that the cinderblocks weighed different amounts, an illogical response, given that each block had a large label stating its weight.

In the pulley exhibit, the information necessary to formulate and solve the problem was presented conspicuously. An effective mediator, even without knowing the answer, would *gather the evidence* by relating the label, "18 pounds," to the experience or by *comparing* the pulleys. Gathering evidence and comparing are essential cognitive acts. Effective mediators *intend* to make children understand the importance of gathering evidence and comparing.

Animation Principle. At CCM, an exhibit called "Animation Station" contained a studio-behind-glass where visitors could animate their drawings. Ginny, age 10, drew a stick figure with arms at its side. Then, she drew several more, identical except that in each drawing she raised the figure's arms just a bit, then a bit more, until after several drawings the arms were upright over the figure's head. After each drawing, Ginny shot the image with a camera. When she played back the images, the figure appeared to be raising its arms. The principle of animation is that you change a detail in a drawing each time you draw it (see zoetropes in Chapter 10). Ginny's mother exclaimed: "Ooh! Look what the *camera* did," not understanding that Ginny's drawings, not the camera, caused the figure to look as if it were raising its arms. If people do not understand the principle, they miss the point.

Language Misheard. Adults may think they know something but be mistaken. The CCM exhibit "Mexico" consisted of many environments—a marketplace, a town center with a fountain and typical buildings, a *Miscellanea* (convenience shop), a mountain log cabin, a rural thatched hut, and so on. At least one guide spoke Spanish. Some adults exclaimed: "Listen, she's speaking Mexican!" The adults had the right idea—it *was* a different language—but the wrong information—Mexican is not a language. In mediation it is important to convey *meaning*—but children's lack of knowledge can be reinforced by adults' misinformation.

Missing Content and Context. The "History of Human Communication" wing at CCM had more than 100 exhibits that together traced the evolution of human communication from cave drawings of 20,000 years ago to video studios and computers. One exhibit reproduced an ingenious signaling device that was used in the mid-1800s before the telegraph was invented—a Chappe semaphore system activated by pulleys that moved huge arms. Semaphores were mounted on stone towers built on high hills so that the arms were visible for miles. Operators moved the arms into a different position for each letter in a message. Google "Chappe Semaphore" and browse around to see a picture or find a simulation of a Chappe semaphore in action.

The exhibit consisted of a realistically detailed mural with a semaphore tower in the foreground and others receding into the distance. Opposite the mural was a stone tower, which felt high to children, with a large semaphore on top. Children climbed the tower's steps, manipulated the semaphore's arms with pulleys, looked through a slit in the stone, and saw the towers in the mural (see Figure 1.3). Attached to the mural was a small-scale working semaphore. Using their hands, children manipulated the small semaphore's arms into the shape representing a letter. Thus, they transmitted messages back and forth between the large and small semaphores—one letter at a time.

The labels were clear and succinct: They named the device, explained its history and use, and showed how to work it. On a chart, each letter of the alphabet appeared alongside a diagram of how to position the semaphores' arms. Yet, many adults exclaimed: "Look! A windmill!" If staff were nearby, they could explain: "That is an old semaphore system. Would you like a demonstration?" The challenge in such an exhibit is what to do if visitors don't read the text and if there is no staff or explanatory video.

If children became absorbed in manipulating the pulleys, a mediator could connect this exhibit to the pulleys across the building in the "Simple Machines" exhibit; thereby, mediators could help children transcend from one experience to

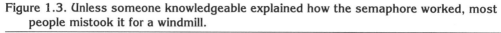

Figure 1.3. Unless someone knowledgeable explained how the semaphore worked, most people mistook it for a windmill.

another, stretching their memory and building a relationship. Mediation is often the determining factor in what children understand or whether they build relationships (*transcend*) from experience to experience.

Summary. These problems confound learning: unfamiliar content; inability to use a particular modality; complex subject matter; and label-dependent, text-based, or static explanations. Keep these problems in mind as, throughout the book, we watch effective mediators overcome problems in order to help children learn to think.

Providing Effective Support

Knowing what to do with a science exhibit or a technical device is not the same as knowing how to climb into a car and grab the steering wheel. Science and technology exhibits contain specific content, rules, and principles, many of which are unfamiliar. In contrast, a car is something most children have often seen maneuvered. To drive a pretend car, children can merely imitate what they have seen. Because different exhibits require different kinds of thinking, it is necessary to use different mediation approaches.

Imitation. Six-year-old Paul visited the grocery store exhibit in a children's museum. Unlike Kim (mislabeled skulls), Frank (pulleys), and Ginny (animation), all of whom faced *unfamiliar content*, Paul (below) faced familiar content but different problems.

Paul's teacher went out of her way to teach him behaviors required for shopping, coaching him every step of the way: "Put the apple on the scale; now put on three more. See?", pointing to the pan, "The pan and the needle have moved." Then, asking Paul to put on three more apples, calling Paul's attention to what he should observe, and alerting him that something has changed: "What does the needle say *now*?" In contrast to teachers' behavior in exhibits on physics, teachers in grocery exhibits simultaneously draw on what children know and add new information while using museums' props to convey their lessons. But, as we shall see, that is still no guarantee that children's thinking will change in one (or more) of the many ways that show a child has learned. In exhibits with familiar content, simply because an adult tightly controls children's behavior does not mean the adult is fostering learning.

Avoidance. Cognitive scientist Rochel Gelman pioneered the study of how, from infancy, children acquire math and science concepts (Gelman & Au, 1996; Gelman & Schatz, 1977). She has conducted extensive research on learning in children's and science museums. Based on her museum work, Gelman says many teachers:

> avoid what they don't know. Despite questions on a math exhibit in big bold black letters, few . . . even read the crucial words "How many?" to call children's attention to a salient fact. [Recall the pulleys.] Yet, in the store, they talked and talked, keeping firm control, giving the child no lead. (quoted in Lewin, 1990, p. 4)

In fact, some adults allow *no* leeway for children to show what they know. When adults overwhelm children with information or avoid topics that are unfamiliar, they unintentionally stymie children's opportunity to build confidence or develop *agency*, the word psychologists use for a strong sense of self. When adults walk right past exhibits on science, math, or unfamiliar content, they miss opportunities to arouse children's curiosity.

Correcting Mistaken Beliefs

Psychologists offer insight about why we don't learn. Powerful, firmly entrenched theories that people develop by age 5—what psychologist Howard Gardner calls "interfering habits of mind"—shape our thinking and are extremely difficult to dislodge.

Interfering Notions. Gardner (1991) explains some hard facts about learning:

> Understanding is a complex process. . . . (I)t seems to require teachers and students to move readily from one form of representation to another and back again. Understanding does not and cannot occur unless the relations among different notations and

representations come to be appreciated, and unless these formal expressions can be mapped onto more intuitive forms of knowing. . . . [G]enuine understanding probably involves some kind of direct confrontation of those habits of the mind that tend to get in the way of a thoroughgoing understanding. . . . (T)hose *interfering habits of mind have not even begun to be understood until recent years.* (p. 179, emphasis added)

Kevin Crowley, assistant professor, School of Education, University of Pittsburgh, and Maureen Callanan, developmental psychologist at UC Santa Cruz, agree:

The way children interpret evidence depends on their current personal theories. . . . When new evidence contradicts a strongly held theory, children sometimes distort the evidence to make it consistent with their theories, or they ignore the evidence altogether. (Crowley & Callanan, 1998, p. 13)

Feuerstein observes that some people feel no need for logical evidence or do not understand its value. They are not disposed to wonder or have no appetite for thinking hard. They pass by things that are strange, beautiful, preposterous, or intriguing, and take no notice or impose irrelevant meaning on something unfamiliar. This is illustrated in the following story of "Suspense," an exhibit on electromagnetism at the Exploratorium, a major science museum in San Francisco.

Misapplied Ideas. In "Suspense," a metal sphere suspended in midair is controlled by a photoelectric cell. When visitors block the cell with their hand, the sphere drops. When visitors place the sphere within the magnet's grasp, they feel and see it again stay suspended. The exhibit demonstrates the effect of interrupting the source of power in an electromagnetic system (see http://exs.exploratorium.edu/exhibits/suspense/).

Sue Allen, educational researcher and project evaluator at the Exploratorium, says:

Observations of visitor behaviors were quite positive: visitors manipulated the ball and magnet successfully, stayed at the exhibit for extended periods, and showed signs of excitement and pleasure. However, when . . . asked . . . what they thought the exhibit showed, many replied it was a model of the solar system with the ball representing the earth. (Allen, 1997, pp. 8–9)

Visitors did not simply miss the point of the exhibit; they imposed an irrelevant concept with which they had some familiarity on content that was completely unfamiliar. This is not uncommon. The brain is driven to see patterns, even where none exists.

Electromagnetic systems involve tough subject matter, complex and unfamiliar. As with pulley systems, the only visitors who thought about what the exhibits were designed to teach already knew the content, had the schemata (psychologists' word for organized mental capacity), and therefore could grasp the principle. As Schauble, Leinhardt, and Martin (1997) explain,

How and what people learn in museums [or anywhere] are very much a function of their motivations (why they have come there), their interests (enduring propensities to engage with a topic), and their sense of identity (who they think they are in relation to museum offerings).

. . . Beyond anything a museum or classroom can do is the question of who a particular student is and the nature of thinking itself. Elementary school children often fail to see what is before their very eyes when they inspect devices that include gears, levers, and inclined planes. Instead, *their expectations and interpretations tend to be driven by familiar mental schemes about the way things usually work.* (p. 6, emphasis added)

Summary: Perceiving and Meeting Challenges

Perkins (1995) says: "In general, performance on activities that demand thought and understanding falls much further below ideal expectations than performance on routine activities [riding a bike, getting dressed]" (p. 139). Perkins (1992) blames the problem on lack of content, naïve theories, ritual knowledge, or answers that sound right but that are based on incorrect logic or content.

Unless children know how to watch their own reactions, they may not even know they are confused, much less resolve the confusion. Or, as in the electromagnetic exhibit, children who know how to watch their reactions draw on content they have learned that is not relevant and connect what is in their head to something unfamiliar.

People may believe that learning occurs as a result of direct exposure. But direct exposure rarely helps children watch themselves think. Children (and adults, too) accept phenomena without feeling any need to explain, understand, or formulate a rule. Moreover, adults may point out only the most trivial things: "Look! What a long tail!" "Gee! What a small car!" Mediation that asks children to compare can help them perceive problems because the act of comparison requires seeking evidence. Mediators can stimulate this by stating explicitly: "Compare what we are watching to what we did in class yesterday." Or, "When you said this engine is powered by gas but that engine is powered by electricity, you were making a comparison. What was the evidence for your observation?" Or, "Put comparison in your arsenal of thinking techniques and remember to use it."

Learning something tough almost always requires mediation. The challenge is for an adult to observe children's reactions and help children focus on what is going on with the intention of encouraging them to think—gather data, compare, analyze, conclude, revise, synthesize.

> Many factors, among them the complexity of the thinking processes, contribute to students' confusion.

RECOGNIZING MYTHS ABOUT LEARNING

Myths prevail because of general confusion about what thinking and learning actually involve. School as we know it is a cultural form only 2 centuries old. Yet, myths about curricula, textbooks, tests, and other school practices seem carved in stone. "Schools have preferred to go with tradition—even if universal education has a very short one, and one fashioned on the model of the mass-production assembly lines of the Industrial Revolution—instead of learning how to apply the discoveries of neurology and psychology to the teaching of children" (Csikszentmihalyi, quoted in Lewin-Benham, 2010, p. ix). Myths about what it means to learn also abound in children's museums, a recent cultural form.

Myth of Discovery

A clever exhibit contrasted water in its three states—liquid, solid (ice), and gas (steam). Sara, age 8, could name each state, but she adamantly refused to believe her teacher, who told Sara that the liquid, solid, and gas were fundamentally the same. No one of any age is likely to *discover* the scientific principles of states of matter without an explanation:

- The same matter can take different forms.
- Water maintains its chemical structure no matter what form, or state, it is in.
- The arrangement of the molecules is always the same, regardless of state.

People tend to believe information they can perceive directly. But it is not possible to discover water's chemical or molecular structure through perception or without using a powerful microscope and knowing how to interpret what the microscope reveals. Water's chemical composition was learned through a series of experiments, first by Antoine-Laurent Lavoisier in 1768, and then confirmed by many more experiments over the next half century by several other scientists (Evan-Moor, 2010).

> Research on cognition shows that children are unlikely to discover ideas such as states or science principles on their own without direct teaching.

Myth of Exposure

The 4th-graders shown in Figure 1.4 enjoyed themselves, spontaneously jumping and dancing in "Strobe Theater" where the wall surface retained their shadows. But on their own they did not wonder why their shadow stayed on the wall, question the role of the strobe light, or think about the light-retaining properties of the wall covering, the relation between a shadow's size and the location of a light source, or where strobe lights fit in the long quest to use a source other than fire to penetrate darkness.

> Exposure without mediation does not "train children's brains" (Posner et al., 2008, pp. 1–10) to question and make connections.

Myth of Activity

This myth says that when we push buttons, pull ropes, climb on seesaws, or ride stationary bikes, we are thinking. In other words, action

Figure 1.4. Children intuitively knew *what* to do in "Strobe Theater," but had no idea *how* the effect worked.

Illustration by Daniel Feuerstein

makes us aware of cause and effect. Most of us, however, think little of cause and effect in exhibits, classroom activities, or elsewhere. Yet, the belief that activity causes thinking is so deeply entrenched that it spawned the epithet "hands-on learning." Watch youngsters who actively push buttons in museums: Their eyes turn toward the next exhibit and off they run *without waiting to see the effect of pushing the button; neither do they form a relationship between the act of pushing and its effect.* They do not wait because they do not know how to look for relationships.

Neither children nor adults are aware of the importance of finding relationships caused by the interaction of two objects (batting a ball, putting yeast in batter), by natural forces (tectonic plates relation to the formation of mountains, the reasons for rain cycle), or by popular opinions (Islam is/is not a religion, HIV is/is not contagious).

> Effective mediation disposes children to compare, contrast, and categorize; to regularly use analytic thinking processes; and thus, eventually, to form relationships.

Myth of Trial and Error

A common assumption is that children will "get" the meaning if they "mess around" with something. Cuisenaire rods, the rage of New Math in the 1970s, were designed to help children learn numerical relationships. Children are given bags full of these satiny-feeling, beautifully colored wooden rods to "play" with. The white rod, the size of a 1-centimeter cube; plus the orange rod, the size of nine 1-centimeter cubes, makes 10. One goal is to position rods of different lengths alongside one another to show all the possible combinations of 10, using the numbers 1 through 9. Eventually, goes the myth, through trial and error, the children would find other numerical relationships, such as the additive property of numbers (1 + 1 = 2, 1 + 2 = 3, 1 + 3 = 4, and so on) or the commutative property of numbers (3 + 3 = 6, 6 – 3 = 3, 3 × 2 = 6, 6 ÷ 2 = 3, and so on)—both basic principles of arithmetic.

To learn from trial and error, children must relate each error to a particular trial, conclude that the trial did not lead to the desired effect but resulted in an error, and try again. But few children *define* what result they are after, and fewer still *summarize* behaviors in terms of whether they achieved the result. That is, they do not relate trial to error! Children "get it" *only if* they:

- have learned how to observe,
- have been coached in how to see the relationship between what they observe and what actually happens,
- feel bothered when a result is wrong, and
- have learned how to correct random trial-and-error actions.

> Teachers who know the specific capacities that are prerequisites for thinking about a phenomenon can better mediate to help children think accurately.

Myth of Intrinsic Motivation

Visitors from age 5 on loved the flower-making activity in the Plaza in the "Mexico" exhibit at CCM. They were highly motivated to turn brightly colored squares of tissue paper into flowers. Some children made eight or ten flowers, but none asked *why* they were doing this activity in this exhibit.

Intrinsic motivation is important in engaging someone's attention. But, beyond engagement, thinking means stretching current understanding to consider new and different content. The flower-makers mastered a technique, but never thought about the attributes, functions, significance, or transcendent meaning of flowers in the context of Mexican culture or in any other context, such as the properties of tissue paper or how accordion folds behave. Mediation could have provided content or sparked children to wonder about context.

> Mediation can help children go beyond mere engagement by encouraging them to think about the relationship between content and context.

Summary: Overcoming Myths

Myths lure many into believing children are thinking or learning when, in fact, they are not. The issue is not how children interact with physical objects but how they use their minds to construct meaning and create relationships. In other words:

- Do they think about what an object is intended to convey?
- Do they observe and compare?
- Do they connect the meaning in a current experience to other experiences?

Myths overlook the role of mediation in learning, but perpetuate the belief that simply by having experiences, we are thinking. Don't we wish learning were that simple!

The two examples at the beginning of this chapter, Hawkins's swinging bobs and the Head Start child and the giraffe, show that mediation involves doing *whatever* is necessary to connect children to ideas. The question to ask of any experience is, How will it pick children up off the ground so that they learn? Examples abound in the next 11 chapters of how mediation helps children expand their cognitive capacities.

Takeaways

1. Children don't learn when they are asked to manipulate unfamiliar content.
2. Children don't learn if the adults who influence them have mistaken beliefs about what learning is, offer incorrect content, or demonstrate inadequate techniques.
3. Without mediation, children are unlikely to learn through discovery, exposure, activity, trial and error, or intrinsic motivation.

CHAPTER 2

The Mediated Learning Experience Defined

If the sun and moon should doubt
They'd immediately go out.

—William Blake, 1803

THE CENTRAL IDEA in this book is that children learn because of mediation by another human. Mediated learning experiences are interactions: Adults intervene in children's experience with the intent of teaching something. The word *mediate* represents the essence of Feuerstein's theory of the Mediated Learning Experience (MLE). Mediation:

- includes a range of techniques to guide any adult/child intervention, and
- involves both cognition and motivation.

Feuerstein considers cognition and motivation two sides of the same coin. He calls motivation the *affective* aspect of cognition, that is, motivation is one's *will* to do something.

In this chapter, we will first show Feuerstein mediating a child and then explain what motivated Feuerstein to develop mediation theory. Next, we present his two theories, Structural Cognitive Modifiability and Mediated Learning Experience. Finally, we describe the key facets of mediation.

FEUERSTEIN: MEDIATOR AND THEORIST

As a mediator, Feuerstein draws on his powerful clinical skills. As a theorist, Feuerstein draws on his lifelong experiences. Here, we see both.

Lewin-Benham's first introduction to mediation was at Feuerstein's institute in Jerusalem. There, more than 100 psychologists, social workers, and other professionals were treating people with a range of learning problems—autism, severe brain trauma, lack of motivation, reading problems, Down syndrome, and other unnamed conditions. Lewin-Benham recounts:

> Feuerstein was mediating 10-year-old Richard from Long Island. Four phones rang incessantly, some calls demanding time, others a few seconds. After each call, Feuerstein resumed the session, Richard's attention focused

as if there had been no interruption. Feuerstein's demeanor—eyes, posture, tone of voice—conveyed his intention: You *will* pay attention! Feuerstein was using exercises from his instruments to assess Richard's potential to learn; he told me Richard was there because he had been labeled "autistic." Children's performance on an exercise in the instrument reveals if, when shown how to do something, the child can remember what to do and use the technique to solve the next exercise that uses the same principle but different particulars.

Intrigued by Feuerstein's ability to keep Richard focused, curious to learn about the theory, and eager to be instructed in how to use the instruments, I returned to Jerusalem for a 2-week summer course given by the ICELP in mediation theory and practices. Psychologists and educators from around the world were present. Over the next decade, I drew Feuerstein into the work we were doing at the Capital Children's Museum and the two schools we were running in the museum's spacious buildings.

Feuerstein's mediation theory sharpened our focus then, and it shapes the two main messages in this book: Mediation can powerfully stimulate thinking, and mediation of museum exhibits is a paradigm for how mediation principles can be applied in any learning situation.

Developing Mediation Theory

Feuerstein explains: MLE theory was motivated by historical events. My ideas about mediation initially grew as part of my theory of human development, called Structural Cognitive Modifiability (SCM).

The Historical Perspective. Many learning theories have come and gone, dating from Plato's Socratic method, "perhaps the first in human intellectual history" (Gardner, 1985, pp. 3–5). Each theory was based on a set of beliefs. The basis for MLE theory is the belief that the brain is capable of change. This was a radical idea when Feuerstein proposed it around 1950. Then, the prevalent belief was that the brain was inaccessible and unchangeable. This widespread belief led psychologists, educators, and the general public to conclude that each person's intelligence was fixed and that intelligence was one single "entity" in the brain and would not change.

Jean Piaget purported that intelligence was not only fixed but that it developed in predictable stages at predetermined times—much like the cycles of a caterpillar turning into a moth or an egg turning into tadpole and a tadpole into frog. Piaget also implied that each stage must be mastered before going on to the next (Gleitman, 1987; Piaget, 1973).

Feuerstein and Piaget. In 1947, Piaget invited Feuerstein to study at his institute in Geneva. Feuerstein had great admiration for Piaget, particularly his insight of working one-on-one with children as they performed exercises. Piaget called this a "clinical" method; he was the first modern psychologist to use such an approach. But, having thought about human development since his early years in Romania, Feuerstein saw restrictions inherent in Piaget's theory.

Piaget and Feuerstein are both giants. The greatest differences between their theories are their beliefs in fixed versus changeable intelligence and in adults' role in children's developing intelligence. Adults, according to Piaget, should not intervene in a child's activity; rather, they are a kind of object that can reveal new information because they have much richer data and experience. The adult is essentially no different from other objects that also provide information.

Hans Aebli was a disciple and collaborator of Piaget and the director of Piaget's Pedagogic Psychology Institute at the University of Zurich. Around 1948, Aebli attempted to use Piaget's theory to teach children. Twenty years later, he recanted: For Piaget, teaching is neither necessary nor possible. Aebli rethought

> the tacit assumption [in Piaget's theory] that experiments simply uncover cognitive structures, which are said to build up during the child's spontaneous activities [and proposed] an alternative conception of developmental processes and of cognition . . . in which an elaboration concept, language, and *social stimulation* are central. (1970, p. 12, emphasis added)

Put another way, other people, most likely adults, are essential in encouraging children to elaborate their thinking and to use language in doing so; in these ways, adults' interactions stimulate development.

Piaget made important contributions by interviewing children to learn about their cognitive processes. In actuality, Piaget was a scientific observer of biosocial phenomena. Both his theory and practice (to the extent that practice existed) reflect his initial training as a biologist. Piaget himself said, "As for teaching children concepts that they have not already acquired in their spontaneous development, it is completely useless" (Hall, 1970).

Sociocultural Theory. Today's foremost theory on human development is sociocultural theory. Yet, it is barely known to the public and rarely used in schools. Lev Vygotsky, father of sociocultural theory, was little known in the West before the 1960s. Vygotsky died of tuberculosis at age 38, too young to expand the powerful ideas he proposed. Moreover, his work was imprisoned during the Iron Curtain years. Today, Vygotsky's ideas are considered seminal and are the basis for research by many psychologists and for many teaching practices (Kozulin, 1988; Vygotsky, 2007).

Alex Kozulin, foremost Vygotsky scholar and director of research at the ICELP, considers Feuerstein's work a robust elaboration of Vygotsky's ideas, although Feuerstein did not know about Vygotsky's work when he proposed his theory in the 1950s. Yet, the wide-ranging work that Feuerstein and his colleagues developed falls squarely within sociocultural thinking. Kozulin says that Feuerstein's work embellishes Vygotsky's as Borodin's music embellishes folk tunes (Presseisen & Kozulin, 1994).

MLE Theory. Briefly, MLE holds that intervention by an adult during a child's engagement with a task or challenge is the catalyst for changing thinking and causing the child to learn. Feuerstein says mediation changes cognitive structure.

Today, cognitive structure means the numerous capacities of the brain to think. Conducting research with squirrel monkeys in the early 1980s, neurologist Michael Merzenich provided the first evidence that brain circuits change in response to activity (Merzenich, 2004). Others replicated Merzenich's findings. Current research affirms that throughout life, the brain rewires itself in response to internal and external forces (Feldman & Brecht, 2005).

The relationship between brain change and Feuerstein's work is this: Feuerstein considers mediation a strong force to change the brain. The large arsenal of activities that comprise Feuerstein's instruments and the varied techniques of mediation, when used intentionally and systematically, bring about changes in behavior that suggest changes in underlying brain functions—hence, the name Structural Cognitive Modifiability (SCM) theory. Feuerstein's two theories, Structural Cognitive Modifiability and Mediated Learning Experience, resonate with the current understanding of how we think and learn.

Structural Cognitive Modifiability

Feuerstein's theory of human development, Structural Cognitive Modifiability (SCM), has three basic ideas (Feuerstein, Feuerstein, Falik, & Rand, 2006):

- Three forces shape human beings: environment, human biology (both in evolutionary terms and in each one's own development), and mediation.
- Temporary states determine behavior: How someone behaves—which means "emotional, intellectual, and even habitually learned activities" (p. 27)— represents a temporary state, not a permanent trait. This means that intelligence is adaptive. In other words, intelligence can change; it is not fixed once-and-for-all.
- The brain is plastic: Because all behaviors "are open and developing" (p. 27), the brain can generate new structures through a combination of external and internal factors (p. 25).

The intersections among biology, environment, and mediation are frequent and complex. They echo throughout all the brain's systems, from how a child responds if he touches a hot radiator to the impact of this action on

- his immediate behavior;
- the neurons (brain cells) that control eye, arm, hand, and body movements;
- the matter inside the brain cells; and
- epigenetic forces, the chemicals that store reactions to an experience and are a vital part of memory. (Kandel, 2006)

Thus, complex networks of systems, each one itself extremely complex, determine how we act, remember, and learn. These forces intersect constantly, with one another and with the outside environment; it is the complexity of these many interactions that makes the brain a *dynamic*—or continually changing—system (Damasio, 1994; Kandel, 2006; Ratey, 2002).

Feuerstein maintains that human cognitive function can be changed regardless of a condition's cause, severity, or a person's age, even if the condition is generally considered irrevocable and irreparable. "Don't tell me what a person *is*," says Feuerstein, "tell me how he is *changeable*!"

> The foundation of the theory of Structural Cognitive Modifiability is belief in the human capacity to change.

THEORY OF MEDIATION

While in the midst of creating Feuerstein Instrumental Enrichment (FIE), Feuerstein saw *Salah Shabati*, a popular film by the prolific, prize-winning author Ephraim Kishon. A line spoken by Topol, the main character—"*Rega! Hoshvim!*" ("A second! Thinking!")—struck a chord with Feuerstein. The line inspired the trademark image and motto for the FIE program: a youngster of indeterminate age and ethnicity, eyes shut in concentration, pencil poised on lips (see Figure 2.1).

"Just a moment! Let me think!" is the first thing students are taught to say as teachers begin to use FIE. The words stifle impulsivity and cue the brain to focus. These two actions are essential for self-regulation and therefore are the first steps in any thinking act.

Understanding Feuerstein's motivation shows how his theories and practices depart from prevalent theories, how his work foreshadowed some current research on the brain, and why his approach has been effective for 50 years. The following background sets the stage for our central idea: Mediation teaches children to focus their attention and perform the thinking that enables them to develop increasingly effective cognitive structures.

Feuerstein's Motivation

In a poignant reflection, Feuerstein described how he began to formulate the ideas that ultimately became the theory of mediation:

Figure 2.1. The logo on Feuerstein's instruments depicts a child thinking.

In my early 20s, while still in Romania, I was responsible for children abandoned when their parents were sent to Nazi work camps. I determined to provide them rich experiences, not only custodial care but reading, hearing and playing music, and using artistic media. When the Nazis closed in and I fled to Israel, because of my experience I was appointed head of psychological services for Youth Aliyah, a position I held for decades in this large effort to integrate youth from throughout the world into the new state of Israel. My charges had been traumatized. Many had grown up with no family, fending for themselves in inhuman conditions. I found that standard tests of intelligence that determine what one has learned and remembers were useless. My children had learned little and remembered mainly horror.

I needed to know: What can each youth learn when taught, and how can each change as a result? Working with Andre Rey, a creative scientist, really a genius, and using test items he and others had developed, we devised a different way to test called dynamic assessment: You test not what children have learned and remember, but what thinking skills they possess. First you test, [then you] immediately (during the testing session) teach the missing skill, [and] then [you] immediately test again to determine a child's capacity to learn. Results showed that, when taught skills they were lacking, youth were capable of immense change. In other words, they could learn.

When I saw that the youth were capable of learning, I realized I would have to develop means to help them do so. This realization led to the creation, over the next decades and continuing today, of the two large bodies of instruments called FIE-Standard [5th grade and up] and FIE-Basic [roughly ages 3 to 10], the latter program designed and produced by Rabbi Rafi Feuerstein.

For 20 years research accumulated, study after study, showing positive change in children with whom our mediation techniques were used. But, by the 1980s some psychologists insisted our achievements were the result of changing the diagnosis, not ameliorating the condition. To counter these critics, we began to work with children diagnosed as having Down syndrome, a chromosomal condition where change could not be considered the result of false diagnosis.

The children with Down syndrome with whom we worked gained unheard of abilities—caring for themselves, reading, and eventually living independently and earning a modest income. These results created a revolution in how Down syndrome children were treated: They were brought out of hiding and made part of their families' lives, and later their community. The history is told in the book *You Love Me! Don't Accept Me as I Am* (Feuerstein, Rand, & Feuerstein, 2006).

In 1990 Elhanon, my eldest grandson, was born with Down syndrome. It inspired Elhanon's father—my eldest son, Rabbi Rafi Feuerstein—to become a psychologist. With continual mediation by the family, by age 15 Elhanon could read and understand the complex texts that make up some of Judaism's great teachings.

Genesis of Mediation

Mediation is mothers' intuitive way of interacting with infants. Mediation is influenced by one's environment.

Mothers as Mediators. Mothers are natural mediators; they convey feelings of self-competence, make children aware of important ideas, and teach essential behaviors. Mediation is the oldest effective way anyone has ever taught anything to another. A mother's mediation, from the moment she first holds her infant, is the strongest shaping force in a child's development.

Stanley Greenspan, an authority on children from birth to 3 years old, and co-author Stuart Shanker say that the newborn "depends on a caregiver's ability to adapt her gaze, voice, and movements in a pleasurable, emotionally satisfying manner to the baby's unique way of responding to and taking in the world" (2004, p. 55). In these first months, physical events become interlinked with emotional responses as:

> the basic unit of sensory-affect-motor response becomes more and more established through infant-caregiver interactions. . . . [W]hat we call emotions and the texture of consciousness is influenced by the qualities of distinctly human interactions characterized by regulation, sensitivity, and a variety of feeling states. Children deprived of these types of interactions do not experience a range of subtle emotions, especially those dealing with caring, love, and empathy. (pp. 289–291)

The earliest months of life set the stage to learn.

Environment as Mediator. Who we are results from complex interactions among culture, education, environment, the people around us, and our own DNA. Today, some children and youth live in toxic situations, for example, destruction of community, war, and immigration. Others struggle with unbearable amounts of stress caused by addicted parents, poverty, and crime. Some youth under-realize their potential. Some fail the increasingly frequent tests that have edged out other classroom activity. Affluence does not provide immunity from a noxious media surround, work-crazed parents, junk food, or overemphasis on testing.

We believe that adult intervention is the only antidote to a disadvantaged environment, no matter what its cause. Further, we believe that effective mediation can help traumatized children learn to focus, stressed-out students to adopt a calmer approach, underachievers to become motivated, failing students to build cognitive skills, and strong performers to become stronger. Because mediation affects motivation as well as cognition, children who receive effective mediation learn to experience joy in accomplishment and as a result become motivated to learn.

Summary: Evolution of a Theory

The genesis of mediation theory was Feuerstein's varied experiences as a youth, in the Holocaust, in his studies, and in his charge in Israel: to make war-ravaged youth productive citizens. This cauldron of experience gave rise to a powerful theory of learning that in time grew into an equally powerful body of practices.

THE THREE PARTNERS OF MEDIATION

Mediation is not just any adult intervention but embodies specific techniques. Mediation has three essential partners—the mediator, the stimulus, and the mediatee. They intersect dynamically and responsively. *How* the partners intersect structures the ideas throughout this book.

The Mediator

The mediator is an agent of change whose interventions are driven by compassion and belief. So, here is 8-year-old Glenna, considered "low-functioning." Her neighborhood is beset by gang-instigated crime, the community is frightened, and tensions are high. In a penetrating glance, the mediator—her teacher—assesses Glenna's state. The teacher feels an urgent need to relieve the anguish permeating Glenna's life. The need has energized the teacher: She believes her calling is to give Glenna and her classmates a chance to escape their neighborhood's hell. The teacher knows her students will succeed only if they feel empowered and believe in themselves, that Glenna and her classmates must each develop an interest that can blossom into a passion, that they will require a multitude of thinking skills to realize their goals. The teacher believes she can help her students acquire a zest for accomplishment and a host of skills.

Glenna's teacher is a mediator; she:

- selects a stimulus and shapes it to grab children's attention;

- presents the stimulus with authority;

- intervenes at the moment stimulus and learner connect, even if the connection is tenuous, and intervenes again when the learner responds;

- responds second-by-second to children's reactions to a stimulus;

- presents a stimulus so that children perceive both its meaning and the mediator's intention in choosing this stimulus; and

- engages responsively; that is, as children grapple to respond, observes in order to determine how she, the mediator, will respond in turn. If learners do not grasp what the mediator intended, the mediator clarifies the meaning for them both.

Mediation is the ultimate responsive behavior—an impromptu dance. The dance is unpredictable because every learner is unique and the "steps" in the "dance," which must change the learner *as he is dancing*, change second-by-second and are different for every child. Mediators' belief that someone can do something is a powerful force in their doing so.

The Stimulus

A stimulus is anything mediators choose as the focus of an interaction with students they are teaching. Stimuli bombard us constantly—random, disordered, varied in intensity, and with unpredictable frequency. Stimuli are so powerful that we protect ourselves by tuning out. If we did not, every sound however slight, every tactile impression however gentle, any smell—all sensory impressions would distract us. Stimuli overwhelm anyone who focuses poorly. Most of us learn to respond selectively to stimuli. In mediated exchanges, adults interpose themselves between child and stimulus, and modify the stimulus, themselves, and the child with the goal of changing how children perceive the stimulus. The stimulus is the source of meaning in a mediated interaction.

The Mediatee: Lesson for Glenna

The mediatee is the focus of a mediator's intervention. Let's watch Glenna. Glenna has learned to tune out. She hardly ever responds, but her teacher has thoughtfully conceived an intervention. She explains:

> I want the stimuli to get through, penetrate Glenna's consciousness, not go unnoticed, but *modify* her. So, I have *planned*; [I have] carefully *selected* a novel, content-rich stimulus, different from the random stimuli to which Glenna is accustomed. How I mediate that stimulus will break through Glenna's tuned out, unfocused state.
>
> Because Glenna consumes her food with great passion, I chose food as the stimulus. My intentions are:
>
> ✓ to encourage Glenna to use comparative behavior, and
> ✓ to make Glenna aware of the concepts of more and less.
>
> I selected four lemon candies [that are] similar looking, but [which] rang[e] from extremely sweet to extremely sour.

The teacher was following these mediation principles:

1. *Preparing the lesson* by selecting a provocative stimulus so that the mediatee feels *compelled* to attend to it.
2. *Changing the mediatee's state of mind.* "Glenna! Look!" the teacher commands as she puts the four candies on the table. Immediately, Glenna is aroused. She comes to attention, now wide awake, not aloof, inattentive, or sleepy.
3. *Ensuring the stimulus is perceived.* If stimuli are not perceived, mediatees won't benefit from them. Choosing an eating experience takes into account Glenna's nature—her preferences, what interests her, and her likely response.
4. *Making sure the stimulus gets through.* In this sense, mediation is an imposition: Don't look *there*; look *here*! Don't do *this*; do *that*! The teacher calls her name imperatively: "*Glenna!*"

The success of mediation depends on mediators' use of specific techniques.

A Dynamic Process. The teacher proceeds by having Glenna taste each candy and then put the candies in order from sweetest to sourest. This causes Glenna to use comparative behavior. In this lesson, Glenna must use a mental operation called seriation—organizing a group from shortest to longest, lightest weight to heaviest, or, here, sweetest to sourest. The ability to make comparisons is the foundation for being able to use seriation.

Feuerstein says making comparisons is one of the most basic and important cognitive functions. It requires:

- focusing on detail,
- attending to two or more things simultaneously,
- drawing on schemata (the brain's organization of concepts), and
- expressing your conclusions. (Feuerstein, Feuerstein, Falik, & Rand, 2006, pp. 242–243)

If children's responses are weak, lackluster, or anemic, it means they lack the ability to elaborate.

Glenna perceives the difference and with minimum coaching responds by describing the four candies: "This one's sweet. This one's *not* sweet. Yuk! This one's *really* not sweet. This one's kinda sweet." The response tells the teacher that Glenna lacks content knowledge: She does not know the word *sour*. The more children receive mediation, the more content they acquire. As content knowledge grows, so will a student's capacity to register and deal actively with stimuli so that he or she can benefit from future encounters.

The Lesson Continues. The teacher uses the word *sour* frequently until Glenna adopts and uses it herself. Then the teacher uses the candies as the stimulus to teach Glenna the concepts of *more* and *less*, the main meaning she intends for this lesson. In a subsequent lesson, she will use a different stimulus—perhaps other candies, perhaps shiny baubles or beads—to reinforce Glenna's understanding of *more* and *less*. She will continue until Glenna uses these concepts spontaneously in situations that differ from the lessons and until Glenna's responses are thoughtful.

If children's responses wander, it shows that, as they *elaborate*, they cannot pick relevant attributes or they fail to make connections. Elaboration consists of one or several different mental acts from among the many the human brain has the potential to perform. Children's responses reflect which "verbal concepts are part of an individual's repertoire . . . [and can be] mobilized at the expressive level" (Feuerstein et al., 2002, p. 139). The ability to express themselves verbally enables children to move to higher levels of thinking. When children cannot explain what they are thinking, it indicates that they are having difficulty in elaborating—using higher mental operations—to think about an experience. Complex thought processes underlie even seemingly simple behaviors.

Summary: The Essence of Mediation

The design of the stimulus, the mediator's tone of voice, the response the mediator evokes—*everything* is deliberate, calculated, and intentional because the purpose is to *change* the child and make the new skill permanent. For Glenna to think, she must learn more content and concepts. Mediators separate the content and concepts of stimuli, determine exactly which bit is problematic for given children, and then figure out effective ways for children to learn the content or form concepts.

The essence of MLE is that:

- change is produced in the three partners—stimulus, child, and mediator;
- the change persists beyond this one instance; and
- the change becomes part of the thinking repertoire, that is, becomes available and increasingly easy to use when students must tackle similar problems in the future.

Mediation enables children to learn to think, initially using fundamental and eventually increasingly higher-level thinking skills. Ultimately, children develop what some psychologists call *metacognition—thinking* about how they are thinking.

> In mediation, tiny bits—mediators' gestures, choice of stimuli, and child's focus—can make huge differences.

Using Stimuli

Where do we find stimuli? What is their precise nature? Why do we select one over another? How do we make a stimulus meaningful in *this* instance? How do we ensure that the mediation will orient students to attend, not just to any stimulus, but to *particular* stimuli?

Stimuli provide the content of mediated learning experiences. They abound in natural and man-made environments and can be shaped in innumerable ways. Selection of a stimulus is a thoughtful process: What is the precise word to state a writer's intent? Should the composer choose the key of C, F, or G minor? What poem should the teacher read to help students understand metaphor?

Exhibit designers are mediators: They design exhibits in order to arrest visitors' attention. Each object, color, placement, word—*everything* in an exhibit—represents the end product of a designer's selection process. Making stimuli available, arresting, and attractive to a student is one of the most satisfying aspects of a mediator's job. A mediator's goal is to select stimuli to make learners stop, focus, and think.

Tom's Story. Ten-year-old Tom is repeating 4th grade. Lewin-Benham is his tutor. She describes the situation:

> Tom lacks both the know-how and the persistence to break a word into syllables; he only pays attention to the first letter. When he reads long words, for example, *appetite,* instead of searching for syllable breaks, he grabs the

first letter or two and utters them as the first sound in a multisyllabic but meaningless "word": *ap-r-mumble*, indistinguishable. For this lesson, I use syllables as the stimulus.

I have chosen the word *appetite*. First, I arrest attention: "Tom!" Next, I ask the meaning; Tom says, "That when you hungry!" This tells me the word is in Tom's "mental dictionary," that if he hears it, he will recognize it.

I cover all the word except the initial syllable, "ap," and explain to Tom: "I am breaking this word into bits because I know you can read bits." Tom succeeds, reading the syllables "ap," then "pe," then "tite" as I move my finger to uncover them one after the other. Tom does well; he even reads the syllable "tite" with the long "ī" sound (as in the word *mine*, not the word *bit*). But he can neither recall all three syllables nor blend them, which means he can't say all of the syllables in order and fast enough to hear the word. So I coach him to recall and to blend, to say all three syllables faster and faster until he hears the word. For months, I continue sounding-out lessons to increase Tom's content knowledge and solidify his sounding-out skills.

Rethinking Labels. Youngsters who are diagnosed with Attention Deficit Hyperactivity Disorder (ADHD) have fleeting attention. They cannot focus on stimuli, much less hold three syllables in mind. ADHD children actually give the same amount of time, attention, and investment to *all* objects. Other children, who for various reasons have limited vocabularies, do not hear three syllables as a word because that word (and many others) is not in their "mental dictionary." Fleeting attention and limited vocabulary greatly limit a child's capacity to learn to read. The theory of mediation does not refer to students like Glenna and Tom as students with ADHD, as slow, or as hyperactive. Rather, in MLE theory they are referred to as students who are unmediated and therefore have not learned how to treat stimuli differentially or use them effectively.

Work done over decades by Feuerstein and his many collaborators has resulted in a wealth of specially designed stimuli. These are the collective FIE instruments, which we describe in more detail in Chapter 3. Courses run by the ICELP and its worldwide training centers train educators and psychologists in mediation theory and in the use of the instruments. Courses are typically held in the summer and are 2 weeks long. The 70 worldwide training centers are listed on the ICELP website.

> Mediation theory is a different lens through which to look at children defined by labels.

Summary: Partners in a Mediated Exchange

We have used many words for "mediatee"—*student, learner, person, child, Glenna, youngster, Tom, ADHD children*. A mediatee is all of these—anyone who is being taught by someone whose intention is to convey meaning, to bridge from this experience to others, and thereby to improve the brain's thinking processes.

As you read scenarios in this book, remember: A Mediated Learning Experience (MLE) has three partners:

1. mediator, teacher, parent, museum guide, or other adult;
2. stimulus (or exhibit or lesson) that is the subject of the intervention and provides its meaning; and
3. mediatee, or the child at whom the intervention is directed.

These are the *who* and *what* of mediation. Next, we focus on *how*.

ESSENTIAL ASPECTS OF MEDIATION

The meat of this book is about *how* to mediate—the gestures, questions, comments, and other encouragement that adults provide to children. Based on lengthy study of what mediators do and how they interact, Feuerstein and his colleagues have developed descriptions of effective ways to mediate. Among them are the three essential acts (or parameters)—intentionality, meaning, and transcendence. If we are missing any one of these acts, the interaction is not a mediated learning experience. We describe these three parameters next. Many other parameters of mediation are identified throughout the book.

Intentionality

Intentionality refers to the mediator's attitude, which should be purposeful, specific, sometimes commanding, and always directed toward a particular end she has clearly in mind. The various aspects of intentionality follow.

Saliency. When I act as a mediator, I aim to make everything I present to the individual *salient*. So, I select color, form, content, or other features as the means to attract children's attention. Saliency is most important in drawing children's eye to the object under consideration. It is the aspect of intentionality that connects mediator, mediatee, and stimulus.

Imperatives. If I speak to you with intention, regardless of subject, I will make sure to arrest your attention. My stance and expression will be imperative. I won't merely put something before you, but I will display it so you cannot help but notice. Because this is my intention, you *will* see it. It *will* penetrate your conscious, whether you want it or not. First, I will modify *myself* by changing my attitude, tone of voice, and the frequency of my words to be sure you notice. I will whisper, sing, chant, shout, clap, wave my arm, do whatever it takes to make my intention known because intention motivates both mediator and mediatee.

Thoughtfulness. Intentionality means changing the stimulus and the mediatee while focusing simultaneously on both: What is the best *time* to see something? What is the most *attractive* way to present it? What is the most *effective* way to make children attend? To present something with intention is to select a goal, clarify it, focus on it, and make it immediate for yourself and for the children with whom you are interacting.

Multimodalities. The intention to mediate can be realized by communicating in any one of a multitude of ways—verbal, gestural, pictorial, or musical. Intention can mean changing the stimulus: amplifying, coloring, or giving it a special rhythm. The goal is to make the mediation conspicuous so that ultimately children can adopt the meaning apart from the lesson. Example: Children are learning a poem. The mediator says it with them, but instead of his usual rhythm, he enunciates every phrase slowly so the children can repeat; changes the flow and rhythm; alters the pitch. An interaction is efficient when it affects mediatees and they, as a result, become modified—or, in other words, learn.

> Intentionality is the most important criterion of a mediated learning experience.

Meaning

Meanings are the essence of stimuli. A single stimulus may contain multiple meanings, subtle shadings of meaning, and even opposing meanings.

Selecting a Meaning. Typically, meaning is thought of as vocabulary, or the definition of a word. Yet, words can have different meanings. The word *note*, for example, can mean a specific musical sound, a short written communication, a paper representing an amount of money, or to pay attention, as in "Take note."

Words in and of themselves may make little sense, as in the idioms "blow my top" and "hit the hay." Mediators are, in a sense, merely dispensers of the meaning intrinsic to objects, utterances, or situations. But, as a mediator, I determine *which* meaning I want to emphasize. Selecting a particular meaning gives value to an activity. When I value something, I embed its meaning in the task.

Conveying Meaning. Mediation of meaning starts the moment you present children with a stimulus. Simultaneously, you (1) prepare children to become open and (2) equip the stimulus to convey your meaning. By selecting a meaning you specify what you want children to attend to, deal with, and understand. *Why* is it important for you to know this? I want you to be able to repeat, use, own the meaning, and ultimately generalize from a single instance.

Instilling a Need for Meaning. At issue is how *much* meaning to impose. Some believe that they should not endow things with meaning, and that doing so disrespects others' individuality: If *I* select meaning subjectively, then I deprive *them* of objectivity. The question, however, is not, Am I disrespecting them? but, What *effect* will this have on them? Taking a step back out of respect creates a vacuum in children's ability to construe meaning. The issue is not whether children want a meaning other than what a mediator conveys, but *whether they develop the need to seek meaning.* When mediators are objective, it negates the orientation to look for meaning in whatever children find in the world—to ask the question, What does this mean?

"Inadvertently," says Feuerstein, "we have bred a generation with a kind of blind existence that is devoid of meaning." They have the human capacity to seek meaning, but

- they do not ask how or why,
- they are unaware of their capacity to attend to or ignore stimuli, and
- they fail to notice.

Meaning and Motivation. The tendency, or lack thereof, to seek meaning depends on how much meaning mothers, the first mediators, convey. Children who are immersed in stimuli without being able to ascribe meaning to them become impenetrable, and therefore unmodified by exposure. Watch youth absorbed in TV or video games. Not only do they fail to grasp meaning in the world around them, they fail to *want* to do so. Underachievers lack meaning-seeking behavior.

In contrast, if whatever we do is imbued with meaning—if we mediate for meaning—we begin to see hints of motivation, then its evolution, and eventually a disposition that inclines children to seek meaning. Offering meaning does not imply that children should keep that meaning throughout their lives. But without the need to find meaning, people feel empty; they lack goals and the energy to pursue them. What for? they ask. Why should I do this? What meaning will it have for me?

Meaning and Media. Many stimuli in today's world are conveyed through the media without meaning. Media dominate many children's lives; for some, it is their primary experience. Lewin-Benham has worked with 3- and 4-year-olds who talk only in the words superheroes use or with the noises of cartoons. As a result, the children are unfocused; each experience is an episode unto itself, disconnected from anything else. The children see no need to pay attention to stimuli, to convey meaning to others, or to fix meanings in their brain as the basis for further—and more advanced—thinking. Neil Postman (1931–2003), author, media critic, and NYU professor, called it "amusing ourselves to death" (1985).

> The purpose of mediating meaning is to instill a need to search for and find meaning and thereby connect individuals to the world around them.

Transcendence

Transcendence simply means that something *goes beyond*. Children connect what they are doing now to something they recall or something they imagine.

Transcendence and Complexity. An interaction usually occurs in response to a need that is created through the intention of the mediator. Mother–child interactions are the source of all human interaction. The child needs to eat, so the mother feeds it. How or where she feeds the child doesn't matter. *When* she feeds it matters because the need to eat is cyclic. The basic need is satisfied—somewhat—by the mere interaction. But transcendence means that, as the mother satisfies the need, she introduces something that has nothing to do with the action at hand. Maybe she sings a song, shows the child pictures, or reads a book.

The mother who simply teaches a child a particular bit of information does very little by way of mediation. But the mother who, along with food, provides information about order, cleanliness, manners, customs, and ideas creates those as new needs in the child. When children are given something that transcends a specific interaction, it motivates and prepares them to deal with increasingly complex situations.

Transcendence and Transfer. Transcending elements are vital in human mediation. They form what is called the "ever-expanding need systems of human needs" that have existed since humans' earliest days. The cat, in training her kittens, shows some intention, for example, making sure the kittens see how to dig a hole to bury their bowel movements. But humans are the only animals who transcend the immediate by expressing the meaning of present experience in terms of something children might encounter in the future.

Mediation for transcendence is a natural means of generalizing, of transferring what you learn to different situations that are somehow connected, but in an entirely different place, time, or context. Thus, over and beyond what is included in the interaction, I incorporate something that prepares children for further development, expectations, other needs, habits, and desires. This is the most humanizing part of mediation. The adult who merely says, "Do it because I say so," dehumanizes children, shuts down curiosity, and sets the stage for power struggles or passive acquiescence, two conditions that diminish spirit, intellectual capacity, and the motivation to learn.

Transcendence and Motivation. The transcendent goal may be the very impetus children need not to give up but to persevere *now*. Steven, age 8, was reluctant to practice skip counting. Lewin-Benham explained that skip counting is fundamental to many things that come later in math. She compared it to the need to know letter sounds in order to read and the need to understand the functions of different LEGO™ pieces in order to create your own objects. The examples made him receptive, and they drilled until he mastered skip counting by three. Transcendence prepares children to extend their need systems to large numbers of activities and interests, even to denial—postponing something pleasurable or foregoing a treat. We all have seen the seemingly inexplicable behavior of a person who has little to eat but spends his meager allotment on a concert ticket rather than a meal.

> Transcendence connects one's life to a past and a future.

Mediation and Motivation

B. R. was a cheerful baby, always smiling and cooperative, enthusiastic as a toddler and preschooler about every experience. At age 2, his smile felt like sunshine. At age 3, he engaged readily, regaling total strangers with songs, stories, or personal episodes; his enthusiasm and joy were contagious. B. R.'s mother was depressed and his father, desiring to help her, decided to make B. R. her constant companion. "She needs him to buoy her up" was how he put it. By age 7, B. R. pouted more often than he smiled, stressed over inconsequential things, and was frequently resistant. By age 10, his lack of motivation was one of his salient characteristics. His sunny disposition had been mediated—for the worse.

J. A., in contrast, by age 2 was intense, focused, with a clear sense of what she wanted. If something did not meet her expectations, she felt distraught and often cried. "C'mon," her father would say, with a huge smile. "Let me see you smile." And, despite herself, J. A. would break into a grin.

From birth through the early years, children learn by observing parents' actions, feeling their emotions, imitating their tone of voice, observing, copying, and gradually adapting—for better or worse—what they observe and how they are treated. B. R. adapted the affect of a depressed mother who at times ignored him and at other times scolded him for reasons unfathomable to B. R. The combination of a depressed role model and irrational (to him) treatment gradually shut down his naturally sunny disposition. J. A. had positive role models whose interactions were pleasant. Her parents respected the intensity in her nature. Her mother enveloped her in unqualified love and her father was able to change her attitude with his own sunny disposition or with subtle cajoling: "Gimme that smile!" With these models, by age 7 she took things in stride. Her intensity had been mediated—for the better. Mediation affects motivation, an important aspect of cognition. The nature of their disposition is strongly influenced by the emotional/cognitive surround in which children live (the nature/nurture dichotomy) during their formative years. For B. R., being the emotional support for a depressed mother was a greater burden than he could bear.

SUMMARY: A PICTURE OF MEDIATION

Mediation occurs in countless situations. In order to deepen understanding of what it means to mediate and to see the theory in action, we provide examples of innumerable situations in which mediation can be applied. Each chapter in this book highlights several parameters of mediation and expands parameters of mediation from the essential three—intention, meaning, and transcendence—across a broad spectrum of ways to mediate. In Chapter 3, we'll see mediation in action as children and their teacher use an FIE instrument.

Takeaways

1. Theory of Structural Cognitive Modifiability

    *   Human development occurs as a result of biology, environment, and mediation.
    *   Behavior represents individuals' temporary state, not their permanent traits.
    *   The brain is capable of change.

2. Mediation is a process capable of changing behaviors that suggest changes in the brain.
3. The *who* and *what* of mediation are its three partners: mediator, stimulus, and mediatee.
4. The *how* of mediation is the three essential parameters—intention, meaning, and transcendence—as well as many others.

CHAPTER 3

Mediated Learning in Action

Who taught him knowledge and showed him the way of understanding?

—Isaiah, 40:14

It is September, a new class, a new subject. On the cover page of an instrument from the Feuerstein Instrumental Enrichment-Standard (FIE-S) are:

- the title Organization of Dots,
- the face of a boy (or is it a girl?),
- five stars in a night sky,
- the words "Just a moment. . . . Let me think."

Twenty-six expectant 5th-graders watch the teacher. She begins: "Who can tell me what is on this page?"

This chapter gives a brief overview of the content of the Feuerstein Instrumental Enrichment (FIE) programs—the series of exercises that build specific and varied thinking abilities or diagnostically pinpoint thinking deficits. The focus of the chapter is on the "texture" of using mediation: what we would see were we to sit in a classroom and watch a teacher interact with students. Our purposes are to show mediation when it is

- the focus of classroom lessons, and
- carried out by pros.

The examples set a standard for the kind of effective interventions that make it likely children will learn.

In this chapter, we first briefly describe the FIE programs, then we observe two lessons.

THE FIE PROGRAMS: AN OVERVIEW

FIE-Standard (FIE-S) consists of 14 comprehensive series of exercises. Each series is called an instrument and is organized systematically according to specific, essential cognitive functions or, in other words, important thinking skills. In each instrument exercises repeatedly engage the *same* cognitive skills but apply them to increasingly difficult and diverse problems. The teacher presents the exercises page by page; pages are torn off a pad to maintain children's focus on *this* lesson rather than on a whole book or a next page. The FIE-S program is typically presented in two 45-minute periods per week over 2 or 3 years.

Feuerstein maintains that in the process of using the tasks, the brain becomes rewired because, through repetition, brain functions crystallize into new, permanently accessible thinking structures, called neuronal networks. Over time, research has accumulated showing that FIE and the underlying theories are effective in building cognition (Ben-Hur, 2008; Kozulin, 2006).

Observing a Mediator: FIE-Standard

The first four instruments in FIE-S are "foundational"; that is, they provide a platform of concepts and strategies essential to all thinking. The instruments are titled:

- Organization of Dots
- Orientation in Space I and II
- Comparisons
- Categorization

The next six instruments build diverse brain functions that are more complex and require operational thinking such as making analogies, inferences, and permutations. The last four require higher-order thinking and involve cognitive functions such as using syllogisms and transformations as well as higher levels of literacy and verbal comprehension.

Toward the end of each instrument, even highly proficient thinkers find the exercises challenging. To the amazement of many educators and psychologists, higher-order functions become accessible to children whose functioning was formerly compromised for one reason or another. "Accomplishments in the earlier instruments have changed their brain!" (Feuerstein, Feuerstein, Falik, & Rand, 2006, p. 212).

There are a great many objectives for each instrument; together, they enable students to use essential thinking skills such as:

> organization, planning, summation, categorization, analysis, both of materials and the sequence of operations. Precision, the use of time and space dimensions, restraint of impulsivity, and reduction of egocentric behavior are also indicated. There is an improvement both in problem-solving techniques and social interactions. (Feuerstein, Feuerstein, Falik, & Rand, 2006, p. 224)

The FIE instruments provide comprehensive and systematic ways to build cognitive structure.

Beginning an Instrument. This is day 1, lesson 1 of the 5th-graders' introduction to FIE-Standard. Organization of Dots is usually the first instrument presented because it establishes the reflective, questioning, intentional approach the teacher will use with all instruments. Beginning with the cover page (see Figure 3.1), the teacher orchestrates a focused conversation with the full class. With younger children or those whose functioning is compromised, the conversation might take place with a small group. With an unfocused child, it could take place one-on-one. The teacher asks questions, allowing answers to continue until all who want to contribute have done so. Typical questions are:

- What is the title?
- What does it mean?
- What does the expression on the figure's face mean?
- What are *you* thinking when you wear that expression?
- What might people be doing when they look like this? Why?
- What is the model's hand holding? Why?
- What are the implications?

The discussion reveals that the stars are *not* a "night sky"; they are clues to a pattern and a main purpose of exercises in this instrument is to find patterns.

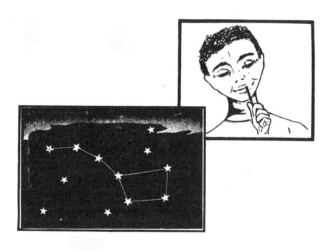

Figure 3.1. The cover page of each instrument has the logo, the thinking child, the slogan—"Just a minute . . . Let me think!", and an illustration conveying the type of exercises in the instrument.

JUST A MINUTE ...
LET ME THINK !

Note the word pattern. Pattern seeking is something the brain does spontaneously to make sense of the world. By making children aware that they are finding patterns, pattern seeking gradually becomes a technique that children use intentionally. In other words, children become conscious pattern seekers because the teacher has "mediated"—brought to children's attention, taught, emphasized, modeled, explained, repeatedly used—conscious pattern seeking as a thinking strategy.

The class is surprised when the bell rings. The students were so engrossed in the conversation, they did not notice time passing. Students' discussions about FIE instruments typically break the monotony of other classes where teachers lecture because in FIE classes students do most of the talking.

The many meanings that students contribute to discussions make students feel that their ideas are valuable. Such lessons are the opposite of "one-right-answer" classroom dialogue. Predetermined answers or formulaic lessons that spell out what teachers should say are not part of mediation. Rather than covering specific content, the goal is to make children conscious and aware of how they are thinking.

Establishing an Approach. At the second session, the discussion is about the meaning of the words "Just a moment . . . Let me think." As students brainstorm, the teacher draws a mind map of their ideas on the board. The exercise grabs students' interest and they become absorbed in describing mistakes they have made or observed others make. Their examples tumble one after another, words and phrases like "careless," "bugs me," "uh-oh!", "gets you in trouble." Gradually, the conversation converges on the thought, aptly expressed by one student, that you make mistakes when you hurry. The group concurs that hurrying and acting carelessly most precisely describe why they make mistakes.

The teacher provides very little information and, without damming students' enthusiasm:

- facilitates the discussion;
- acts as recorder;
- ensures that students listen to one another respectfully;
- sees that everyone participates;
- makes it clear that ridicule is inappropriate;
- takes care that no one dominates;
- keeps remarks focused on the topic or, in some way, related to it; and
- encourages the students to be more and more precise.

At the end, she asks students to summarize what the exercises are likely to involve and how they will be likely to think as they do them.

The conversation sets the tone for the entire instrumental enrichment program —students' deep engagement. The teacher has established an atypical norm:

- *Students'* ideas are the focus.
- The teacher does not lecture.
- Answers lead to more discussion.

The teacher has "mediated" careful observation, attentive listening, precise expression, and summative behavior. The class's motivation remains high when, during the third session, the teacher hands out the first page of exercises and says, "Let's begin."

Using the Exercises. The instrument Organization of Dots has 13 pages with 8 to 22 exercises on each page. In all exercises throughout this instrument (except the last three pages), students confront clouds of dots among which they must discern specific shapes that are presented in a model at the top of each page. Exercises on the last three pages use three-dimensional shapes. The shapes "become more intermingled and require progressively higher levels of discrimination, precision, and segregation. . . . A great deal of mental power has to be invested in scanning, focusing, transporting, planning, and anticipating" (Feuerstein, Feuerstein, Falik, & Rand, 2006, pp. 219–220).

On page one, the model shows two squares and a right-angle isosceles triangle. Many exercises follow, each with an amorphous cloud of dots. In that cloud, students must discern the pattern and, with a pencil, connect the dots that are *exactly* the same shape and size as the shapes in the model (see Figure 3.2). The catch is that the shapes are rotated in many orientations and may overlap one another. As clues, such as boldface dots, cease and rotations and overlapping increase, it becomes harder to distinguish which dot goes with which shape. As shapes become more complex, exercises quickly become difficult. By page six, students are seeking a four-pointed star and a compound shape made of a rectangle and semicircle.

The tasks require:

- projection of virtual relationships,
- conservation of constancy across positions of the figures,
- visual transport of the model into the cloud of dots,
- precision and accuracy,
- summative behavior,
- planning,
- restraint of impulsivity,
- discrimination,
- segregation of proximate [nearby] elements. (Feuerstein et al., 2006, pp. 215–219)

As the teacher "mediates," she brings to students' conscious awareness the many functions of the brain that they are using.

Page One: Organization of Dots. The teacher does not set the students to work in silent isolation. She places a transparency of the page on an overhead projector, switches on the lamp, and throws a huge copy of the image on a screen. The teacher has the class work together and think aloud. They group-solve the problems, as they did in the discussion about the cover page.

The teacher's first question is: "What's going on here?" She calls on Vernon, whom she knows can do the problem but who does not use words precisely. Vernon answers: "You make 'em like those." Motioning Vernon to the projected image, the teacher says: "Come show us." The first example is easy; the dots correspond

Figure 3.2. In the first exercises on page one of the instrument Organization of Dots (FIE-Standard), the extra-large, boldface dots guide children in how to solve the challenges.

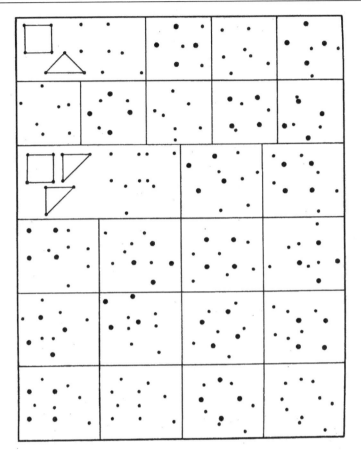

exactly to the positions of the figures, and Vernon rapidly and correctly traces all three figures.

The teacher calls on Jenny, who may not solve the problem but might be more articulate. It is an easy problem because, among the cloud of dots, the four that together make a square are oversize; they virtually jump off the page. "Jenny," she says, "do just one figure and talk to us as you do." Jenny responds: "I'm looking for a square and it's right here, so I'll draw from here to here, to here, to here," correctly connecting dots that make the same square as in the model.

The teacher then calls on a student who is very articulate: "John, talk us through the next." John, punctuating each movement with verbs and nouns, says: "I found the top of the triangle right here and am now connecting the first side, the base, and the third side."

> How students *phrase* problems and solutions to themselves is as important as their performance.

The teacher next calls on students she hopes will use the word *corner*, or who will count the dots, since some of the more advanced exercises have more dots than required. A more difficult Organization of Dots task is pictured in Figure 3.3.

Beginning Independent Work. As students show that they have developed an effective approach to the task, the teacher suggests that they work independently. She continues using new examples with the remaining students. If some fidget because the pace is too slow, the teacher suggests that they work on their own. The teacher continues with an increasingly smaller group. In this way, the teacher gives more support to students who require it. Eventually, all students are working independently at their own pace, the teacher circulating to observe and intervene as necessary. If the teacher sees need, she calls the entire class's attention to concepts, strategies, or vocabulary. The mediation of problem-solving approaches is an important teaching strategy.

Concluding a Session. The teacher stops students about 10 minutes before the end of class and triggers a debriefing with questions such as:

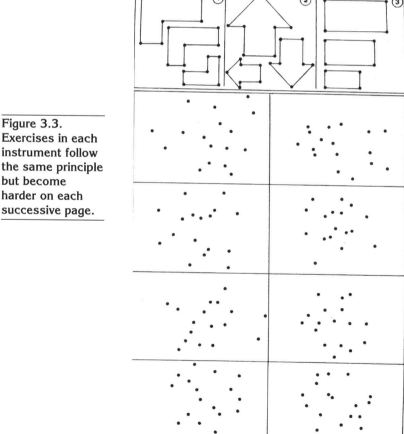

Figure 3.3.
Exercises in each
instrument follow
the same principle
but become
harder on each
successive page.

- How did you do the task?
- Where did you have difficulties?
- When you confronted difficulties, what strategies did you use to solve the problem?
- What does this remind you of?
- What have you learned from this?
- What kinds of thinking are you using?
- Can you think of another class in which a problem required you to use the same kind of thinking?
- To what other problems could what we learned today apply?

The last five questions are transcendent, that is, they stretch students' consideration of how this problem relates to others they may or may not have confronted. Again, the teacher notes on the board what students say, and students debate their increasing number of ideas, continuing the debate as they leave the room.

Teacher/mediators make sure students understand the value of what they are learning and the role the brain plays in everything they do. The interactive, responsive teaching is like mortar: It makes the elements of MLE theory into a cohesive structure. The goal is for students to succeed, and the mediator does whatever is necessary toward that end. David Perkins (1995) reviews four robust approaches to teaching intelligence, FIE among them. Perkins says: "Feuerstein conceived students' difficulties as attitudinal as [much as] cognitive. He wished not only to equip students with better cognitive skills but to instill in them positive, proactive attitudes toward thinking and learning and self-reliance as thinkers and learners" (Perkins, 1995, p. 188). FIE exercises are presented so that students not only become conscious of what thinking processes they are using but also enjoy learning to learn.

Observing a Mediator: FIE-Basic

The FIE-Basic program (FIE-B) is designed for children as young as 3 or 4 and up to age 9 or 10. FIE-B can be used diagnostically when teachers, parents, or psychologists suspect that a child may have learning problems. And FIE-B can be used with children whose progression is varied, which is typical of children in early grades. Because many cognitive skills are embedded in each exercise, FIE-B can be used with children who:

- have been diagnosed as having one or more learning difficulties,
- are stuck because they are "blind" to a cognitive skill that is essential to move to higher-level thinking,
- have not developed cognitive functions because of circumstances such as economic poverty, war, immigration, or other social forces.

A Diagnostic Tool. FIE-Basic (and FIE-Standard) can be used diagnostically to pinpoint students' thinking deficits. Teachers can move backward or forward through an instrument to find just where a child is stuck. For example, in Orientation in Space-Basic, a 5-year-old was unable to locate an object with a large black circle above it. So the teacher questioned and observed the child with the intent of determining if he knew this content:

- the adjectives *large* and *black,*
- the noun *circle,*
- the preposition *above.*

Learning that the student did know the content, the teacher concluded that the command *find* was causing the problem. Indeed, the teacher observed that the student lacked the ability to scan, that is, to systematically explore a page to find one particular image, so he taught the student to scan.

Another child lacked the ability to remember the adjectives *large* and *black* and the preposition *above.* The teacher repeated these words in game-like activities until the child used them readily.

> Because FIE-Basic instruments pinpoint problems, they are valuable for students who are either suspected of having problems using one or another cognitive function or who have been determined not to be able to use one or more cognitive functions.

A Cognition-Building Tool. Most FIE-Basic exercises picture compelling situations, some humorous, others preposterous, that mediators use to stimulate discussion. Through discussion, children develop basic cognitive skills such as:

- reciprocal exchange,
- learning to ask questions,
- learning to make comparisons,
- spotting the absurd,
- assessing another's emotions,
- orienting oneself in time and space.

The instruments build essential brain functions—focusing, scanning, labeling, positioning. The content and functions learned from FIE-Basic can be generalized to any subject.

At this writing, FIE-Basic consists of 11 instruments with others in development. Because it addresses basic skills, FIE-Basic contains far more content than FIE-Standard in which content is minimized in order to focus on cognitive processes. FIE-Basic also emphasizes the acquisition of an increasingly large vocabulary. The program has been tested in Israel, Belgium, Holland, Canada, Chile, Alaska, and elsewhere. "Research suggests that it is possible to significantly improve fluid intelligence in children with cognitive impairments using a comprehensive program such as [FIE-Basic]" (Kozulin et al., 2009, p. 9). A recent study confirms earlier findings (Salas et al., 2010).

Content and Concept Formation. It is essential to learn content in order to form concepts. And concepts are essential to establish relationships. For example, when you know the concept of color, you can think of the virtually limitless number of colors that exist, how paint behaves when you mix colors, why colors harmonize or clash, the ways different artists have used color, how color warns of danger, its meaning on flags and family crests, how the brain's visual system interprets color, or any of the limitless meanings that color brings to human experience.

Concepts are ways to organize the world; without concepts, content remains merely episodic. Episodic onetime experience is unlikely to turn passing thoughts into crystallized thinking. Crystallized thinking that is universally applicable is made possible by the creation of new neuronal pathways. Crystallizing thinking results from repeated experience.

> FIE instruments are organized to build systematically from content-laden, lower-level brain functions (FIE-B) to increasingly abstract thinking (FIE-S).

FIE LESSONS BY MEDIATORS

In both FIE-Basic and FIE-Standard, exercises are grouped logically by content, concept, or thinking skills and students repeatedly practice the same principle but meet the principle in varied exercises. Because exercises vary, they are not boring. With enough practice, the cycle of repetition/variation corrects deficient cognitive functions or strengthens fragile cognitive functions.

Spatial Organization in FIE-Basic

Eight-year-old Walter has a hard time following instructions because his sense of spatial relations is weak and, although he knows many nouns and verbs, he confuses spatial concepts, mixing up front and back or right and left. Moreover, he has difficulty following a sequence of instructions that depend on spatial relations. When a teacher says, "Bring your cards to the front of the room and stack them face-down on the right-hand side of the top shelf," Walter is lost. In the brain, the representation of space is closely aligned with movement centers. Sequencing is a motor activity that "involves maintaining and organizing the serial order of information and integrating this information with previously learned data. . . . Without this ability we would not be able to remember, learn, or even think" (Ratey, 2002, p. 177).

Walter's teacher, trained in FIE-Basic, knows that the instrument called Orientation in Space-Basic (see Figure 3.4) develops young children's competence in using spatial relations by helping them

- recognize, differentiate, and label positions in space;
- develop a vocabulary rich in spatial references, especially prepositions.

Having observed Walter's confusion using spatial references, the teacher begins by helping Walter learn these concepts—in, above, under, outside, behind, inside, in front of, and next to (Feuerstein & Feuerstein, 2003). If Walter grasps these quickly, the teacher will move on to inside, outside, and between.

Figure 3.4. Exercises in FIE-Basic use far more pictures than abstract symbols.

Some approaches to teaching spatial concepts have children use 3-D objects. Feuerstein prefers to use pictures because they enable teachers to be more precise and require children to translate words into images or vice versa. Translating words into images is a form of representation that requires switching modes. Therefore, it is a higher-level cognitive challenge than manipulating objects. Much thinking requires spatial representation.

Pinpointing Walter's Problem. The teacher directs Walter's attention to page one in Orientation in Space-Basic (see Figure 3.4). First, she makes sure that Walter is able to scan a field of information—in this case, the picture in the first exercise—in order to locate one particular thing. Scanning is an essential skill; children who cannot scan will not be able to focus. "Walter," she commands, "find the dog." Walter easily locates everything she names, including tiny details such as the red triangle on the flag and the lines that represent light coming from a lamp post. As she assesses Walter's scanning ability, the teacher also assesses whether he knows the names of shapes and colors and the concepts of color and size. He does. He easily finds all the objects, and uses their correct names and precise adjectives and adverbs. These are essential skills for proceeding with the exercises. Because Walter has these skills, the teacher moves ahead.

The second picture is the same as the first, but it abounds with shapes—a total of 31 circles, squares, and triangles plus one rectangle and four diamonds—in six different colors and two sizes. "Walter," she asks, "can you tell me where a large black circle is?" Walter intently scans the picture, quickly finds a black circle, and answers, "It is on the boy's head." The teacher continues: "And, can you tell me where a large black square is? " "Here," says Walter, "on the roof." From these two answers, the teacher sees that Walter's use of the word *on* is imprecise. The shapes are actually above, not on, the boy's head and the roof. The teacher continues with this page, observing and assessing Walter as she teaches him the precise location that each of the eight prepositions represents. After two lessons, Walter uses the prepositions quickly and precisely.

The exercises continue, with pairs of pages, identical except that assorted shapes abound on the second page of each pair. Once Walter uses prepositions fac-ilely, the teacher returns to the first page in the pair and says: "Make a mark *above* the motorbike." Mark-making requires representation that is more difficult than merely pointing. When Walter makes marks easily, the teacher gives him more dif-ficult challenges, to *draw* shapes of particular color and size at specific locations: "Make a big black triangle above the car." This requires accuracy in:

- visual tracking,
- spatial orientation,
- motor planning,
- coordination. (Feuerstein, Feuerstein, & Falik, 2004)

When they use Orientation in Space-Basic, children internalize a vocabulary that enables them not only to orient themselves in space, but also to represent relation-ships among different things with great precision.

Stretching Walter's Capacity. Exercises continue in seven pairs of pages with increasing difficulties—a denser field of objects, some irrelevant objects, more ab-stractions, more details. The spatial representations become more differentiated—for example, *between* and *in the middle*. Some require children to use *relational* concepts—high*er*, high*est*. As exercises become harder, children must both scan more carefully and use what they have just learned. The final pair of pages requires children to consolidate the concepts they have used in the first six pairs (Feuerstein, Feuerstein, & Falik, 2009).

> FIE-Basic exercises build a deeper understanding of concepts.

Spatial Organization in FIE-Standard

In FIE-S, spatial orientation exercises begin with pictures that require chil-dren to represent relationships among figures on a page—a house, bench, tree, and flowers—and a human figure facing in different directions (see Figure 3.5). In the first exercises, there are four figures, each facing either front, left, right, or back. For example, in the problem on the first line of exercise 1, children must state where the house is in relation to the figure in position 2 (the answer is behind). In the problem on the second line of exercise 1, children must state where the flowers are in relation to the figure in position 3 (the answer is to the right). As exercises become more difficult, children are challenged to represent increasingly difficult spatial relations. The hardest exercises are abstract: Dots represent objects and arrows represent the direction in which the figure would face if the dot were to the left, to the right, and so forth (see Figure 3.6).

Figure 3.5. Beginning exercises in Orientation in Space (FIE-Standard) use easy-to-recognize pictures—a child, a house, flowers, and the like.

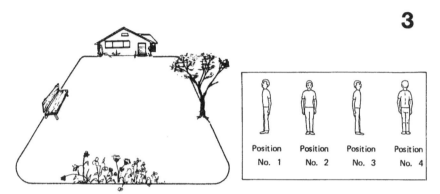

I.   Where are the objects located in relation to the boy?

Position	Object	Direction in Relation to the Boy
2	The house	
3	The flowers	
1	The flowers	
4	The tree	
3	The bench	
3	The tree	
1	The house	
4	The bench	

II.   What is the object?

Position	Direction in Relation to the Boy	Object
1	right	
2	front	
3	left	
4	back	
4	front	
3	back	
2	left	
1	back	

Figure 3.6. Later exercises in Orientation in Space (FIE-Standard) use abstract symbols—in this example, arrows and dots.

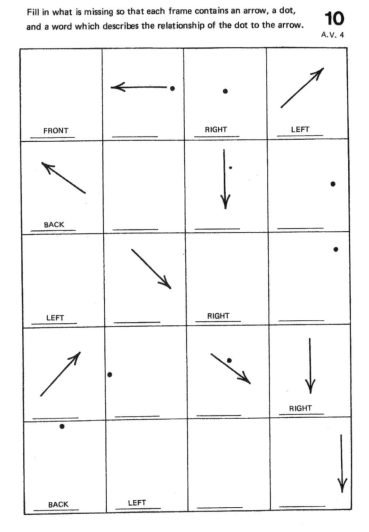

Fill in what is missing so that each frame contains an arrow, a dot, and a word which describes the relationship of the dot to the arrow.

10

A.V. 4

Initially, one's own body movement serves as the basis for the discrimination and division of the world into dimensions of left/right or front/back. Symbols force a detachment from using one's body to orient in space. The axis of the body continues to serve as the basis for the distinction, but is no longer the sole criterion. Tasks are again varied and the level of abstraction increases as tasks cease to depict concrete objects (Feuerstein, Feuerstein, Falik, & Rand, 2006).

Each FIE instrument addresses different clusters of brain functions to help children gradually master them.

SUMMARY: IMAGINATIVE, AUTHORITATIVE, AND RESPONSIVE TEACHING

The textbook on Instrumental Enrichment, with oversize pages and many figures, devotes 98 of 476 pages to FIE-Standard, and includes applications to special populations such as the blind or youngsters in early grades. Two-week summer training courses, held in different parts of the United States and other countries abroad, instruct participants in the theory and use of the instruments. Check it out online by Googling *Feuerstein* or *ICELP*.

Mediators, tutors, teachers, exhibit guides, parents, or other adults create an orientation to learn: The adult establishes the nature of interactions, manages their flow, and ultimately guides students through a learning process. The process literally "trains" (Posner et al., 2008, pp. 1–10) the brain so that children learn how to learn.

The mediation techniques we have seen in this chapter are:

- slowing down or speeding up children's pace;
- increasing children's feeling of competence;
- teaching with intention, meaning, and transcendence;
- training children to take a moment to think;
- asking children to seek patterns;
- learning how to make mind maps;
- labeling precisely;
- concluding experiences by thinking about summative questions;
- orienting oneself in space with increasing precision and abstraction;
- solving novel and complex challenges.

These techniques are all examples of different parameters of mediation.

"Activities that challenge your brain actually expand the number and strength of neural connections devoted to the skill" (Ratey, 2002, p. 37). The more a strategy is repeated, the more likely it is to become habituated. Once it is habituated, children can use the strategy confidently in situations that require the kinds of novel, challenging, and creative solutions portrayed in this book. In Chapter 4, we will watch master teachers in three different lessons.

Takeaways

1. Effective lessons first introduce children to how to approach an exercise.
2. Children learn from listening and responding to one another's thoughts.
3. Specific cognitive deficiencies—such as a lack of systematic seeking or disordered spatial relations—require point-blank attention with teaching and exercises (or stimuli) designed to address and "fix" the deficiency.

CHAPTER 4

Expert Mediators

Let knowledge grow from more to more.

—Alfred, Lord Tennyson, 1849

IN THIS CHAPTER, we use three scenarios—two classroom experiences and a museum exhibit—that show the three defining characteristics of mediation—intention, meaning, and transcendence. Mediation is an intervention: An adult interacts with a child with the intent of helping the child learn something specific. Mediation is fundamentally about change. Theory and practices aside, mediation is only effective if a teacher *believes* that children can change. Overwhelmed that 1.5 million children were murdered and a generation was essentially wiped out in the Holocaust, Feuerstein knew the Jewish people could not afford to lose even one additional child, that every child still alive needed to be reclaimed, to return to a normal life, to think, sing, live, love, experience joy. The intensity of this need *compelled* him to believe that he could change children. "If you believe a child can change," he says, "you will do something to make sure he does. If you don't believe, you don't do." "Among all the things we can learn from Feuerstein," says Lewin-Benham, "perhaps the most important is to consider, as we approach a child, what we believe about him, what we hope for her."

Mediators can be parents, museum guides, school teachers, or any adult who wants to teach something to a child. Mediators must select a specific stimulus with the intention that children:

- become aware of the stimulus;
- perceive all aspects of the stimulus;
- understand what the mediator intends to convey by using the particular stimulus;
- realize that a stimulus can be transformed, that its value transcends to other situations.

The following stories show what it means for teachers to use the three key parameters of mediated interactions:

- intervene in children's activity with intention,
- convey a particular meaning of a stimulus,
- make stimuli so powerful that both the immediate and transcendent meanings are apparent to children.

Contrast the experiences of two children in light of their teachers' beliefs and hopes. Eight-year-old Jimmy has an engaging personality, great sense of humor, talks articulately and passionately about deep interests, and revels in describing inventions he will make, people he knows, stories he's heard. He is a 3rd-grader but is more typical of a 1st-grader: He squirms on his chair; if he remembers his papers, they are scattered about. His handwriting is imprecise, only passing resemblance to letters or numbers, barely related to the position of the lines on the paper. His teacher only sees his negative traits—disorganization and reading skills that are not up to those of his peers. She has bought into the school's drill/kill program; her room is mainly silent as she paces the class through lessons in the teacher's guide. If passion for engaging children's minds brought her into teaching, it is not evident. She merely wants her children to pass the state tests. Most of her effort focuses on test prep.

In the 3rd-grade classroom next door, Laura's reading skills are the least developed. Unlike Jimmy, she has a meager vocabulary and is unable to retell facts from well-known stories like "Jack and the Beanstalk." Her teacher has taught the children to work independently, speak without shouting, walk rather than run, put things away, and not fight. He has organized both the classroom and his time so that he can instruct children one at a time and thereby focus his full attention on each child individually. He has many materials that challenge children to think and can be used independently by a single child or by a small group. His rules are clear: Put it away when you are finished; ask John if you may join him. The children have been trained in where things go, how many can play specific games, what voice level to use, and other rules that make the system of individualized instruction possible.

The time the teacher spends teaching writing, reading, or math skills to individual children is efficient because he works with just one child. When the teacher singles out Laura, he focuses on specific thinking skills such as building memory for logical sequence. He does this by, for example, asking what's wrong in a series of pictures with an absurd element—the top not screwed on when the milk is returned to the refrigerator, the leash put on the dog after its walk. When the teacher made a presentation to a civic group, volunteers, attracted by his organization, offered an hour per week to support children who work independently. The teacher wants to prepare his children to reach high academic goals. Jimmy's teacher has not been exposed to techniques of mediation; Laura's teacher is a natural mediator. Neither Jimmy's nor Laura's teacher has heard of mediation or Feuerstein. But if training in Instrumental Enrichment were offered, we can guess who would enroll.

MEDIATION IN TWO CLASSROOMS

Two scenarios show how teachers who excel as mediators use intention to help children focus, meaning to build diverse capacities, and transcendence to help children build relationships between past, present, and future experiences. One scenario takes place at the Model Early Learning Center (MELC), the other in a

Reggio Emilia (Italy) school. The MELC was a school for Head Start–eligible 3- to 6-year-olds located in the "slums" near the U.S. Capitol in Washington, D.C. Most MELC children began with limited language—sparse vocabulary, few concepts—circumstances caused by economic poverty. Practices throughout the school were based on mediation—teachers' intentional intervention in all children's activities. The following example shows how the children's interest in their own and their friends' birthdays became the stimulus to build vocabulary, develop awareness of others, and become able to conceive an idea and realize it in three dimensions by collaborating with others. The second school example shows a project that motivated children to solve a big challenge. Clay was the stimulus.

A Year of Birthdays

The MELC developed elaborate birthday routines that continued throughout each year and became a favorite activity. Mediation involved *intentional* use of varied stimuli to convey the *meaning* of birthdays and to *transcend* from birthdays to the meaning of friendship. The experience was effective because it used something of keen interest to children and their families and provided limitless ways for children to express themselves.

Universal Interest. For anyone, his or her own birthday is special. The MELC teachers involved parents in deciding how to hold celebrations that would affirm each child's specialness but not burden families. The decision was to hold parties at school in which a small group of a birthday child's best friends, in collaboration with a teacher:

- determined the birthday child's favorite activity,
- decided what gift to make to reflect the favorite activity,
- considered how best to make the gift and then did so,
- figured out what all other party arrangements should be,
- carried out the arrangements.

Limitless Modes of Expression. Children vary greatly in all ways, including expressive capacity. One of the MELC's goals was to increase this capacity by helping children learn many varied means of expression. The renowned educators in Reggio Emilia, Italy, call these means of expression "100 languages." Psychologist Howard Gardner calls it "multiple intelligences." Feuerstein calls it learning "modes of expression" and believes that learning different ways to express an experience ultimately leads to insight. Gift-making fulfilled the goal of helping children expand the number of ways in which they could express themselves. The gifts were complex—so competently executed, you had to remind yourself how young the children were who made them (Lewin-Benham, 2008).

Children developed their ideas and executed the gift-making and party-giving after extensive conversation orchestrated by their teacher. Through conversation they expressed opinions, exchanged ideas, argued, debated, and resolved differences, all influenced by one another. The children's interest was intense because:

- The ideas for gifts were theirs—to make a turtle for Howard because he was fascinated with how turtles move.
- They used an endless variety of materials to express their ideas—cardboard for Ronald's robot, large sheets of colored tissue paper to hide Galeesa's surprise bundle of balloons, paper they painted themselves to wrap the book they made for Frank of his friend's photos.
- There were opportunities to use complex and demanding tools and materials—fine-point markers to make precise lines, decorate, or write messages; scissors, hole punch, or with the teacher, paper cutter or ice pick.
- Their teachers were expert mediators.

The gifts the children made reflected tremendous achievements, as these examples show:

- creative expression in the pocketbook for Lorian, textured in papier-mâché, painted a rich pink, her favorite color, and finished with a wide ribbon for a strap;
- the ability to analyze and make appropriate choices like boxes in sizes to represent a robot's body, Ronald's gift;
- competence using many different tools such as rulers and stencils that demand tremendous hand control and some understanding of numbers, the latter usually with a teacher's help since few children of this age understand rulers' numerical properties;
- understanding of others' mind-sets as reflected in the utter delight with which all children received their gifts;
- skill at collaborating, as shown in the children's ability to work in small groups to produce gifts for 36 different classmates.

Children's work was significant—original, creative, complex, competent, and joyfully executed and received.

The experience continued over several school years. The next year, the gift was a portrait and written description of the birthday child. The year after, it was a song, and the year after that, a dance—all conceived and made by small groups of best friends to represent each birthday child's specialness.

Mediation at Work. Gift-making required children to be aware of and to use:

- dimension, as in the fire engine that Willie and Akil made for DeMarcos;
- color, as in the calendar four girls made for Cemetria with a beautifully painted picture for each month;
- materials' different attributes, as in the necklace made for Latricia from papier-mâché beads, seeds, and other materials that could be hole-punched and strung;
- assorted mark-makers, as in the writing materials assembled and packaged for Angela, who loved to correspond;

- glue, as in the truck for Xavier, large and elaborate, with features—glued on—that every boy yearns for on a truck;
- scissors, as in the drums for Otis decorated in lively cut-paper shapes.

The use of so many materials and tools required precise movement and varied skills involving hand/eye/brain/body coordination.

The project required children to:

- concentrate intently on what they were making;
- express empathy through their perception of friends' deep desires;
- use receptive capacities to distinguish subtleties in materials;
- use expressive skills in widely different modes—graphic, figural, auditory, tactile, visual, verbal;
- represent ideas by transforming them into words, drawings, and 3-D objects.

Transformation from one mode to another is a high-level brain function that requires holding some aspects of an idea constant while varying others or changing the form (recall the word/image transformation, Chapter 3). The principle of transformation lies at the heart of most scientific processes.

The teachers' *intention* was to support children's efforts to create something complex by a particular deadline. They focused the children on the *meaning* of:

- understanding another individual's interests,
- imagining how to embody that interest in a "thing" their friend would like,
- selecting the most suitable materials to make the thing,
- turning an idea into a reality,
- collaborating,
- being aware of passing time.

Teachers developed the *transcendent aspects* of birthdays, with an emphasis on the relationship between birthday celebrations and friendship, through frequent discussions with the children. Children were "mediated" in many ways to feel competent; share behavior; seek individuation and psychological differentiation; set, plan, and achieve goals; focus; select stimuli; and schedule complex acts (Feuerstein, Rand, & Feuerstein, 2006).

> Mediation made the children aware of the complexities of producing diverse objects, established a disposition to enjoy 3-D problem solving and appreciate hand skills, and laid the groundwork for engaging in productive work throughout life.

Horses and Riders

Intention, meaning, and transcendence may be part of a teacher's repertoire, but if not used *consciously* or *systematically*, may fail to affect children's thinking.

The intention to mediate heightens teachers' consciousness of all their actions. Being conscious is a cognitive act; it's the impetus that propels a person—teacher or child—to do something or think something through. Cognition concerns the structure of how the mind is involved—thinking about *what* I do, *how* I do it, and the *when* and *where* of actions.

Many teachers are natural mediators; growing numbers of them have been trained in Feuerstein's theories and techniques in formal courses offered by the ICELP, Feuerstein's own institute, or by other organizations certified by the ICELP. Worldwide, there are 70 Authorized Training Centers (ATCs) where teachers can train. Teachers in the many Reggio Emilia schools, though they are unfamiliar with Feuerstein and MLE theory, are a rare cluster of exceptional mediators. Consider this story from a Reggio class of 4½- and 5-year-olds.

A Difficult Challenge. The teacher had given four children a challenge with clear *intention*: Make a clay horse and a clay rider to seat on its back. The medium was low-fire clay, an artist's material requiring competent hands and some familiarity with techniques for working clay. Artists' clay is a satisfying medium for persons of any age. Unlike play-dough, a more commonly used material, artists' clay requires some oomph to fashion it—fingers to pinch, gouge, smooth, or coil; hands to squeeze, pull, push, pound, or roll in order to work the clay.

The *meaning* in the project was clear: The shapes of horses and people are constrained by nature and a sculptor must adhere to those constraints in order to make a horse that will support a rider and a rider that will sit upright on a horse's back. The children's challenge was to deal with those constraints.

Many *transcendent principles* could be drawn from the lesson:

- balancing one figure on another is a function of the shape, size, weight, and position of both figures;
- focus and scheduling are essential steps in a process;
- it takes time to accomplish big things;
- difficult challenges have periods of frustration;
- when challenges are met, it is intensely satisfying.

The lesson began with the teacher's announcing in the commanding tone typical of Reggio teachers, *"Alora! Attenzione!"* Such announcements engage the brain's attention systems. Four good-sized hunks of clay, each as large as a big loaf of bread, sat on the table along with tools to shape clay and wooden slats to support figures. There were many possibilities for integrating the figures, but also much danger:

> Tomas and Fabio had each made a horse of sorts. "Thicker here," said Tomas, adding a hunk of clay between his horse's two hind legs, making its rear more like a tree stump. Fabio had his own problems. His horse stood, but he could not imagine how to seat the rider. Realizing he needed more stability, he pushed the horse's back almost onto the table, and commented, "It's better like this."
>   Vea, the teacher, watched the progress, knowing what experiences these children had and having used clay with many other children over 20

years. . . . "What have we here, Tomas?" asked Vea, looking at his tree stump. She left the room, returning shortly with wooden support pieces. Tomas took one, wrinkled his face, removed the offending hunk of clay, reworked the legs to their original shape, and quickly shoved a support under the belly. "Ah!" exclaimed Vea with pleasure, "now the horse stands like a horse."

Fabio protested: "But horses do not have wood underneath. . . ." "*Mine* does," said Tomas, pleased with the shapely hind legs and proud his horse was standing. Fabio, unsure about the wood, turned to Vea. "Yes," she nodded matter-of-factly, "the wood is alright." Still not convinced, Fabio pounded his animal's back [until] it was spread so flat the horse shape was barely recognizable. "And, Fabio," Vea asked, "how will such a horse hold a rider?"

The Challenge Is Met. In Vea's selecting the problem, in her interactions with the children, in her support and challenges, we see highly skilled mediation.

By morning's end, Tomas had gone back and forth from shapely to stumpy legs, settling at last for a horse with rather stumpy legs with wood supports, but a horse that would support a rider. Fabio solved his problem by incorporating wood supports for rider *and* horse. Vea had questioned, encouraged, and provided materials, some requested by the children, some suggested by her (Lewin-Benham, 2006).

Mediation at Work. The *meaning* of the project is that children analyzed a tough problem in the medium of clay and solved the problem. The *intention* is the many specific cognitive processes the children used to solve the problem, to name a few:

- focus in moving forward with a task despite frustrations;
- mental representation to envision what the words horse supports rider or rider on horse might look like shaped in clay;
- sequencing in making horse first, then rider, then joining the two;
- planning to determine how much clay to use for different body parts or how a horse must be shaped to support a rider;
- analysis to balance one clay figure upon another, or determine the relative size of each;
- anticipation of consequences such as a horse buckling under the weight of a rider or a rider flopping or falling off a horse;
- "hand smarts" in learning to make two complex figures from a medium as demanding as artists' clay.

The project's *transcendent aspects* are (1) the varied solutions and explanations offered by each child and countered or affirmed by the other children and the teacher, and (2) how, on subsequent days and at other times, Vea will build other experiences on this one.

> Effective mediators stimulate competent work by interacting with *intention*, conveying *meaning*, and making stimuli so powerful that both the immediate and *transcendent* meanings are apparent to children.

MEDIATION IN AN EXHIBIT

At the Capital Children's Museum (CCM) we created "Remember the Children," an exhibit on the Holocaust. Here, we use the exhibit to show what it means to intentionally imbue stimuli with meaning and transcendent meaning. In a later chapter, we use this exhibit to show how to evoke young children's empathy, a higher-level brain function.

The "Remember the Children" Exhibit

The purpose of the "Remember the Children" exhibit was to stimulate young visitors to grapple with the meaning of prejudice. The exhibit was later adopted by the U.S. Holocaust Memorial Museum (USHMM) in Washington, D.C., as its permanent children's exhibit, where it is called "Daniel's Story."

The CCM exhibit incorporated many mediation techniques:

- intentionally using extremely varied stimuli—video, audio, numerous re-created environments, discussion, activities such as painting a porcelain tile, writing a comment, or using symbols to express the meaning of the experience;
- conveying the meaning of one particular story;
- transcending the story to show its relation to the universal human condition.

The exhibit was effective. As demonstrated here, it arrested visitors' attention, caused cognitive dissonance, and provided varied ways to resolve the dissonance.

Cognitive Dissonance. The experience was startling. Led by the voice of a 10-year-old Holocaust victim, visitors walked down a typical street of gracious townhouses, through a beautiful home, then onto a street swarming with children, suitcases in hand. Visitors were then herded into a walled-in area teeming with people. Finally, they entered a cramped, decrepit ghetto apartment (see Figure 4.1). Obviously, something terrifying had happened. The contrast between the beautiful home and the ghetto apartment made visitors hyperalert emotionally. They felt sympathy and identified with the victims, realizing that what had happened here could happen anywhere, could happen to me! In this anxious state, visitors were compelled to seek resolution, to lessen or dispel their anxiety.

Resolution. The exhibit offered many ways to resolve the conflict. Visitors could:

- Snuggle against comfortable pillows in a library-like area to read and discuss one of many books about children's experiences in the Holocaust. Like Anne Frank, many children who lived through the Holocaust wrote diaries; hers became the best known.
- Record thoughts, stirred by the exhibit, in a special book.
- Paint a ceramic tile as a memorial to children murdered in the Holocaust.

Figure 4.1. Visiting the decrepit room in a ghetto apartment strongly roused children's empathy for victims of the Holocaust.

- Hear a Holocaust survivor speak.
- Question survivors about their experiences.
- Watch a computer print out continually lengthen as each minute the computer printed several new names of children who were Holocaust victims.
- Observe a large electric counter that began at number 1 the moment the exhibit opened and continued counting to 1.5 million, the number of children murdered in the Holocaust.
- Study a bulletin board of news clips on current instances of human rights violations and their impact on individuals, families, neighborhoods, nations, whole regions, or the entire world.
- Manipulate a hands-on exhibit on prejudice and discuss it with a museum guide or other adult.

Because children were engaged in varied, repetitive ways to confront and overcome emotional conflict, they learned. This was evident in what children wrote in the special book that stood on a spot-lit pedestal just outside the ghetto environment—remarks such as: "Why did this happen just because someone was Jewish?" Or, "I hope such an awful, terrible thing never again happens in the world." What children learned was also evident in the ceramic tiles they painted as a memorial to Holocaust victims. Their strong images expressed empathy, anger, hope, dismay—a whole range of emotions.

The Exhibit's Hallmarks

The techniques the museum staff used in creating the exhibit reflect central principles of mediation and show mediation at work. The techniques are:

- incongruence in the difference between the beautiful home and decrepit ghetto apartment;
- repetition in the numerous yet varied ways to process emotions and thoughts aroused by the exhibit;
- transformation in turning fear into positive responses through discussion, reading, writing, drawing, or in other ways processing the experience.

The museum's experiences required visitors to:

- concentrate on the story line and details of Daniel's life;
- receive information in varied modes—visual, auditory, kinesthetic (movement), music;
- orient themselves in space by following the sinuous path through changing exhibit environments;
- overcome fear by engaging in various activities to analyze emotions thoughtfully;
- express empathy by using Daniel's story as a lens through which to view their own experiences at home, on the playground, in the classroom, or in viewing the news.

To convey intention, meaning, and transcendent ideas, museum staff designed the exhibit by consciously using:

- dimension in re-creating all aspects of several environments in which Daniel lived;
- light to change the mood in different environments or draw attention to an object, such as the spotlight that shone on the book in which children wrote comments;
- color, which segued from the black-and-white introductory film to the full-color images of the neighborhood where Daniel lived, or from Daniel's warm and inviting home to drab ghetto apartment;
- analogy in applying the idea of prejudice, aroused by the exhibit, to circumstances in one's own experience;
- contrast in the varied ways each visitor reacted to the exhibit or to the changes in Daniel's life;
- music that changed in mood and key as it played in the different environments to accompany changes in Daniel's life;
- storytelling in Daniel's story, in one of the many books written for or by children about the Holocaust and available in the exhibit library, or in the experiences of Holocaust survivors who told and discussed their own stories as part of the exhibit experience.

Human Mediation

Well-trained staff and volunteers, including Holocaust survivors, were integral to the experience. Each group of children listened to a survivor tell his or her story, and the children were encouraged to ask questions about the survivors' experiences and the exhibit. Children were "mediated" to confront the past experience of the Holocaust, to face the present reality of sarcasm or prejudice in their own lives, to face the realities of persecution or genocide, to perceive feelings of others they knew or had read about, to form values about how people treat one another, and to represent the future in their expressions of hope for a better world. These are all parameters of mediation (Feuerstein, Rand, & Feuerstein, 2006).

Mediation was the keynote of the exhibit and was successful because visits were planned with as much time for discussion as for experiencing Daniel's story and engaging in the various exhibit activities. Discussion was the main technique to encourage visitors to reflect, analyze, summarize, disagree or concur, and through common experience, share their reactions.

> Principles of mediation can be adapted to any situation where one wants another person to learn something.

SUMMARY

Throughout these stories, we have woven labels for different criteria of mediated learning experiences: *awareness* in the Holocaust exhibit, *sharing behavior* in the birthday gifts, *competence* in the working of clay, *focus* in all the stories. Such descriptive words are mediators' tools—concepts that enable them to apply these techniques in different situations. "Representations without concepts are blind. Concepts without representations are empty" (Kant, 1991). Concepts organize the world and enable people to experience "cognitive distance," going beyond the immediate experience and using creativity, fantasy, intuition, or imagination about the wider world.

Feuerstein says:

I did not invent mediation. My mother knew it long before I was even born. I merely watched what she did and followed her steps. Mediation is the way generation after generation has improved its life by using experiences of the prior generation. Humanity's progress is assured by the fact that experiences are transmitted to the next generation. Mothers are natural mediators and the foremost transmitters of culture, ideas, and values. They do so in the most wonderful ways.

Feuerstein spent a year in residence at Yale, where he and James Comer, professor of Child Psychiatry and a leader in his field, became friends. Feuerstein relates how Comer told him that as a child he questioned his mother about how she could be a housekeeper. She taught him, Comer explained, that the work you do does not matter so much as *how* you do it, and to strive for perfection no matter what you do.

Takeaways

1. Mediation can help adults guide children to develop increasingly sophisticated thinking, values, and feelings.
2. Mediation is a way to generalize thinking so that children acquire an approach to learning and the ability to use specific thinking skills in a variety of experiences.
3. FIE is one way, but only one, to stretch children's thinking; examples throughout this book show others.

CHAPTER 5

Four Essential Cognitive Acts

Like a long-legged fly upon the stream
His mind moves upon silence.

—William Butler Yeats, 1946

A T THE CAPITAL CHILDREN'S MUSEUM (CCM), 7-year-old Rachael
learned that the world is round. Her uncle was an avid traveler. From infancy she had heard, "Uncle Eddie's going around the world." At age 4,
when asked what that meant, Rachael answered, "My uncle is going away." Or,
"He is taking a suitcase." The words *around the world* had no meaning.

Visiting CCM, Rachael's mother pointed to a globe hanging from the
ceiling—making sure Rachael was paying attention—and told her it was the
world. Rachael exclaimed, "Oh! Uncle Eddie's going *around the world*!" This
was an "a-ha" moment when, in a flash, something Rachael had heard acquired
meaning. Psychologists say Rachael built a new schemata—a way for her brain
to organize experience—because her mind was prepared and she had been mediated in these ways:

- She had often heard the words around the world.
- The words were motivating because they were used about someone she loved.
- Her mother carefully alerted her to look at a powerful stimulus.
- Because the stimulus was a concrete example, it gave the experience meaning.

In this chapter, we look at four cognitive acts that underlie all thinking: attention, imitation, spatial orientation, and movement. We first examine the behavior
of children who are weak in these areas, then describe how to build strength so
that children form new schemata.

ACQUIRING BASIC COMPETENCIES

Learning is most likely to occur if (1) a mind is prepared by past mediation so
that it is accustomed to observing, comparing, making analogies, and building
relations; or (2), if an adult intervenes at a propitious moment when children are
engaged and are curious, struggling, perplexed, or in other ways open to receive

mediation. If children have not been mediated in the past to notice and to seek explanation, or if too many perplexed moments pass with no one to mediate, the chance of learning is greatly diminished.

The lower-level, or essential, skills children are most likely to learn in museums are to:

- maintain attention even with enormous distractions (provided they're not dragged off to see something else);
- rehearse actions that, through play and imitation, develop procedural memory;
- orient spatially, a skill that, ultimately, enables us to take another person's perspective;
- master movements that build specific skills and, as a result, self-confidence.

"Lower-level" does not mean less important; in fact, it's just the opposite. Lower-level skills are essential for children to develop higher-level, efficient thinking and to form *schemata*, psychologists' word for mental images, models, or concepts. Schemata do not resemble real objects; they are not "little pictures in the brain," but are neurons that trigger responses in other neurons. Perkins (1992) says schemata are "a holistic, highly integrated kind of knowledge. It is any unified, overarching mental representation that helps us work with a topic or subject" (p. 80).

Sometimes children fail to learn because they:

- have blurred perception and unfocused attention,
- imitate without awareness or consciousness that they are doing so,
- are spatially disoriented, or
- have motor deficiencies that prevent their learning.

Here, we elaborate each of these circumstances.

Attention: The First Act in All Learning

Paying attention involves numerous brain systems, each consisting of many other complex systems that perform myriad actions, each orchestrated by the brain to occur in logical sequence so that brain and body function smoothly and seamlessly. Failure in any single action, no matter how trivial it seems, can cause blurred perception. We are reminded of the anonymous couplet:

> The massive gates of circumstance
> Are turned upon the smallest hinge.
> Thus some seeming pettiest chance
> Oft gives our life its after tinge.

"Chance" in the brain is not accidental; it is the firing of neurons that, through repetition of the same experience, have learned to fire together. Otherwise, the couplet is a good metaphor: Seemingly small things in the brain can have tremendous consequences in a child's understanding, behavior, and motivation. Here, we focus on one aspect of attention, what Feuerstein calls "blurred perception."

The Limitations of Blurred Perception. This means that children do not look closely enough to see all aspects of an experience's salient features. For example, children:

- watching a ball on an incline would not notice the incline's pitch;
- watching a boiling pot would not notice the steam;
- pouring water into connected vessels would fail to notice the level of the water equalize;
- trying to find their way through a maze would not conceptualize orientations such as right, left, ahead, or behind;
- doing a paper and pencil task would fail to read all the instructions;
- searching for an example would not scan systematically.

Children with blurred perception may not:

- see all dimensions of an object;
- connect two or more pieces of data;
- notice the cause(s) of an effect.

With blurred perception, children see a person facing backward in a saddle and do not perceive it as a problem. They would not predict how a cube might behave differently from a ball on a runway. They would not perceive outcomes such as losing equilibrium if you walk in a room with a tilted floor or having your hair fly awry if you walk in front of a fan. They neither recognize illogical actions nor know how to build a logical sequence of actions.

Strategies to Reverse Blurred Perception. To overcome blurred perception, someone must call children's attention to—or mediate—the salient features of an experience and encourage or demonstrate how to seek and recognize salient features. Parents and educators can do this by guiding children to

- direct their attention: "Tom! Follow my finger!"
- identify what they see: "Mary, name the shapes, their size and color."
- use comparative behavior: "Find the object that is bigger than all the others."
- precisely describe what they see: "How would you describe this room to someone who has never seen it?"

Overcoming blurred perception requires teachers to help students focus by maintaining their attention, noticing salient features, remembering salient features, and relating what they notice through comparison and repetition. These words, although written succinctly, suggest a process that is not succinct: One-on-one interaction for however long is necessary—1 year, perhaps 2 or 3. The process requires patient, persistent intervention by a teacher whose intention, in each lesson, is clear, focused, reflective, and varied; by a teacher who is clever at keeping attention focused, inventive in selecting stimuli, and generous in praising each success, no matter how small the progress may seem to be. In the child's brain, which is being "trained" by the teacher/mediator, seemingly small progress may indicate massive realignment of neurons. Using diverse stimuli and techniques enables mediators to work with children of widely varied abilities.

Imitation: An Inborn Way to Learn

Children imitate naturally, but some are unconscious of the fact and imitate without knowing they are imitating. Other children are selective and imitate only someone they identify with or objects that attract them. Others lack the cognitive ability to select a stimulus on which to focus. To overcome children's lack of awareness that they are imitating or imitating in a limited way, a mediator must:

- direct children to focus on how they are attending to a stimulus: "Marcus, be sure to look at all three angles of the triangle."
- encourage children to observe how they are performing (or failing to perform): "Shameka, listen carefully so you can repeat exactly what I say."
- guide children to analyze which specific behaviors one uses when imitating: "Johnnie, watch yourself as you mimic Rob and describe everything you do."

Children with ADHD may not have been taught to focus on stimuli or to be conscious of the detailed actions that make up the process of imitating. These children can be helped if mediators consistently and repetitively raise children's awareness of:

- the mental actions involved in particular thought processes: "Nan, describe what you say to yourself when you add 32 and 44."
- the sequence of those actions: "Harry, what exactly do you do when you begin your homework?"
- the techniques of self-observation such as taking notes, making a recording, perhaps looking in a mirror or having someone observe and report.

Mediation for consciousness and awareness requires one-on-one attention, teacher to child, to help a child focus, maintain awareness, observe, remember, compare, repeat, and be self-aware.

Spatial Orientation: A Foundation for Thinking

Lack of spatial awareness is seen in children who represent something by movement rather than with words. For example, if young children are asked to show something, they might walk to it, lead you to it, or point to it, but not use words to say where it is. If you ask older children for directions, they might take you to the location rather than telling you how to get there or drawing a simple map. Many people actually turn in one direction or another to visualize how to reach a location; they are unable to divorce directionality from movement. Some children, especially young children or those who do not readily perform basic cognitive functions (such as focusing, remembering, or comparing), even if they actually move or imagine moving, become disoriented when they attempt to find their way. Spatial orientation is at the basis of many thought processes.

As described in Chapter 3, exercises in FIE-Basic and FIE-Standard have been designed to build the capacity to use spatial thinking effectively. Typical classroom print-based activities are not designed to pinpoint or ameliorate spatial deficits that underlie many kinds of confusion. Raising children's awareness of the spatial component in thinking is how to begin to mediate children with weak spatial skills, as examples in a later section of this chapter demonstrate. Effective mediation requires that teachers make children aware of the great degree to which thinking is dependent on spatial orientation. Look again at Figure 3.4 to see the relation of spatial thinking to many cognitive activities.

Movement: A Substructure of Human Thought

Movement is a fundamental basis of learning because it is a major aspect of experience every second of every day. Without the fine-motor control we have over our vocal chords, for example, speech would be impossible. Motor memory is important for purely "mental" tasks, from doing long division to sequencing the steps in a management problem (Ratey, 2002).

Children's clumsy or imprecise movements are evidence of movement deficiencies. Some children lack a goal or have no organizing principle behind their actions—for example, children who try to fit pieces in a puzzle but do not coordinate their movement with their perception and thus cannot orient the piece correctly. Their eyes may not follow their hand, or their hand may not go where their eye wants to. There are a myriad of movement deficiencies. Some result because children have not been taught how to:

- gather data,
- perceive spatial clues, or
- respond to temporal requirements such as the necessity for logically sequencing movements.

Observing movement functions as they emerge in infants and young children can reveal potential problems.

Overcoming movement deficiencies requires making children conscious of the *temporal* dimension of all actions: "Not *now* but *later*" and "Not *before* but *after*." Adults laugh at the expression "Ready, fire, aim." Humor can help children see illogical actions. Discussion, as shown in Chapter 3, can train children to spot *illogic* and become aware of logic. Practice in thinking about *when* events occur and about the relation of one event to another helps children gradually internalize an awareness of how to sequence movements logically. Re-evoking past events and projecting future events helps children organize, sequence, and understand relationships among temporal events (Feuerstein, Feuerstein, Falik, & Rand, 2006). Understanding time concepts (now/then, first/later) and the relation between time and logical sequencing makes movement a conscious act.

> Attention, imitation, spatial orientation, and movement are essential to all thinking acts.

INTERSECTION OF BASIC COMPETENCIES

Children's competence is linked to attention, imitation, orientation in space, and movement. How do these functions intersect? What impact do museum experiences have? What does research on the brain show? We address these questions next.

Learning to Focus Attention

Research reveals the importance of attention in every thinking act. Museum exhibits provide mediators with many hooks to focus attention.

Using Exhibits to Focus Attention. Designers use many techniques that give mediators ways—stimuli—to engage attention. These include movement, lighting, sound, color, isolation of one object, density of many objects, and repetition of the same idea in varied ways. Mediators can use such stimuli to focus children's attention:

- How does the speed of the big gear relate to the speed of the small gear?
- Why is the light shining *here*?
- What would you learn from this exhibit if there were no sound?
- Why is this display bathed in *blue* light?
- What is the meaning of the head mounted on the pedestal?
- How can you spot the carnivores in the mammal hall?
- Where else do you see this same idea?

Possible questions are endless. The challenge is to use stimuli in museum exhibits to hook those things already in children's brains (like Rachael's memory of the words *around the world*). Children who do not pay attention can be guided to focus on those aspects of stimuli that attract. This requires alerting children to notice stimuli. Museum exhibits offer numerous handles for focusing children's attention.

The Brain and Attention. High-level attention is required while connections among neurons are being formed. Thus, there is a strong relation between attention and learning.

Forming Schemata. Sometimes called neuronal networks, schemata are groups of brain cells that, through repeated use, form a pathway in the brain that eventually becomes habituated. "Habituated" means that the brain uses this pathway automatically, with little or no conscious attention. Examples are dressing, eating, working a long division problem, dribbling a basketball, maneuvering a car, and hundreds of other procedures many of which we use regularly.

Consider buttoning your shirt: Because this activity is automatic, while you are buttoning your shirt, you can concentrate on finding matching socks or on the words for the spelling test. But at some point, buttoning your shirt demanded intense focus and repetition; it occupied a lot of real estate in areas of the cerebral cortex that are devoted to higher-level thinking acts such as analyzing, scheduling, and imagining outcomes. Once you mastered buttoning procedures, they were stored in "lower" regions of the brain, freeing the cerebral cortex to concentrate on *other* high-level thinking. Your buttoning without thinking about it shows that the brain rewired and formed schemata (Ratey, 2002).

While a procedure is being learned, the brain's attention systems—sometimes called "executive" or control systems—are heavily involved. These systems are responsible for: (1) a basic level of arousal and alerting; (2) a selective focus on specific stimuli and signals; (3) further processing of these signals either in passing "or in a sustained manner" (Neville et al., 2008, p. 107). Attention includes some of the neural equipment we are born with, functions that infant researchers call "core knowledge" (Spelke & Kinzler, 2007).

Research on Attention. "Attention and consciousness are the foundations on which we create an understanding of the world" (Ratey, 2002, p. 111). Recent research (Gazzaniga, 2008) has identified the neural networks that connect the areas in the brain that are responsible for attention.

> Extensive studies on the processes of attention used by infants and children have established that the attention brain network is related to self-regulation of cognition and emotion. It is involved in attending to high level skills, including making word associations . . . and delay[ing] rewards. (Posner et al., 2008, p. 3)

Implications for Schools and Museums. Museums' diverse exhibits are novel and likely to alert children's brains. As you observe children, consider: Are children engaged in a new activity that requires high-level attention? explanation of new content? demonstration of an unfamiliar procedure? schemata formation? If so, mediation is called for. Schools' everyday routines provide the repetition that is essential to practice and consolidate new skills.

Yet, Mihaly Csikszentmihalyi (1990) has shown that typical classroom activities bore students. When someone is bored, the brain's reticular activating system shuts down. This is the part of the brain stem that receives input from most of the senses and from other parts of the brain. If classroom lessons are mainly mechanical, with limited data and no new elements, the brain feels a lack of activity that, in many cases, induces a state of sleepiness, manifest as boredom. Feuerstein says, "The kinds of variety, novelty, and challenge found in exhibits overcome boredom."

> Understanding how different environments impact the brain enables teachers to use experiences to best advantage in helping children learn to think.

Making Imitation a Conscious Act

The design of some exhibits, particularly in children's museums, spurs children to imitate. Imitation is a primary means through which humans learn.

How Exhibits Spur Imitation. Children's museums re-create many familiar environments—grocery store, hospital, city, street, kitchen, classroom, home—where children can imitate what they have observed. Other museums re-create entire environments where visitors can experience the aura and see the artifacts from bygone eras or inaccessible places such as scientists' labs or lunar capsules. Such exhibits stimulate mental actions, some imaginative, some imitative.

Feuerstein says, "There must be enough familiarity [in experiences] to feel comfort, enough novelty to feel accomplishment" (Feuerstein et al., 2006, p. 76). Csikszentmihalyi (1990) says when we have the right balance between familiarity and challenge we get into a *flow state,* so concentrated that we lose all track of time. Vygotsky refers to the right balance between familiarity and novelty as the "zone of proximal development."

Museums' opportunities for imitation mix familiarity—"drive" a vehicle—with experiences unknown to children—operate a cockpit's controls or construct a building. Imitating requires what psychologists call "procedural" knowledge—enacting specific sequences of actions. Perkins (1995) says that making specific actions is like "knowing how, [like] having appropriate information and mental processes at your fingertips" (p. 241). In some exhibits, children reenact—or imitate—what adults do commonly, but children do rarely, if ever. In other exhibits, those with an unfamiliar procedure, imagination drives children's actions. Or, children may employ familiar actions that have no relation to the meaning of an exhibit. Feuerstein says: "We view imitation as one of the major mechanisms for building cognitive schemata" (Feuerstein, Feuerstein, Falik, & Rand, 2006, pp. 94–95). The question is, What are children imitating? Are they imitating actual procedures? fantastical actions? television? Each involves different networks in the brain. Careful observation as children imitate can show teachers what children may be learning or if they are learning.

Learning by Imitating. The more familiar the environment, the more realistic the imitation. Young children "play" school, faithfully imitating their own classrooms—or play "home" while at school. As playtime is replaced by formal instruction, imitation is restricted—or is seen as cheating. Yet children imitate, for better or worse, copying clever actions, disruptive antics, and especially anything new. Imitation of new behaviors, including speech, is the reason Twitter quips and Facebook blips "go viral."

Katherine Greenberg, professor of Educational Psychology at the University of Tennessee in Knoxville, and longtime follower of Feuerstein's practices, tells of a 4th-grader who was very unhappy because she had no friends. In the child's school, teachers practiced mediation, so the child had learned techniques to analyze her own behavior; to observe, compare, and find different paths to the same place; and to think about how she was thinking. "The children who have friends," the child told her mother, "have short hair; please cut my hair." Her mother did cut the girl's hair, but short hair did not garner friends. "The children who have friends raise their hands a lot," so she raised her hand a lot, but it didn't garner friends. "The children who have friends smile a lot." So she smiled a lot, and in a short time she made lots of friends. Loris Malaguzzi, founder of the Reggio Schools, understood:

> We must stress that, even if children are naturally endowed with the art of making friends or acting as teachers among their peers, they do not improve this art by means of instinct or books. They steal and interpret patterns from adult teachers; and the more these adults know how to work, discuss, think and research together, the more children get. (1991, p. 17)

By watching how children imitate, we can determine how well they have observed, whether they attend to detail, understand logical sequence, and make appropriate connections. Ann recalls:

> From age 2 to 4, my grandson Sheppy's favorite activity in the preschool area of the Memphis Children's Museum was having me wait in a cubby-like space while he went back and forth to the kitchen, far across the exhibit, to bring me lunch. Over 3 years, what I ate changed from a random assortment of lettuce or cookies, to proper sandwich and beverage followed by dessert. The change showed that Shep had consolidated his knowledge of what constitutes a meal, one of thousands of complex behaviors children must master.

Feuerstein says that deferred imitation, which takes place after exposure—maybe minutes, maybe days—shows that the model was interiorized. Imitation gives children practice in mastering complex routines.

The Brain and Imitation. In 1996, while working with macaque monkeys, neurophysiologist Giacomo Rizzolatti and his group at Parma University, Italy, found in the motor region of the cortex a new set of neurons that control the hand and mouth. These neurons were active both when the macaques performed *and* when they *watched* an action (Gallese, Fadiga, Fogassi, & Rizzolatti, 1996). *The New York Times* reported:

> A graduate student entered the lab with an ice cream cone in his hand. The monkey stared at him. Then, something amazing happened: When the student raised the cone to his lips, the monitor sounded—brrrrrip, brrrrrip, brrrrrip—even though the monkey had not moved but had simply observed the student grasping the cone and moving it to his mouth. (Blakeslee, 2006, p. 1)

The responsible neurons, dubbed the "mirror neurons," have comparable functions and positions in the brains of macaques and humans. As further tests by Rizzolatti's and others' labs showed the same results, the significance became clear: Mirror neurons enable humans to learn by imitation. Scientists say the findings have enormous implications; continuing research could confirm that we have found the neurophysiologic substrate for speech perception (Gallese et al., 1996).

> The discovery of mirror neurons . . . is one of the most important findings of neuroscience in the last decade. . . . Today, mirror neurons play a major explanatory role in the understanding of a number of human features, from imitation to empathy, mindreading, and language learning. (European Science Foundation, 2008)

Mirror neurons function in all behaviors—speaking, hearing, seeing, smelling. The neurons fire when making an action as well as when watching another make it. "The process," says Feuerstein, "is not merely a generalization; in essence it is a kind of translation from what a person perceives to what the person does or thinks about doing."

The implications are that students can be encouraged to notice classmates' actions: Who provides effective evidence when they answer questions? Who finds strong sources of research? Whose presentations are powerful visually? Who uses strong analogies? Whose oral delivery excels? Who manages computers facilely? Who makes clever props? Once aware of what others do well, students can be encouraged to imitate consciously and critically. Schools have a monopoly on students' time. By encouraging thoughtful imitation, teachers help students use time to advantage.

Broadly Applying Spatial Orientation

There is more opportunity for spatial thinking in museums than in classrooms. Here, we provide examples and explain the significance of spatial thinking.

Exhibits and Spatial Orientation

We describe a few favorite exhibits based on spatial factors.

Rollways and Mazes. A familiar exhibit is a tall sculpture-like structure with intricate rollways for balls (see Figure 5.1). Children revel in watching the movements, some predictable, others random (see Chapter 12).
Lewin-Benham recalls:

> Sheppy, age 6, spent 1½ hours at the Boston Children's Museum making rollways from PVC pipe (see Figure 5.2). He made subtle changes to give the ball greater momentum or make the rollway more complex. When we visited the next year, he said: "I've been dreaming about this exhibit all year." "Why?" I asked. "Because," he said, "you can do so many things." He spent the entire morning configuring a rollway that traversed the entire wall and adding special effects. With every roll, the weight of the ball skewed the pipes, requiring continual alignment, subtle design shifts, and total concentration—all cognitive processes. He was engaged in high-level thinking as his brain built, enlarged, and stored effective procedures for making a complex rollway.

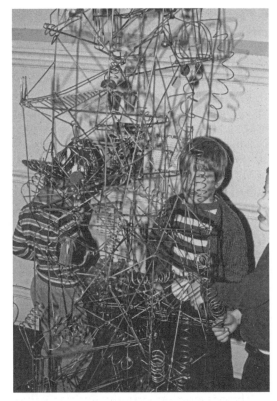

Figure 5.1. Children
are mesmerized by
the movement of balls
that fall through a
complex maze of wire
loops, tracks, and
collectors.

Figure 5.2. The child has arranged the pipes and connectors so that, when the ball hits the
three bells, they play the opening notes of "Three Blind Mice."

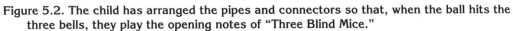

Spatial thinking enables children to navigate mazes. Remnants of ancient mazes and labyrinths testify that spatial challenges have fascinated people for millennia. The spatial and movement modalities of mazes and rollways satisfy the brain's need for novelty and complexity.

Climbing Structures. These elaborate exhibits challenge children to orient themselves in physically complex spaces, to employ right, left, front, back, before, behind, and many other positions that represent the subjective reference system humans use to locate themselves in space (see Chapter 3). Children who innately understand these references display what Gardner calls "spatial intelligence."

Tangrams. This ancient Chinese game has seven geometric shapes—one square and six triangles—to arrange in 100s of different designs, some realistic like boats or hats, others abstract. Every design uses all seven shapes. Some children are uninterested; some place the shapes only with guidelines; others, quickly and without guidelines, make complex abstract figures. Teachers can determine if children think spatially by observing their use (or lack of interest in) tangrams. Play tangrams at one of many sites on the Internet.

The Brain and Spatial Organization. Spatial orientation is an essential aspect of intelligence; yet, outside physical education classes it is rarely a conscious part of the school curriculum. Gardner (1983) enumerates cognitive acts that depend on spatial thinking:

- recognizing the same element in different orientations, such as tipping a rectangle until it looks like a line;
- transforming elements—for example, cutting circles or squares into other shapes;
- forming mental images and transforming them—for example, thinking of a bird as it takes flight or a flower bud unfolding;
- recognizing scenes, like a neighborhood or a movie setting;
- orienting in vastly different spaces—a room, an entire building, an ocean, forest, or desert.

Perkins (1992) says that knowing something "means understanding the piece in the context of the whole and the whole as the mosaic of its pieces" (p. 75). These ways of knowing depend on spatial orientation.

The following examples show the importance of spatial thinking.

Prepositions. Math teacher Eleanor Wilson Orr (1987) provides examples of urban high schoolers who cannot solve math problems because they incorrectly use the little connecting words that show relationships. Prepositions—*of, on, behind, near, under, between, beside*—define spatial relations. Psycholinguist Steven Pinker (1994) calls prepositions "one of the major syntactical categories" (p. 512). Without them, thinking would be impossible. Challenge students to interpret a written passage with no prepositions. Confusing prepositions impacts reading, science, math, following directions, and many basic thought processes.

Metaphors. Throughout the history of science, many towering figures have expressed their insight spatially:

- Lewis Thomas's analogies between microorganisms and organized society,
- Darwin's image of the "tree of life" to represent evolution,
- Freud's vision of the unconscious as a submerged iceberg,
- Dalton's description of the atom as a solar system,
- Kekulé's structure of the benzene ring,
- Watson and Crick's double helix to represent DNA,
- Einstein's vision of riding a light wave to describe the relationship between space and time,
- Szilard's conception of a chain reaction as the mechanism of an atomic bomb.

Drawing metaphors is spatially based (Gardner, 1983).

Spatial experiences enable children to acquire concepts and vocabulary essential for precision in the output phase of mental acts (see Chapter 6). Remember Walter (Chapter 3), who did not distinguish between *on* and *above* until a teacher mediated? Good thinking depends on using prepositions and other spatial references precisely.

Feuerstein says that changing children's ability to represent space is:

critical for two reasons. First, it is linked to correct perception of objects over a wide range of situations. Second, good articulation of representational space can be used as an efficient . . . [way to develop] rational abstract thinking and . . . [to correct] a host of deficient cognitive functions. (Feuerstein, Feuerstein, Falik, & Rand, 2006, p. 228)

Students should be taught what it means to think spatially and be encouraged to use spatial thinking often—critically, consciously, and precisely.

Logically Sequencing Thought Through Movement

There is little opportunity for movement in classrooms, plenty in museums, and strong research supporting the relation between movement and brain function.

Movement-Based Exhibits. Movement is represented in logically sequenced processes that take place across time. Reread the examples in this chapter and notice that movement is integral to each experience. Focusing attention is movement dependent: Children must inhibit some movements and emphasize others, such as holding the head steady on the neck, keeping eyes trained, retaining posture. Every cognitive act depends on underlying abilities to use or control different aspects of movement.

Internal Representations. Ask children to represent something by drawing it—not a refined drawing, but simple lines to show the connections in what they are describing. The movement required by drawing is an internal representation; drawing turns an experience into a mental organization (schemata). As children embellish an explanation with a drawing, they must represent movement internally by describing or visualizing it. These acts consolidate experience so that the thought processes are available for future actions. When coaches show tapes of athletes' expert performance or teachers demonstrate how to do long division, outline a paper, or follow a science process, the internal representations that they build are all based on movement. Cognitively, these processes require "planning, calculating, and forming intentions" (Ratey, 2002, p. 148), all functions carried out by *"the regions of the brain responsible for actual movement"* (p. 147, emphasis added).

Ratey continues: Accumulating research "shows that movement is crucial to every other brain function, including memory, emotion, language, and learning. . . . [O]ur 'higher' brain functions have evolved from movement and still depend on it" (p. 148). "Whether the activity is maintaining body temperature, moving like Michael Jordan, or learning to read, movement cannot be separated from other brain systems. A lot of brain function is, essentially, movement" (p. 155).

Herein lies one of the major differences between learning in classrooms and in museums: In museums, there are possibilities to make something move, to observe things moving, or to move yourself. The implications for classrooms are to find ways to incorporate movement, especially when lessons are new or complex.

The Brain and Movement. Effective mediation builds children's cognitive capacity by making them aware that movement is part of everything they do and of the widespread role of movement, from focusing attention to understanding math. Neurophysiologist Frank Wilson describes physical development early in one's life: Motoric mastery

> is one of the earliest maturational imperatives in the human nervous system. . . . [T]he baby will play [movement] game[s] and rehearse . . . [reach and grasp] movements endlessly as it gives itself things to do with its body that are more and more difficult. These games are created by the nervous system in order to teach itself a concrete, experiential sense of physics. (1998, p. 104)

Wilson says that the connections between movement and brain are so synergistic and thoroughly integrated,

> that no single science or discipline can independently explain human skill or behavior. . . . The hand [for example] is so widely represented in the brain, the hand's neurological and biomechanical elements are so prone to spontaneous interaction and reorganization, and the motivations and efforts which give rise to individual use of the hand are so deeply and widely rooted, that we must admit we are trying to explain a basic imperative of human life. (1998, p. 10)

Beyond requiring focus, motoric mastery requires children to maintain alertness, rapidly integrate visual and spatial information with physical responses, and orient themselves in complex spaces. Lest these seem unrelated to school tasks, consider that children who cannot do these things also cannot respond to teachers' instructions: Write your name in the upper left-hand corner; turn over the paper and do the problems from the middle of page 20 to the bottom of page 21.

Young children solve spatial challenges by actually moving. This trains the motor neurons in the brain to make the body move, to see part/whole relationships, to sequence logically, and to realize an intent. FIE exercises for older children require them to simulate movement mentally (see Chapter 3). Gradually, movements become increasingly facile.

Perkins (1992) calls facile acts "understanding performances"; the word *performance* means "action." Understanding is not

> a state of possession but one of enablement. When we understand something, we not only possess certain information about it but are enabled to *do* certain things with that knowledge. These things . . . that exercise and show understanding are called "understanding performances." (p. 77)

SUMMARY: MEDIATION—THE CONNECTING LINK TO LEARNING

Museums offer a wealth of stimuli that teachers can use to mediate so that children focus attention, engage in imitative play, and orient their body in space—all movement-based acts.

Jot down these four essential brain functions:

- attention
- imitation
- orientation in space
- movement

All higher-level brain functions depend on them. Look for them on your next visit to a museum, a playground, or any complex, content-rich experience. Seek occasions to make them part of your teaching. Make children aware of when they are using or could benefit from using these functions. Making children conscious of how their brain is thinking is a powerful form of mediation. Building consciousness—sometimes called metacognition—connects experience and brain so that learning lasts. Consciousness enables children to become their own mediators.

Mediation involves doing *whatever* is necessary to connect children to an idea—even picking them up off the floor, as we saw in Chapter 1. It is an apt metaphor: An environment must provide the stimulus to arouse children's interest, and the mediating adult must provide the question, suggestion, gesture, action, raised eyebrow, or other interaction that stimulates children to make a connection between the stimulus and something already in their heads. When they make connections, children learn.

Takeaways

1. When teachers ask children to focus, they draw on what researchers call the "executive" or attention systems in the brain.

2. When children imitate what they see others around them do, they are using one of the brain's most elemental ways of learning.
3. When children play games with prepositions, they exercise one of the brain's spatial functions, the systems that enable us to understand how the world is organized.
4. When teachers ask children to incorporate movement in their thinking, they engage the brain's movement centers, the basis for virtually all thinking and learning.

CHAPTER 6

Defining the Effectiveness of Learning Experiences

And gladly would he learn, and gladly teach.

—Geoffrey Chaucer, 1387–1400

FEUERSTEIN'S WORK offers two tools that are useful in any situation where an educator wants to determine what a student might learn from a museum exhibit, how a lesson is structured, or what handles an experience offers to foster learning. One tool is the Cognitive Map. The other, Thinking Deficiencies, categorizes cognitive structures that in some specific way block a student's thinking capacity and can be changed through mediation. Here, we describe these tools and introduce two additional techniques to help students learn efficiently: how to explore systematically and recall explicit information.

The Cognitive Map is a tool to analyze the challenges in a task. If a student does not meet those challenges, the list of Thinking Deficiencies can help pinpoint why. This latter tool describes aspects of individual cognitive structures that are related to learning certain types of skills: Do children perceive in an episodic way so that, if the task requires linking things together, they will fail because they only look at certain aspects or altogether miss others? For example, in the analogy "Green is to grass as _____ is to sky," a student who perceives episodically might ignore the second part of the analogy, think instead of what goes with grass, and answer "cow." This answer would be logical if the task was to make associations with grass, but the answer does not fit the analogy given. Taken together, the tools described in this chapter support effective mediation.

THE COGNITIVE MAP

The Cognitive Map describes seven different aspects of a task, the specific kinds of challenges the task presents. Thus, it provides a framework for analyzing a learning experience. The framework helps adults think about what takes place in children's brains as they use museum exhibits, hear lessons at school, or engage in other experiences. Mediators use the contents of the Cognitive Map as handles to analyze and interpret the structure of an experience (Feuerstein, Rand, & Feuerstein, 2006). Feuerstein calls these handles "parameters." They comprise content, modality, phase, cognitive operations, complexity, abstraction, and efficiency.

Content

Content means "the subject matter addressed by and involved in a mental act" (Feuerstein, Falik, & Feuerstein, 2006, p. 7). Content is what one knows about anything—a 4-year-old about colors and shapes, a 94-year-old about historic events in his lifetime. What people know is determined by their own experiences, culture, and brain. If the content in a task is too unfamiliar, the task will be too hard. It can be difficult, even impossible, for mediators to distinguish between children's lack of familiarity with content and their failure to perform a cognitive operation.

Without knowing content, understanding is severely limited, if it is even possible. For example, read and explain this sentence: "The length of a Cepheid's cycle from dim to bright determined its average luminosity, or the average amount of light it gave off" (Kupperberg, 2005, p. 24). If you are unable to explain the sentence, it might be because you do not know:

- content—the meaning of the words *Cepheid*, *cycle*, or *luminosity*;
- concept—how astronomers determine the distance of stars from Earth or from one another;
- context—the passage is about astronomy.

Lack of content, concept, or context—important aspects of cognition—can swamp the ability to identify, organize, analyze, synthesize, or use any other thinking process.

Another aspect of content is domain—does the content fall in geography? history? biology? sports? algebra? music theory? Within a domain, you must determine the context: If you are talking about dogs, are you referring to different kinds of breeds or the process of training? the role of dogs in the lives of children, invalids, or the elderly? related members of the canine family? how dogs were domesticated? traits of different breeds? or other?

Children's lack of content knowledge may have nothing to do with their ability to *perform* the task. If children are missing content, the teacher must figure out which content is missing and teach it! Feuerstein recalls a group of Moroccan children who, on first seeing snow, scooped it up, put it into their pockets, and took it inside! In order for anything to have meaning, children must understand the broader content.

The Cepheid example is from a field that requires broad content knowledge in order to process the facts and perform cognitive operations. If children know nothing of constellations, stars, and light waves, they will fail tasks that involve astronomical principles. *Children engaged in a task cannot function unless they know the content.* It is unfair, Feuerstein says, to call children failures if they cannot perform because they do not know the content. Mediators' first priority is to determine whether children's failure is lack of content knowledge or lack of ability to perform the cognitive function(s)—the thinking process(es)—the task requires. Knowing content *and* using one or more particular cognitive functions may both be essential in a given task. If a teacher does not first analyze whether a child is stymied by lack of content or by not knowing how to use a particular thinking process, the meaning of the lesson may escape the child.

Modality

Modalities are the huge variety of ways in which individuals *receive information and express the results of* mental acts. Feuerstein's use of the word "modality" is different from its more common meaning as a form of sensory perception or motor activity. In using the term *modality*, Feuerstein makes a distinction between the sensory act of perception and the cognitive act of interpreting what is received through the senses. Modalities include figural, pictorial, numerical, verbal, symbolic, or any combination of these or many other "languages"— literally, any form of expression that can be understood in a particular culture. These languages are the diverse ways that "input" triggers the brain and the equally diverse ways in which a thought, after being elaborated in the brain, is expressed. Howard Gardner calls these languages "intelligences." They are an essential aspect of thinking.

Each modality "speaks," as it were, to

- different clusters of networks in the brain;
- visual, auditory, tactile, and other senses;
- movement centers;
- memory centers; and
- other centers involved in anything the brain processes.

> A goal of mediation is to increase the number of modalities children can use and their facility in each.

Every culture develops its own modalities; think, for example, of the variation in traditional dance, music, gesture, dwellings, writing, sports, and kinship systems.

Some people excel in certain modalities, but barely function in others, effectively modality-blind. For example, some children can add numerals correctly and read graphs, but do not comprehend if the addition problem is stated in words. Schools use mainly linguistic modalities, expressing most things in words. Museums use a great range of modalities.

Phase

A phase is any one of the three levels, or parts, of a mental act: input, elaboration, and output. All mental acts consist of these three phases: Briefly, the first is data gathering, the second is organizing and analyzing the data, the third is expressing what is concluded. For example, I see a drawing of a giraffe, but it has the head of a dog! (input phase) Why did the artist draw the giraffe like this? I must solve this problem! Could it be an imaginary creature? Could it be wearing a headdress? Why? (elaboration phase) "I think the drawing is imaginative and fanciful." (output phase).

Boundaries between phases are fluid. Mental processes particular to one phase may be essential in the others as well. The idea of phases is a device, yet the device can help teachers understand where children are stuck in their thinking.

Input Phase. Some mental acts required at the input phase are:

- careful data gathering,
- systematic comparison,
- spatial orientation, and
- simultaneous consideration of two or more sources of information.

Operations in the input phase are relatively simple; for example:

- perceiving ("See car!" 2-year-old)
- identifying ("It's green!" 3-year-old)

Elaboration Phase. Children assemble the data they gathered in the input phase, identify the problem, and draw inferences from the data. What we generally call "good thinking" depends on good processing during the elaboration phase or, more precisely, efficient use of data. For example, some mental acts required in the elaboration phase are:

- identification of the problem,
- selecting relevant cues,
- putting data together,
- spontaneously using comparative behavior,
- pursuing evidence logically,
- forming and testing hypotheses, or
- sequencing tasks logically.

Psychologists Brown and Burton (1978) analyzed how 2nd-graders subtract by listening to their self-talk, observing their actions, eliciting their explanations, and studying their answers. They found that children performed subtraction problems in more than 200 different ways! The research demonstrated the very varied networks of neurons the brain creates to perform the complex mental operations that occur in the elaboration stage of a mental act and that children use to make relationships.

Failure in the elaboration phase may result in "an impoverished response, a personalized or bizarre response utilizing data that is only meaningful to the respondent, or perhaps no response at all—a blocking in anticipation of complete failure" (Feuerstein, Feuerstein, Falik, & Rand, 2002, p. 140).

Output Phase. Children combine the result of input and elaboration into an expression. Some mental acts required in the output phase, where communication skills are essential, include:

- ability to be precise and accurate,
- discipline to discern and resist trial-and-error responses,
- capacity to transform a mental process into a modality in which it can be communicated, and
- capability to stifle impulsive responses.

The three phases are highly dependent on each other; elaboration, for example, is determined by input. So, if John and Sam are arguing over who caused the pitcher of juice to drop, Bill, who is trying to resolve the conflict, must know whether John bumped into Sam accidentally, tripped him intentionally, or was trying to take the pitcher in his own hands but missed. The evidence will be what Bill saw himself, whether other children's observations confirm or contradict Bill's story, or Bill's understanding of John's and Sam's different abilities to handle a pitcher full of liquid. In the input phase, students must be aware of what to pay attention to so that they have the information required for the elaboration phase.

> The distinction among the three phases of a mental act is a didactic device—a way to help a teacher get a handle on the enormous complexity of any mental act. In real time, thinking is a dynamic process among the three phases.

Cognitive Operations

These are functions of the brain in which it organizes, analyses, transforms, deduces, or in any other ways manipulates information *during the elaboration phase* in order to generate new information. Examples (Caution—these are a tiny sample of a limitless number of possible cognitive operations; ages depend on different children's ability and can vary considerably):

- *Comparing*—making a relationship between the commonalities and differences in two things. "This more 'en that." (4-year-old) "The leopard has spots, the tiger has stripes." (5-year-old) "I'll put the zoo animals here and the farm animals here [different location]." (5–6-year-old)
- *Counting.* "Two, four, six, eight, ten, twelve . . ." (5–6-year-old)
- *Inferring.* "A horse is bigger than a sheep." (5-year-old) "Tom is taller than Joe, Joe is taller than Bob; therefore Tom is taller than Bob." (10-year-old)
- *Ordering.* "Going up the scale I sing do, re, mi, fa, so, but coming down the scale I sing so, fa, mi, re, do." (8-year-old)
- *Making analogies.* "Zebras have stripes; leopards have spots." (4-year-old) "Stripes are to zebras as spots are to leopards." (6-year-old)
- *Deducing.* "If that animal is about the size of a horse but lives in the wild and has black and white stripes, it must be a zebra." (10-year-old)
- *Finding progressions.* "If I see 5, 10, 15, the next number will be 20." (5-year-old) "If the number pairs I see are 1, 1, 2, 3, 5, 8, 13, 21, then the next number pair must be 34, 55." (10-year-old) In progressions, children must find the formula by which the line of numbers is organized. To do so, children must deduce a relationship.
- *Seriating.* "I laid the stones from little to big." (4-year-old) "We lined up from short to tall." (5-year-old) "I put the colors from dark red to pale red." (7-year-old) "I rearranged the series: BAD, ADB, DBA, BAD." (9-year-old).
- *Syllogisms.* "All mammals have hair; the rabbit is a mammal; therefore, the rabbit has hair." (8-year-old)

The age at which children can perform a mental operation depends on what content they know. So long as children know the content, they can be shown the operation. Piaget's notion of stages proved to be wrong when 3-year-olds were found to be capable of making analogies *if they knew the content*. Young children's thinking is hampered by the vast number of things they have not yet encountered. A toddler who loved orange juice stood at the window, pointed at the pelting rain, and delightedly squealed, "Onj joos!" He made an analogy, recognizing that juice and water have something in common. But lacking specific content—in this case, the word for "rain"—substituted words he knew. Adults do not always understand what such utterances represent in terms of children's cognition and merely find them charming or amusing. Fortunately, we don't grade toddlers or test them on how they're learning to speak.

Think of the field geologist trying to identify the minerals in a new rock specimen, or the computer programmer trying to find the bug in a line of code. In such complex tasks, even an expert who has the mental capacity to analyze, deduce, and interpret new information may be stymied by unfamiliar contents or modalities or overwhelmed by the volume of information. When Craig Venter's team of brilliant scientists was sequencing the genome of the fruit fly, one wrong direction at line 678 in 150,000 lines of code overwhelmed the program (Shreeve, 2004). If content is unfamiliar, students cannot accomplish cognitive operations.

Complexity

Complexity refers to the quantity of information to be handled in a mental act and how familiar the information is. When you are learning, every piece of a complex act must be understood on its own. Think of the number of acts in reading:

- hearing the phonemes in a word;
- isolating each individual sound;
- associating each sound with a letter;
- blending letters into a sound that has meaning (a word);
- holding all the sounds in mind as you blend them;
- learning (by memorizing) those words in which the sound does *not* represent the phoneme—words such as *there, who, why, was, been, they*— and recognizing (from memory) enough words so that you can read a book.

For example, a beginning reader confronts this sentence: *He pitched the ball home.* Assume the student has learned one sound for each letter:

- If she only knows how to pronounce "e" as it sounds in *get* but not in *he* or *her*, she will not be able to read the word *he*.
- If she only knows how to pronounce the letters "t," "c," and "h" as they sound in *tip, cat,* and *hop*, she will not know how they sound when blended together as "tch" in *pitch*.
- If she only knows how to pronounce "a" as it sounds in *ham*, she will not be able to read *ball*.

- If she only knows how to pronounce "o" as it sounds in *hot*, she will not be able to read *home*.

And, because there is no phonetic attack for the word *the*, it must be memorized, something a beginning reader may not yet have done.

Reading the sentence is challenging because every word deviates from a consistent phonetic sound. The number of units of unfamiliar information makes the five words in the seemingly simple sentence unrecognizable. Thus, the sentence is complex and difficult. A beginner might read it as: Heh pit cuh hed tuh huh eh baal hahm eh.

Moreover, assume the child has no knowledge of baseball, and therefore no context for understanding the meaning, even if she were able to read the words correctly. With no context, she might form a mental image of someone (blank)ing a ball where he lives. Or, consider the 2nd-grader to whom English is a new language. It is no wonder children have reading problems; it is a wonder anyone learns to read at all. Because there are large amounts of data to be remembered and thinking processes to be mastered, beginning reading is complex. As children learn each process and remember increasing amounts of data, the complexity is reduced.

Abstraction

This means how close a mental act is to the subject at hand; in other words, how closely is the idea or object associated with a specific instance? Are we talking about a feline (abstraction) or about my housecat Bootles (specific instance)? For example, "least abstract" means something is concrete, such as an animal's track in soft earth, the aroma of baking bread, or the effort required to lift a brick. Something that is somewhat more abstract is a picture of the animal, the bread, or the brick. Still more abstract is a symbol for an idea such as a country's flag. Most abstract is a mark, such as a letter in a phonetic alphabet, a numeral, or some other symbol that by itself has no meaning (see Chapter 8).

Consider abstraction in dividing 6 by 2. A young child can push six cars into two groups of three using perception (what he sees) and motor performance (moving objects). This may seem simple, but it requires many neuronal networks in several systems in the brain—vision, movement, and separating an entity into parts—at the time of life when *integrating* varied brain functions is a high-level challenge. Toddlers use concrete tasks to express the abstract idea of division. Older students, who solve the problem mentally with no reference to concrete objects, use abstract thinking.

Try this: Envision six cars and mentally arrange them into three groups. Envisioning objects is less abstract than dealing with the numerical expression $6 \div 3 = ?$, which mentally involves two abstractions. The numbers stand for quantities and a non-numerical symbol, the question mark, stands for a missing number. Yet even this numerical expression is less abstract than the algebraic expression, $n = x \div ?$, which removes all numerals, uses *only* abstract symbols, and therefore is the most distant of these examples from the concrete objects. If children have difficulty with abstract tasks, teachers must reduce the level of abstraction.

A chair is a concrete object. The word *furniture* is less concrete because the concept applies to many kinds of objects in addition to chairs. The phrase *home objects* is even more abstract because it includes furniture, plumbing fixtures, kitchen equipment, locks, knobs, and more. *Artifacts* include all the above *and* the variety of built structures in which they are found. The higher the category, the more abstract it becomes. *Animals* include many different classes; *living things* include far more.

To think abstractly means to ignore the difference in individuals or subgroups and construct a group irrespective of differences among the objects included. Lower categories have more commonalities, higher categories fewer. Abstraction is the capacity to go beyond objects that are immediately at hand. The capacity to think abstractly involves knowing large numbers of different types of objects; comparing, contrasting, and grouping; or, in other words, thinking conceptually.

Efficiency

Efficiency is a matter of speed, accuracy, and a perceived level of difficulty. These elements change as children learn how to do tasks that begin with simple operations and gradually become more complex. As you teach children mental operations, you reduce complexity and abstraction. Efficiency both relates to the task and is a function of how children perform the other acts of the Cognitive Map.

Children who perform tasks accurately and speedily perform efficiently. As complexity and abstraction decrease, so does children's perception of how difficult a task is. Mediators assess or observe several factors to identify how efficiently students perform a task:

- how *readily* they attack the problem,
- whether they are *eager or resistant*,
- how *fast* they perform,
- how *accurately* they perform, and
- how much *energy* they expend in solving the problem.

Different tasks require different kinds and amounts of mental effort in each phase of a mental act. Efficiency may be a function of any of the other aspects of the Cognitive Map.

An affective—or emotional—aspect is part of every cognitive act: "Fatigue, anxiety, lack of motivation, the amount of investment required, or numerous other factors may affect the individual in the performance of a task" (Feuerstein, Feuerstein, Falik, & Rand, 2002, p. 135). What and how much you do are the cognitive aspects of a task. *Why* you do it is the emotional aspect (Feuerstein, Falik, & Feuerstein, 2006).

Using the Cognitive Map

You are standing with James, an 8-year-old, at an exhibit: A small plastic beach ball bobs continuously above a small table; how the ball is held aloft is not visible

Figure 6.1. The
allure of batting a
ball suspended by a
stream of air eclipses
children's interest in
the question of *why*
the ball stays up.

Illustration by Daniel Feuerstein

(see Figure 6.1). James runs to the ball. He does not have to inspect the situation closely to realize that a stream of air is directed at the ball from a blower below. James immediately punches the ball away from the stream and it lands on the floor nearby. The game intrigues him and he continues punching the ball out of the stream for several minutes.

"James," asks the teacher, "what's going on here?" He immediately answers, "The air is pushing the ball up." "Why?" she inquires. James shrugs his shoulders, too absorbed in punching to wonder about the relation between the air and the ball and running and punching too frenetically for the teacher to explain. The activity engages him, not the science of Bernoulli's Principle.

Bernoulli's Principle deals with the pressure of moving fluids and gases and the force they exert relative to objects they move through or around. The principle accounts for lift on an airplane's wing or flow of water or gas through pipes. Google phrases such as "gas flow interactive demo" to find dynamic images that can be manipulated to develop understanding of the principle. Look at the eight simple experiments using readily available materials that are on the website of the University of Minnesota, School of Physics and Astronomy, and at the video of easy to do experiments by Scott Thompson; both are on the web.

Applying the components of the Cognitive Map to James's experience, we see:

- *Content:* James knows nothing about the content in the experiment, and does not know the meaning of the words *fluid, gas,* and *pressure.*

- *Modality:* The modality is the ball's continual movement, the exhibit's main attractor. James's modality is physical action, typical of children who enjoy this common exhibit—blocking the air current so the ball falls, or snatching the ball and trying to toss it through the current to a partner. A nearby label (verbal modality) names the exhibit "Bernoulli Effect" and explains that the velocity and pressure of a fluid passing through a pipe decrease as the pipe narrows. The label contains a diagram (graphic modality) and a formula (symbolic modality) to further explain. If he sees the labels at all, James ignores them.
- *Phase:* James did not formulate or elaborate a problem or express a solution. It is unlikely that James even noticed that the exhibit had anything to do with science, other than knowing he was in a science museum.
- *Cognitive Operation:* James synced his movements to dislodge the ball and catch it. This would challenge a 3-year-old, the age when children try to master the demanding acts of catching balls. At 8 years old, James's actions are mainly the physical pleasure of playing with a ball.
- *Complexity:* Had the exhibit included the kinds of animation that can be found on certain websites, had there been nearby exhibits that were based on Bernoulli's Principle, even ones as simple as the ping-pong ball experiment that you can watch on the web, James's curiosity might have been aroused to think about the effect. For example, there could have been balls that differ greatly in size or weight; visitors could have increased, lessened, angled, channeled, or stopped the air flow altogether. Paper could have been available to crumple and place over the air flow or to fashion into airplanes to fly over the stream of air or in a simple wind tunnel. Or, plastic bottles, ping-pong, and golf balls could have been on hand with explanations of simple experiments. If there were different effects to test, children could experience various conditions in which objects that usually fall down stay up! Find a website with science projects that show video of this scientific principle.
- *Abstractness:* The explanation of Bernoulli's Principle was verbal with a number of words 8-year-olds might not know; it contained a graphic, also beyond 8-year-olds' comprehension, and a mathematical formula, an abstract expression beyond the ken of most museum visitors, other than physicists or mathematicians. Thus, the likelihood of most visitors' understanding the science was small.
- *Efficiency:* The exhibit is highly motivating. But the activity it motivates has nothing to do with the science.

> The Cognitive Map can help teachers determine how readily children might understand an exhibit and how it could be more understandable if children had mediation as they manipulated related exhibits.

THE THINKING DEFICIENCIES TOOL

Along with assessing tasks' difficulty, Feuerstein assesses individuals' performance. Assessments reveal what Feuerstein calls *deficient cognitive functions*. The cognitive map describes the nature of the task confronting an individual; the deficient cognitive functions describe the inappropriate or inefficient responses of the individual to the task. The combination of both factors—task and individual— illustrate the reasons for success or failure with the task. As teachers know well, any child may have deficient functions in some instances and well-established functions in others, depending on the demands of the task.

For example, in tasks requiring children to identify objects, they will not be able to do so if they don't examine the object completely and perceive all its characteristics clearly and sharply. If they merely sweep over the object (or environment or text), they will receive inadequate input to do the task. When a teacher clearly identifies and describes a deficiency, it increases the likelihood of helping children overcome it.

Or, for example, object conservation means that children maintain their perception of an object even if the object is presented in a different orientation. Children cannot conserve an object if they do not *compare* on relevant dimensions such as form, shape, length, girth, and the like. Comparison is an elaboration phase function; observing specific details of an object is an input phase function. The teacher may need to give a lesson showing a child exactly what to look for: "See? The object (a circle cut from cardboard, for example) is perfectly round. I'll put another circle on top of it (input phase, data gathering). Now watch," and the teacher tips the circle so that, from the child's perspective, it no longer looks round, then says, "Remove the top shape. What does it look like?" (elaboration phase, analysis). When the child answers "Circle" (output phase, expression), the teacher proceeds to analyze the circle's characteristics, then tips it again and asks, "What has changed?" With the child, she determines that, even though the circle *looks* different, only the position has changed.

The level of cognitive function children can use is strongly affected by whether their data gathering (input phase) is efficient. For example: Watch how young children or children who find it difficult to make comparisons explore an object. They might palm or partially touch it instead of using careful fingering or keeping one finger in place as a point of reference. When children's exploratory behavior (input phase) is partial, fragmented, or unsystematic, they may fail if tasks require them to recognize objects they are trying to hold in mind, or they may inaccurately estimate size or other attributes (Feuerstein, Feuerstein, Falik, & Rand, 2002).

There are many implications. For example, in matching games children might fail to recall an object. Or, without an accurate description, children may retain the object incorrectly in their "mental dictionary," or retrieve it inaccurately, and thus be stymied in trying to use it later in higher-level thinking tasks. Children who fail to use systematic exploratory behavior may miss clues or perhaps the entire meaning of an experience. Observing how children explore is one clue to the nature of their responses. If, in analyzing children's responses, adults notice that many responses are incorrect, they could alter the experience:

- Does content need to be fleshed out?
- Do children need to be taught exploratory techniques?
- Is there opportunity to explore the material?

The list of cognitive functions that can impair learning is presented in Appendix A. The list can help teachers recognize deficiencies as a first step in overcoming them.

Teachers can mediate classroom lessons or museum exhibits to:

- present unfamiliar content so that it is accessible;
- use varied modalities to reach children whose learning approaches differ;
- hold attention long enough to engage all three phases of the mental act—input, elaboration, and output;
- inform children of what cognitive operation(s) is/are required (more on this in later chapters);
- cause children to deal with complexity by using multiple examples of the same principle and placing the examples in close proximity both in space and time;
- ensure that abstractions, if they are present, follow logically from concrete experience that is present or nearby in time and/or space;
- focus children's attention so that it is directed at the principle the exhibit or lesson is designed to convey.

Realizing that thinking is challenging and that children may not understand the ideas in an exhibit means that teachers must entice children to explore and make children aware of their own thinking as they explore, which is the essence of metacognition and the foundation for self-mediation.

> Identifying deficient cognitive functions helps teachers understand where mediation is needed. In other words, if we know what is deficient, we can target it for change.

TWO TECHNIQUES TO ENHANCE LEARNING

Effective teachers have a large repertoire of techniques with which to help students learn. Maria Montessori was a giant among educators; she devised many techniques, and the following two are universally applicable. Both exemplify mediation that enables children to be precise during the input level of a mental act (Feuerstein, Rand, & Feuerstein, 2006).

Enabling Precise Exploration

Montessori teachers use a specific technique to introduce geometric shapes, leaf contours, letters, or anything that must be recognized by its outline: They guide children to use their "two feeling fingers" (index and middle) to carefully trace the outline. For example, in presenting geometric forms (circle, ellipse, quatrefoil, and so on), leaf forms (cordate, ovate, linear, and so forth), or letter forms (single letters or blends), the teacher engages the child's attention and focuses it on her (the teacher's) feeling fingers as she (the teacher) carefully traces the edge. Then the teacher hands the child the object to finger trace himself. The beauty of Montessori objects—polished wood, deep color, glossy finish, satiny feel—attracts children. With sandpaper letters and numbers, teachers show children how to trace *on* the symbol itself. The implication for exhibits is that adding outlines for children to trace can help them attend to details that are important in identification. The technique is especially helpful for children who are younger or have difficulty grasping or remembering information. The anatomy exhibit (Chapter 1) would have been more effective if children traced an outline of the distinct features of each jaw.

A teacher, working one-on-one with a child, first demonstrates and, if a child fails to explore systematically after being shown how, gently takes the child's hand, touches the tips of his "feeling fingers," identifies them to the child as "feeling fingers," and moves the child's fingers around the form (see Figure 6.2). Thus, the adult both provides the specific information about a defining characteristic and teaches a widely applicable technique for systematic exploration.

The teacher also determines whether children fail to:

- identify a shape because at the input stage their attention wanders;
- transport the image to their mental data bank as they elaborate; here, the clues are children who are distracted, hurried, imprecise, or resistant;
- repeat the exercise enough to associate the object with its name and therefore cannot recall the name in the output phase.

Figure 6.2. The tactile effect of "tickling" the tips of a child's "feeling fingers" sends a strong impression to the brain. Once children identify their feeling fingers themselves, teachers show them how to trace edges or lines. The three modalities—visual, auditory, and tactile—reinforce a lesson's content.

Illustration by Daniel Feuerstein

Feuerstein says that careful fingering is a technique children can apply in many different situations. It slows impulsive children, focuses inattentive children, engages the hands of children who learn by moving. For all children, the technique brings together the networks of neurons that are necessary for coordinated functioning of eye and hand. The precision instilled by this technique overcomes deficiencies in focus and replaces sweeping perception with mindful attention. Challenges to museum designers and lesson planners are (1) to identify what content lends itself to exploration by feeling, and (2) to add elements that can be felt.

> Improving processing at the input phase improves all three phases of a mental act.

Acquiring Unfamiliar Content

A stumbling block for people of any age is not knowing the meaning of things. For young, low-functioning, or environmentally deprived children, this is a huge issue for, as the nursery rhyme says, "The world is so full of a number of things . . ." That number is vast. Montessori teachers use a technique called a "three-period lesson" to help children learn to identify and recall specific content.

Period One: Identification. The teacher, working one-on-one or with a group of two to four children, presents three objects, says their names, traces their edges, and otherwise explores them manually. Then the teacher has the children do the same. The teacher's actions simultaneously engage a number of brain systems:

- *Visual*—calls attention to the object and ensures that children focus on it;
- *Auditory*—alerts this system by saying the object's name, perhaps three or four times;
- *Haptic (tactile/movement)*—runs children's "feeling fingers" around the edges or manually explores the object.

This multimodal approach arouses the brain's attention and processing systems. Several senses, the motor cortex, and the mirror neurons fire rapidly. Simultaneous use of several senses amplifies the input and, if children are "blind" in one modality, engages alternate pathways in the brain.

Period Two: Association. The teacher engages children in playing games with the three objects: The teacher might shift the objects' position, name one object, and ask a child to point to it; shift the objects again, and so on. Or, the teacher might say, "*Hand me* the circle." Or, "*Put* the obtuse-angled isosceles triangle on top of the equilateral triangle." Games can be quite elaborate: *Carry* the ellipse across the room. *Hide* the pentagon near the bench. Games in Period Two continue for a long time—days, weeks, or more. As they repeat varied activities (touch, carry, put, hide, find), children gradually associate objects' names with their attributes and thus, in time, consolidate their content knowledge.

Period Three: Recall. The teacher holds up an object and asks children to name it. If the children cannot recall, the teacher returns to Period Two, or perhaps reintroduces the objects (Period One).

Repeated identifying, associating, and recalling eliminate deficiencies in knowing specific content. If children fail nonetheless, it may be because the adult:

- omits an introduction,
- provides an imprecise identification,
- hurries through one of the periods, or
- asks children to recall without allowing enough time to make an association.

Feuerstein calls this process mediation of "association and application" (Feuerstein, Rand, & Feuerstein, 2006, p. 424); it is one of the many categories of mediated interactions.

In learning to read, if children have never been taught the sounds of individual letters or have been taught letters only by their *names*, they cannot be expected to employ letters' *sounds* to "sound out" words. (If you know "c" as the "s" sound, "a" as in m*a*ke, or "n" as "en," you might say "sayin'" for "can.") In any situation, a person of any age is stymied by tasks that contain unfamiliar content. When reading, the mind stutters when it comes across an unfamiliar word. Children who do not look it up or somehow find the meaning may miss the sense of the passage. Thinking deficiencies are not limited to children who are young, economically disadvantaged, diagnosed with any specific disorder (Down syndrome, autism, ADHD), or uninitiated thinkers. A cognitive problem can occur in anyone at any time.

> Techniques that enable children to fasten meaning in memory can improve all aspects of their thinking.

THE CASE FOR MEDIATION: DEMETRIA'S STORY

Lewin-Benham relates:

> Demetria, whom I was tutoring, had just turned 11, was repeating 3rd grade for the third time, and was finally reading. At least she was decoding common words. But words such as *fragrant, ravine, far-fetched,* and thousands of others were unfamiliar, so classic stories, like "Aladdin's Lamp" or "Aesop's Fables," were meaningless. Demetria had a poor vocabulary and only rudimentary knowledge because she had little exposure at home and her school offered little beyond rote lessons, dull textbooks, and test prep. She had never visited the city's zoo or been to its museums. Her three older siblings had all been placed in special education classes.
>
> Demetria was attractive, neatly groomed, affectionate, and polite. Moreover, she was enthusiastic about our tutoring sessions and, most important, was cooperative. I worked with Demetria 1 hour per week during 2 school years. Many days were lost because tutoring did not begin until 6 weeks into the year or was eliminated during long periods of test prep.

Children who spend considerable time watching TV—as Demetria did—lack the content that children gain from outdoor activity, imitation of friends, physical challenges, collaborative games, and conversation with adults. Their conversation mainly repeats words heard on TV. The issue with children like Demetria is how to make up the deficits begat by economic poverty. Overcoming the paucity of children's earliest years requires enriching their experiences and teaching them techniques to explore precisely and to acquire new information. Tools such as the Cognitive Map, analyzing cognitive deficiencies, careful exploration, and increasing content knowledge build any student's ability to learn increasingly complex and abstract cognitive skills.

SUMMARY: ANALYTIC OBSERVATION TOOLS

Fortunately, the majority of children are not as seriously challenged as Demetria. Keep in mind that the tools presented in this chapter, when used systematically, can help children grasp the meaning in experiences, overcome deficits in understanding, and thereby increase the likelihood that they will learn.

As you take children through a museum, linger at those exhibits the children want to see. Scan the exhibit using the components of the Cognitive Map—in other words, assess whether children are likely to know the *content*, whether there is a *modality* the children use naturally, how *complex or abstract* the exhibit is. Then observe your children. Spot how they approach the exhibit by asking yourself questions such as:

- Do they focus or glance and run?
- Do they explore systematically, or does their gaze dart hither and yon?
- Are their remarks pertinent to what is in the exhibit or irrelevant?
- If you engage children in stating the message of an exhibit in simple, easily understood words, or in diagramming or drawing a mind map of their comments, does it spark responses that relate to the exhibit's content?

Your answers give you a sense of how difficult it will be to engage children in an exhibit so that they "get" its meaning.

Takeaways

Children will get the most meaning from an exhibit or lesson if you:

1. Use the Cognitive Map to understand the nature of the challenges in a task.
2. Use the list in Appendix A to help pinpoint where a child might be stuck.
3. Guide children in learning to explore systematically.
4. Help children acquire new content by using a three-period lesson.
5. Make children conscious of the specific cognitive tasks they are using and encourage them both to use the tasks repeatedly and to recognize the brain functions each task engages.

CHAPTER 7

Creative Use of Effective Exhibits

> Problems are often stated in vague terms . . . because it is quite uncertain
> what the problems really are.
>
> —John von Neumann (in Macrae, 1992)

THIS CHAPTER HIGHLIGHTS several techniques used by museums to make exhibits compelling and explains the relation between each technique and learning. We describe museum techniques so that you will notice and therefore use them.

Museums have both a mandate and the means to create experiences that capture attention. They do so in many ways: by making exhibits that offer rich experiences, presenting conflict-producing ideas, and drawing on multiple intelligences. They use human intervention. We describe these techniques here.

LEARNING FROM RICH EXPERIENCES

Rich experiences are diverse. Occasionally, they kick cognitive functions into gear on their own. More often, they are effective because of mediation. Rich experiences are:

- *repetitive*—meeting an idea again and again;
- *varied*—keeping a principle constant but varying the example;
- *in different modalities*—using images, tactility, varied sensory experiences, or other varied means to elaborate or express information;
- *detailed*—providing many handles on an experience;
- *redundant*—offering a profusion of similar examples;
- *aesthetic*—appealing to the senses.

Discussion of each point follows.

Repetition: Meaning Through Variety

Repetition means doing something again and again with the purpose of making children familiar with specific content, procedures, or principles. Repetition that requires skilled movement builds hand/eye/body coordination. Repetition with mediation develops logical thought processes and other analytic skills.

Example: Pulleys. Pulleys were used everywhere at the Capital Children's Museum (CCM) in:

- the "Simple Machines" exhibit (Chapter 1);
- a semaphore system, ca. 1880 (Chapter 1);
- the exhibit "Mexico" on an old-fashioned water well;
- "Science Hall;"
- "Sound and Silence," an exhibit on hearing impairment that enabled children to finger spell by using pulleys to manipulate huge wooden "fingers."

In each application, pulleys achieved a distinctly different effect. Moreover, exhibits were spread over a huge building, so coming upon pulleys again and again felt like meeting an "old friend." Had there been a thematic floor plan of the museum, you could have taken a "pulleys tour." Repetition makes the underlying principle apparent: Pulleys make work easier.

Example: Communication Systems. At CCM, communication systems were used repetitively: In many different exhibits you could make telephone calls, send messages, use computers, or decipher codes. Codes varied:

- a Morse code key to "operate;"
- Fresnel lenses—a system that uses a strong light—set in facing windows so children could blink light signals across a large courtyard;
- the Hobo code, set in a detailed mural, and below it a translation of the many signs that, for example, showed if someone in the cottage would feed you, shelter you, let you work for food, pay you, or chase you away;
- a quipu (knotted string cord) from Mezoamerica that, prior to the 1980s, was a mystery scholars had not unraveled;
- the Mixtec code, also from Mesoamerica, presented in a 6-foot-high, 16-foot-long mural. The colorful figures, long chains of geometric symbols, and other mysterious marks, have not been unraveled yet.

Children, especially boys from 8 to 12, revel in sending coded messages. Life-long interests are sparked when adults plant ideas such as: "Many have tried but no one has ever deciphered this code although it has been around for hundreds of years. Maybe *you* will do it."

Repetition and Learning. Repetition is essential to learning. Through repetition, the brain consolidates thought processes into new understanding. But, if repetition is dull, lacks movement, is in only one modality, or is too complex or abstract, students will resist. Many exhibits are far from dull and excite children to:

- do something again and again,
- manipulate,
- compare,

- describe,
- question.

Innate human imperatives drive children to repeat. As they do, they build a mental model of how a bit of the world works, check the model to see if it continues to work, and thereby establish their own rules (albeit sometimes fuzzy, imprecise, or just plain wrong). It is important for children to repeat until they stop on their own. Urging them on to another exhibit when they are still engaged both kills concentration and hampers consolidation.

Effective mediators (1) observe children and converse with them to determine the level of their understanding; (2) provide facts, demonstrate, and repeat to alter incorrect conclusions; (3) engage children in comparing, analyzing, and summarizing what they have done; (4) find different exhibits that contain the same principle in order to make the principle clear; (5) transcend the exhibit: "Let's find other machines that make work easier." Or, "What other uses can you find for codes?" Simple statements—"pulleys make work easier"—when repeated, sink into the brain. There, they act as handles to provoke thought and provide openings for further discussion (Feuerstein, Rand, & Feuerstein, 2006). Encouraging repetition is one of the most important kinds of mediation.

Variation: Antidote to Boredom

Richness means variety. Here, we see an example and examine how variety impacts learning.

Example: Printing. Behind the "Print Shop" in the "History of Human Communication" wing at CCM was a "Print Workshop." In changing activities, children printed by:

- stamping;
- engraving wood blocks;
- rolling ink or paint onto paper;
- marbleizing paper;
- using brushes, feathers, or sponges;
- impressing images into wood, copper, or foil.

Activities conveyed the idea that there are numerous ways to print. The variety ensured that printing was a novel experience.

Variety and Learning. Variety is an essential antidote to boredom because it keeps the brain alert; thus, it is an effective technique in many learning situations. A teacher toured the "Communication" exhibit, encouraging students to find many varieties of printing: words, pictures, signs, symbols, handwriting, newsprint, engraving. He urged students to notice differences, question techniques, and compare results. The students concluded that the *constant factor* in all printing is that it leaves marks on surfaces.

A constant in a collection of leaves is that they all have stems and veins. A constant in arithmetic is that numbers can be recombined to increase or reduce quantities. Mediators can use variety to challenge children to find constants. Finding constants provides a way to organize thoughts.

> Repetition without variety shuts down the mind; variety without repetition robs experience of meaning.

Modalities: Different Pathways

Richness means using different modalities. Humans are capable of receiving, elaborating, and expressing ideas in many different modalities, but often use only a fraction of that capacity. Meeting ideas in varied modalities stretches children's minds.

Example: The Scriptorium. Near the "Print Shop" was a "Scriptorium," a re-creation of the Middle Ages environment where monks hand-copied manuscripts. The low arched doorway announced: Pay attention! Opposite the entry, the shape of the door was repeated in an arched window with faceted panes that broke sunlight into separate shafts of light. Interlocking tiles played a symmetrical pattern on the floor (see Figure 7.1). Gregorian chant, the 5th-century musical reading of the Bible, resonated in the background. A page from an illuminated manuscript was chained to a heavy pedestal, a common practice in the Middle Ages. A massive oak table held ink pots, quills, and paper for visitors to write. On the wall hung a historical engraving that named the objects in a Scriptorium.

Figure 7.1. The Scriptorium was a richly detailed exhibit of another time and place. Children's perceptions were reinforced by mediation that encouraged them to spot similarities and differences and make other comparisons.

Illustration by Daniel Feuerstein

The brain was alerted

- visually by the entire surround;
- auditorily by the unfamiliar chants;
- spatially by the arrangement of objects, repeated in a different scale and modality in the engraving;
- kinesthetically by writing with unusual implements; and
- tactilely by feeling chain, quill, paper, ink, and the room's varied surfaces.

The small room felt far removed in time and space, and provided a mental image of an environment few ever see. The ambiance was otherworldly, like falling down the rabbit hole or finding yourself in Lilliput.

From the great choice of stimuli in the Scriptorium, an adult could select a stimulus with specific meaning and use its novelty, diversity, particular aesthetic quality, or modality to engage children's thinking.

Modalities and Learning. A teacher focused the attention of four children on the shape of a window pane. He asked them to find an *exact match*, which they did easily. Then, he asked them to find something *similar*. One chose a detail from the engraving, another chose a floor tile, yet another saw similarity in the shape of a letter in the manuscript. Each time, the teacher asked children to explain what made the items similar. Next he asked children to find *different* examples, always asking them to explain the reasons for their choices. The teacher encouraged children to draw examples from the tonality of the chant, the weight of the chain, the movement of quill on paper, and other aspects of the Scriptorium. Becoming aware of modalities establishes a basis for metaphor. Can you hear how *heavy* the music sounds? See the *rhythm* in the floor tile? Feel the *drag* of quill against paper?

Modalities and Comparative Behavior. In progressing from exact to similar to different, the brain goes through a process:

- Enumerate the features you are comparing.
- Systematically explore the features.
- Precisely describe similarities and differences.
- Project a relationship.

The process leads from concrete (the objects compared) to abstract thinking because relationships only exist in the mind. "Comparative behavior," says Feuerstein, "is essential for the establishment of relationships and is thus one of the basic cognitive functions" (Feuerstein, Feuerstein, Falik, & Rand, 2002, p. 145). Finding same, similar, and different among varied modalities builds meaning, invites analogies (a is to b as c is to d), and extends children's cognitive repertoire. Varied modalities provide a basis for metaphor, deduction, syllogism, and other higher-level cognitive functions.

The teacher used many words—*compare, systematic, precise, similar, related, concrete, abstract*—that describe thought processes. Each time, he told his students what processes they were using and encouraged them to use those words themselves to describe how they were thinking. In doing so, he "mediated" not only meaning, intention, and transcendence, but also the selection of stimuli, verbal stimulation, short-term recall, and association and recall (Feuerstein, Rand, & Feuerstein, 2006, pp. 423–424).

Detail: Entry Points

Detail grabs the brain's attention. Noticing details and their variations sets the stage for encouraging children to build coherent concepts from a large number of instances. This is inductive reasoning.

Abundant Examples. Different children are drawn to different things—subtle shifts in the symmetrical patterns of mosaic tiles, varied percussion instruments in a jazz riff, miniatures in a Victorian dollhouse, realistic landscapes with electric trains, historical costumes, facial expressions, masks. Detail says, Look at me! Detail provides entry points for children with varied interests.

Museums excel in offering detailed visual experiences. For example, watch "Calder's Circus" (Whitney Museum). Examine the "Thorne Rooms" (Chicago Art Institute). Peer at the intricate re-created environments in the "Modern History Hall" (Royal British Columbia Museum). These and other exhibits can be found on the web; Google the name—for example, "Calder's Circus"—along with the museum's name. Add your own favorites. Such images are mind-stretching for children who have never seen them, especially when a teacher stimulates discussion about them.

A rich array of details makes it more likely that children will find something that interests and thereby "hooks" their attention. Once children find an entry point, detail provides a basis for building higher-level concepts as children organize the details in their mind.

Detail and Learning. A teacher showed his students Albrecht Durer's charcoal drawing, "Portrait of Durer's Mother," and James Abbot McNeill's painting "Whistler's Mother." When he asked students to compare the paintings, they mentioned facial expression, skin texture, darkness, lightness, and more. Then the teacher asked them to *categorize* their comments; they mentioned emotion, color, and line style. Thus, they moved from concrete details to general ideas, a higher-level mental process. Images of reproductions or actual great works of art themselves are easy to find on the web. Be sure to browse several and, if possible, show children an original in a museum.

Focusing students on detail:

- enriches their visual imagery,
- expands their vocabulary, and
- provides a basis to compare, contrast, and categorize.

Details offer entry points to observe and, with mediation, to use inductive reasoning. When teachers use the words *observe*, *compare*, and *categorize*, and encourage children to use these words to describe their thinking, children acquire these thought processes.

Redundancy: Profuse Examples

Redundancy is a form of richness. At CCM, we presented different cultures redundantly.

Cultural Examples. In the permanent exhibit "Mexico" and in changing exhibits on Thailand, India, Japan, or Israel, you could prepare food, shop, dress, make crafts, make music, and more. Engaging in activities common to different cultures, visitors repeated the same things in varied ways. Eating tortillas, roti, na'an, rice crackers, and matzo tastes different; wearing serape, pha sin, sari, obi, and talis drapes differently; and these foods and garments have different functions and symbolic meanings. Mexican paper flower decorations, Thailand's phuang malai garlands, India's masses of orange chrysanthemums, the scalene form of Ikebana, and flowers hanging from a Succoth immerse you in color and aroma that differ markedly and embody vastly different cultural meanings; for example, the chrysanthemums symbolize death and the next life, the Succoth symbolizes life and plenty.

> Rich environments challenge children to "search for novelty and complexity" (Feuerstein, Rand, & Feuerstein, 2006, p. 423).

The objects illustrate the principle of *redundancy*—a lavish outpouring of similar things that vary in marked ways. Redundancy makes experiences novel and complex. Feuerstein ranks the search for novelty and complexity among the most powerful ways to learn and, therefore, an important parameter of mediation.

Redundancy and Learning. Tennis coaches lob continuous streams of balls with different trajectories (maybe obvious, maybe imperceptible). Historians analyze cycles that repeat in different eras. Sociologists contrast cultures with varied patterns of kinship, ritual, or food gathering. Museum designers show common threads among diverse cultures. *Redundancy provides a focus for comparison.* Teachers can ask: "What do these have in common? How do these differ? Precisely what is different? What is typical of Mexico as compared to Japan?" Examples accumulate until the brain has a profusion of instances that expand meaning. Expanded meaning establishes a basis to develop understanding. As British philosopher/psychologist Kenneth Craik (1914–1945) said, "You cannot wring the truth out of a particular observation of a particular event" (in Collinson, 2002).

When children make meaning from one example, mediators can encourage them to apply that meaning to other examples. But, to ensure that children learn, the mediator's voice must intervene and not leave learning to chance or to direct exposure—children's deriving meaning on their own is a myth we debunked in Chapter 1. Guiding children's attention is an essential part of mediation.

Aesthetics: Sensory Delights

Aesthetics enriches human experience, enlarges children's perspective, and provides pathways to learn. "Man is not a creature of pure reason; he must have his senses delightfully appealed to" (Lamb, 1913, p. 40).

Example 1: Lewin-Benham Recalls

> As a child, I was mesmerized by a small work of art, at the time attributed
> to Italian goldsmith and sculptor Benvenuto Cellini, standing in its own case
> in a main hall at the Metropolitan Museum of Art. The ornate vessel, in the
> shape of a shell, is perched on a coiled serpent that rests on the back of a
> turtle. The gold is inlaid with enamel, but the handle, fashioned as the bust
> of a beautiful woman whose body terminates like a mermaid, is enameled in
> rich, multicolored hues and inlaid with a huge pearl and other gems. To me,
> she was the most beautiful woman in the world.

Feuerstein says:

> The fact that, as a child, Ann self-mediated—outlining the shapes, perceiving
> the intricacies, enjoying the harmony of a small sculpture—was a product of
> many experiences in which her mother mediated, causing Ann to be aware
> and instilling a tendency to seek aesthetic experience.

Example 2: Object as Pathway

An arrestingly beautiful object can spark as many paths of inquiry as the famed
12 gates to the city of Jerusalem have sparked metaphors in art and literature. Following are examples of a few paths of inquiry the "Cellini" cup could spark.

Actually, the "Cellini" cup was a forgery by the masterful 19th-century German goldsmith Vasters. When the forgery was discovered, the cup was renamed
the "Rospigliosi Cup" (Stone, n.d.). This true story could spur children to study
the history of forgery or great stories of crimes of deception and detection. This
could lead to reading Wilkie Collins's novel, *The Moonstone* (1998/1824), considered the first suspense novel, a tale of how each person who steals the moonstone
is cursed. Reading the novel could lead to finding out about precious gems. Each
brain makes its own chain of connections as it transcends, seeking to relate ideas
from past, present, and future.

Example 3: Literature as Pathway

The autobiography of Renaissance master and rogue Cellini suggests other
paths of inquiry. In his autobiography, Cellini describes the creation—and near
disaster—as he cast the famed bronze sculpture *Perseus Holding the Head of Medusa*,
considered by some the height of Renaissance sculpture. The piece has stood, since
its creation in 1554, in the Piazza della Signoria in Florence, Italy. Cellini's life in
the tumultuous 16th century, known through his autobiography, was filled with
fighting, imprisonment, and the creation of some of the most famous masterworks
of the Italian Renaissance.

The Autobiography of Benvenuto Cellini. Some literature buffs believe Cellini's autobiography contains the best stories ever written. One tells how Cellini
escaped from prison by stealing pliers, extracting the nails from the hinges of his

cell door, and replacing them with candle wax (Turismo. intoscana. it, n.d.). This tale of escape is as fine as those of the great Harry Houdini or Jean Valjean, hero of Victor Hugo's novel *Les Misérables*, who was thrown into a dungeon for stealing a loaf of bread. What teacher would not want to rouse children's desire to read such literature! As children read great novels, they transcend earlier experiences, carrying ideas along new paths and exercising high-level brain functions such as analogy and metaphor, deduction, transformation, and imagination.

Greek Mythology. The Greek myth tells how Perseus decapitated the hated Medusa whose eyes turned men to stone. Perseus's cap of invisibility and his mirror-like shield enabled him to cut off Medusa's head without looking at her eyes. Such stories lead, for children who have not been there, to Greek mythology, source of inspiration for theater, music, painting, sculpture, literature, and psychology. Cellini's *Perseus* has stories carved in every facet, including, some say, a small sculpture on the back of Perseus's neck that might be Cellini himself. More stories to whet children's appetite and a photo of Cellini's *Perseus* can be found on the web; some travel sites have excellent images. Telling children these stories expands their minds, builds bridges to new worlds, and provides the impetus to make connections among diverse ideas.

> Beauty in any modality—visual, linguistic, auditory, spatial—fills children's minds with sights, sounds, and stories that epitomize human achievement.

Summary: Museums' Rich Cornucopia

Museums bring together rich experiences that contain thoughtfully chosen subject matter that repeats itself with great variety, in many modalities, minute detail, redundantly, and with beauty. Richness enables mediators to branch readily from exhibits that seduce children's imagination to other subjects that, with mediators' intervention, lead the mind along diverse paths. When mediators use rich experiences, they bring complexity into children's lives; this keeps the brain focused and expands the meanings children can glean. Mediation induces a mind to explore. Calculated questions—"Can you imagine . . . ?"—may be all it takes to launch children on a reading adventure. Or, intentional remarks—"Suppose this happened because . . . !"—may set children on a quest that, in time, makes them their own mediators.

Museum exhibits offer entry points to vast areas of scholarship. The difference between a theme park and a museum is that scholarship informs the museum exhibit while physical sensation drives the thrilling theme park rides. The thrill of a mind to powerful ideas is the "exciting ride" offered by museums.

PROVIDING CONFLICT-PRODUCING IDEAS

Conflict causes "cognitive dissonance," which means that the brain is in a state of disequilibrium. Disequilibrium arrests attention, leaves one off balance, and makes one anxious to reestablish equilibrium. Disequilibrium creates "teachable moments"—and a strong desire to find an explanation—even if it is faulty! The brain seeks patterns even when they don't exist. Caution: "Truth" cannot be grasped merely through perception. Reread the myth of discovery in Chapter 1. Mediation that occurs when children are in a state of disequilibrium can *permanently* change how children think.

Falling Objects

This common science exhibit should cause cognitive dissonance: Press a button to watch objects of different shape and composition—a feather and a rock—drop in a vacuum. Watch the objects hit bottom together. The effect in the vacuum of a feather and rock hitting bottom together is counter to everything we have experienced about falling objects since, as infants, we dropped spoons from high chairs. The exhibit illustrates that, in an *airless* environment, falling objects behave differently than in our air-filled world where the rock would hit ground before the feather.

But the exhibit is not likely to make visitors wonder, much less cause disequilibrium, because complex factors interfere:

- Children (and adults) don't usually notice or think about the speed at which different objects drop.
- Many do not know that a vacuum means the absence of air.
- Most are unfamiliar with how objects fall in a vacuum.
- Few consider the fact that *air resistance* plays a major role in how fast objects fall in air (but not how fast they fall in a vacuum).

Because of these interfering factors, seeing the rock and feather reach bottom together does *not* set up a conflict in the brain, does not trigger the thought "something is wrong here," and does not cause cognitive dissonance or mental disquietude. Without a mental model of how falling objects behave and of the different effects of air and no air (vacuum), the exhibit will have no meaning and without mediation will not impact thinking. Understanding science phenomena requires diverse thinking processes with numerous steps and often prior knowledge. Perkins (1995) says that people who don't notice effects "tend to think by default in ways that are *hasty, narrow, fuzzy,* and/or *sprawling*" (p. 153).

Rethinking the Exhibit

Using the Cognitive Map (Chapter 6), the exhibit could be changed to involve children more and give mediators better handles to build understanding. Mediators might lack the background to help students think through the science. But the first step is to *recognize* the dissonance! Even without knowing the scientific principles, mediators can point out cognitive dissonances that children fail to notice.

Here, we apply the parameters of the Cognitive Map to the vacuum exhibit. Note the different mediation techniques:

- Test what happens in air-filled space to a ping-pong and baseball, a shoe and sheet of paper, a shoe and *crumpled* sheet of paper. (A shoe will hit before a sheet of paper but a shoe and crumpled paper will hit together.) This is a redundant experience in *visual, kinesthetic, baric,* and *haptic* modalities, with unexpected effects!
- Use a *kinesthetic* modality. *Handle* pairs of different objects in which both objects have the same dimension:
  - ✓ metal and Styrofoam rods of the same length and girth,
  - ✓ bocce ball and Nerf ball of the same diameter,
  - ✓ a brick and a cardboard box of identical measurement (variety, kinesthetic modality, comparative behavior).

First, experience the contrast in weight, then drop the pair of objects. These props *seem* to demonstrate that in air-filled spaces heavier objects reach ground before lighter ones. (Actually, this is a misperception because various factors affect the rate at which objects drop.)

- Focus on the stages of a mental act:
  - ✓ Input: Encourage children to observe closely, to remember by writing notes, drawing pictures, or photographing the pivotal moment as two objects fall (verbal or graphic modality, attention, comparison, association of ideas). (Feuerstein, Rand, & Feuerstein, 2006, p. 424)
  - ✓ Elaboration: Have children work together and talk out loud as they collaborate on their own experiments to test if heavy and lighter objects fall at the same or different speeds (verbal modality, hypothesis testing, sharing behavior). (Feuerstein, Rand, & Feuerstein, 2006, p. 423)
  - ✓ Output: Ask children to compare what they initially thought with what actually happened then restate or redraw the effect accordingly (verbal and graphic modalities, comparison, goal seeking). (Feuerstein, Rand, & Feuerstein, 2006, p. 423)
- *Engage mental operations.* Ask children to *predict* what will happen when two objects are dropped. Or, ask them to *deduce:*
  - ✓ by handling identical objects with different weights, then with the same weight but different amounts of air resistance;
  - ✓ by thinking about air resistance—examples: boxy versus sleek cars; coasting faster on a bike by bending over the handle bars (verbal modality, various analytical mental operations, search for logical evidence at input and output phases).

Children's responses reveal what they understand.

- *Analyze the exhibit's complexity* by asking children to consider what information they have, what they lack, and how it impacts their understanding of the exhibit (verbal modality, problem solving).

- Make the experience more *abstract* by having children imagine how living in an airless world would affect their daily activities (verbal or visual modality, transcendence).
- *Ask children to analyze their own mental state.* Did they think the ideas in the exhibit were difficult? What was familiar? What factors impacted their will to tackle and solve the problems? How would *they* change the exhibit to better understand it? (Verbal modality, cause and effect relationships.) (Feuerstein, Rand, & Feuerstein, 2006, pp. 423–425)

Even with excellent and multiple forms of mediation, in order to overcome intuitive but incorrect observations *children need to try experiments again and again and discuss them with someone knowledgeable.* As clever or enticing as exhibits—or any experiences—may be, they will not create conflict if children are unfamiliar with a phenomenon. Nor will manipulation alone enlighten children who are science-phobic or science illiterate. But, for those children who *do* feel disequilibrium, the way is paved to replace misunderstanding with the kind of thoughtful observation that is an essential part of thinking and the basis for learning.

For children who do *not* feel disequilibrium, the mediator's role is clear:

- Challenge children to discover "What Is Wrong Here!"
- Help children compare, contrast, use logical evidence, and in other ways explore systematically (Feuerstein, Rand, & Feuerstein, 2006, p. 425).
- Encourage children to express what they are doing in one or several modalities, verbally or nonverbally (p. 424).
- Make children conscious of how they are thinking by naming each mental act their minds perform.

Key Points
1. Science principles often involve two or more factors that are counter to perception.
2. The variables in an experiment must be identified—are we talking about weight? size? density? distance? speed?
3. Conditions must be identified—are we talking about air-filled spaces or vacuum chambers?
4. In complex phenomena (most natural phenomena are complex), isolate and explore one factor at a time.
5. Mediators need not know "answers" to help children learn analytic processes—but they do need to be inquisitive!

APPEALING TO MULTIPLE INTELLIGENCES

Children differ in how they absorb information. Some are visual, some auditory. Others process information through movement. Gardner (1983) named these different capacities "multiple intelligences." He says that museums may be the only places where people who are not linguistic or mathematical can successfully show off their skills. Museums

> offer kids lots of different ways to learn about things. They don't assume if you can't get it from a lecture or a book, that you're stupid. . . . Language is not [always] the best way to present everything, and yet in school, that often is the only way things are presented. . . . Because [museums] are open-ended institutions—as a visitor you're not told exactly what to do—you have a chance to figure out which way of learning about things is comfortable for you. (1992, p. 3)

Watch what happens in the following exhibits that draw on different intelligences.

Musical Intelligence

"The Invisible Harp" at CCM was a large electronic exhibit (see Figure 7.2). By waving your arms through an open space, you broke light waves, thus causing notes to sound. Musically inclined children quickly realized that placing their arms in particular places produced familiar tunes. Their success offered a model for other children to imitate (Feuerstein, Rand, & Feuerstein, 2006).

Current research is exploring the connection between music and various brain capacities. A comprehensive study by the Dana Foundation on the relation between arts experiences and attention found:

Figure 7.2. Children with musical intelligence intuitively understood that they could "play" music simply by moving their hands. Few, however, understood—or cared—that the effect was caused by breaking a beam of light on this harp with no strings.

Illustration by Daniel Feuerstein

In children, there appear to be specific links between the practice of music and skills in geometrical representation. . . . Correlations exist between music training and both reading acquisition and sequence learning. (Gazzaniga, 2008, p. vi)

Intelligences Observed

Some children know their own mind and go about their activities purposefully. Others resolve disputes or are naturally powerful convincers. Gardner (1983) calls these *personal* intelligences.

Teachers on field trips express surprise: "She knew just what she wanted to do!" (intrapersonal intelligence). Or, "Ronald can't be dumb if he can find his way around here!" (spatial intelligence). Or, "I thought Barbara was slow, but she solved that puzzle before anyone else" (spatial and kinesthetic intelligence). Such comments reveal that adults improved their opinion of children from seeing children's performance at a museum. Likewise, teachers of FIE are surprised when children perform tasks that even adults find difficult. Gardner says it is most important at elementary school age and the early years to have "opportunity to work intensively with the materials that nourish the various human intelligences and combinations of intelligences. . . . [T]he impact of encompassing milieus . . . [is that] the messages of learning and work are manifest and inviting" (1991, pp. 203–204).

Mediation does not directly depend on the modality or language in which the mediation is expressed. Gesture, mimicry, even silence as a teacher observes may be as potent ways to mediate as speech, although language, naturally, may be the most economic and efficient transmitter of learning (Feuerstein, Feuerstein, Falik, & Rand, 2006). Selecting a specific mode of instruction for a particular student shows a mediator's intention (Feuerstein, Rand, & Feuerstein, 2006). Explaining to children *why* you, the teacher, are using a particular mode makes children aware that they, too, can select a mode, either verbal or nonverbal, in which to express themselves (Feuerstein, Rand, & Feuerstein, 2006).

Feuerstein and his colleagues have observed that sometimes the worst performer becomes the best. Feuerstein says such children, especially low performers, are often intimidated by what they do not know. Why do they star after using FIE instruments? Failure may have resulted, not from inability to perform mental operations, but from inadequacy in the linguistic modality that predominates in school, or from being unfamiliar with content, or having no knowledge of the context. Content-free material gives children a new start in exercising their intelligence without triggering a prior failure syndrome.

When they observe children's behavior, mediators can see which modalities are effective with different children. The mediator's role is to:

- observe which modalities different children use naturally,
- provide experiences that engage those modalities,
- make children aware of their success.

This is particularly important for children who lack self-confidence (Feuerstein, Rand, & Feuerstein, 2006).

SUMMARY: MEDIATING EXHIBITS

Zen Rose, at age 5, was mesmerized by this diorama at the Denver Museum of Nature and Science: a mountain lioness with her fangs in a fallen deer and her kits watching from respectful distances. Countless times, Zen Rose positioned herself in front of the kit farthest from the lioness and pushed a button to hear the kit's mewing. Pointing to the lioness, she told her mother, "That's *you* bringing home dinner" and, pointing to the kit, "that's *me* waiting for you to feed me."

Zen Rose established a relation between the necessity of feeding the kits and of herself being fed. In doing so, she transcended the situation portrayed in the exhibit to a different—and very personal—instance of this universal need. Her mother, as her mediator, showed intention in bringing Zen Rose to see this exhibit often, conveying the exhibit's meaning, and encouraging Zen Rose to transcend the experience by engaging her in conversation about the animals' behaviors.

Museums' arsenal of clever techniques can powerfully attract the human brain and engage its capacity to change and propensity to learn. The magnet that aligns these two forces—museum exhibits and learning—is an adult's effective mediation.

Takeaways

1. Repetition is necessary to learn most things. When children become involved, don't hustle them on but let them continue until their interest wanes naturally.
2. Watch for examples of the same idea repeated in different exhibits; discuss the differences and similarities; form a relationship.
3. Keep an eye out for effects that are not what you would expect. The unexpected makes us notice and thus alerts the brain—a good state in which to learn something!
4. Watch for children's particular learning styles. Is she auditory? Does he learn by looking at sketches? Does she learn from having specific examples? Does he need to move? Go with the way children learn best, but also encourage them to try alternatives.
5. Learning does not always "show" immediately. Sometimes ideas are planted that do not sprout for some time. Revisit the museum experience by discussing it and thus encourage ideas to spout.

CHAPTER 8

More Essential Cognitive Acts

Train up a child in the way he should go, and when he is old he will not depart from it.

—Proverbs, 22:6

THE 3-MONTH-OLD infant was wailing, her crying reverberating throughout the large room. Charlie, 13 months old and newly walking, pointed at her, looking rapidly from the crying infant to his mother's eyes until he caught her attention. "Do you want," she asked Charlie, "to see that baby?" Charlie nodded emphatically, continuing to point and look at his mother's face. She picked him up and carried him across the room. Charlie immediately leaned toward the baby as far as his mother's arms would let him, reached the baby's head, and stroked it, cooing soothing sounds as he did.

Children are naturally empathetic, but may have little outlet to express empathy or little adult nurturance of this innately human trait. Children's natural sense of empathy can be fostered, especially if experiences are made meaningful by mediation. In this chapter, we describe four essential skills that are important parts of both lower- and higher-level thinking: empathy, new skill acquisition, thinking in varied modalities, and collaboration.

EMPATHY

Children's deepest feelings of empathy were evoked by the exhibit "Remember the Children" (see Chapter 4), an exhibit created by the Capital Children's Museum in Washington, D.C. The exhibit showed how the Holocaust changed the life of a child who was a victim. Visitors told us the exhibit stimulated soul-searching classroom dialogue that stimulated children's thinking about big ideas like prejudice, human relations, war, cruelty, bravery, and survival. We recommended the exhibit for children 8 or older and suggested that adults visit first.

"Remember the Children": Another Visit

Most youngsters are not exposed to cruelty; they trust adults and expect them to keep children safe. When young visitors learned how cruel the Nazis were to children, it came as a shock.

The Exhibit Experience. The exhibit begins as Daniel, a 10-year-old and a survivor of the Holocaust, narrates a film about the Holocaust from a child's perspective. Exiting the small theater, visitors find themselves on a street of townhouses in a pleasant neighborhood, any town, in any country of the world. Around a corner, we find ourselves in Daniel's living room: Classical music plays; sunlight streams through lace curtains; the furniture is plush. Brass candlesticks and silver-framed family pictures sit on the antique sideboard; books line floor-to-ceiling cases. Daniel's voice recounts their daily life—hot chocolate, skating parties, singing by firelight.

Daniel's narration continues describing how he and his family are forced to leave their home. Visitors encounter a second environment, a crowded street with many young children carrying large suitcases. Shortly, visitors reach another street, this one walled-in and crushed with people. Each time, the music changes—pleasant, then plaintive, then somber—and Daniel's narrative, about how his family is forced to move and where they are herded, becomes grimmer.

Finally, visitors arrive in a ghetto apartment—peeling paint, broken pipes, the one window barricaded with warped plywood. Furnishings are an old iron bed, dirty mattress, and broken cupboard, bare except for a few dented tin dishes. Here, Daniel and his family must crowd into a cramped ghetto room with ten strangers. On a high ledge are some books, a pair of brass candlesticks, and a couple of framed photos, reminders of the beloved home, grabbed in haste as the family fled. The contrast between the beautiful home and the decrepit room left many visitors in tears.

Processing the Experience. Outside the walk-through environments was a large, leather-bound book in which to write impressions. Nearby was the Eyewitness Chair, where a Holocaust survivor sat to discuss his own experience. During one of his many visits to the museum, Feuerstein took the chair. Sixty children sat gathered on the floor at his feet. His wife, Berta, of blessed memory, and Ann stood on the periphery with other adults. As Feuerstein spoke of his experiences fleeing from Romania, the list of youth resistors hidden in the lining of his shoe, Berta gasped and whispered: "He has never spoken of this before!"

The exhibit had evoked Feuerstein's own powerful memories and, decades later, telling his experience to strangers, many of them children who had just experienced the emotionally compelling exhibit, was a cathartic experience for this psychologist, an opportunity to use his own life story to mediate these children's grasp of a horrific historical experience, portentous human responses, and powerful emotions.

Talking with a survivor was one of numerous ways visitors could process the conflict they felt at the thought of unbounded adult cruelty to children. The remarks youngsters wrote in the leather books were empathetic: "What a horrible, cruel, unjust thing was done to the Jews." Or, "Why does there have to be prejudice?" In time, remarks filled many books, showing that visitors learned what prejudice is and the cruelties it can provoke. Youngsters' empathy was roused by the story of cruelty to children who had done nothing except be born Jewish. An idea repeated throughout the exhibit was the universality of human experience—the archetypal story of a beautiful existence turning into a nightmare.

We only scheduled groups when a survivor could talk with them face-to-face. The varied exhibits within "Remember the Children," the live interpretations, and meeting a survivor were mediating factors that fostered children's empathy. The evidence was children's fervent expressions of hope that the prejudice and cruelty of the Holocaust would never resurface.

Empathy-Evoking Exhibits

Many museums evoke empathetic responses. The National Civil Rights Museum (Memphis, Tennessee) features the balcony where Dr. Martin Luther King, Jr., was assassinated as the culmination of walk-through environments that powerfully re-create pivotal events in the civil rights movement of the 1950s and 1960s. On reaching the motel room where King stayed before he was shot, visitors become overwhelmed, tears stream down their faces. With great intention, the museum focuses visitors on instances of current human rights violations. Visitors relate the empathy triggered by the emotionally evocative story of Dr. King to the other examples of human rights abuses.

The New York Tenement Museum restored a multistory building built in 1863 that, between then and 1935, housed 7,000 immigrants as they arrived in America, began to make a living, settle their family, and educate their children. Five different tours take you through careful reconstructions of their crowded apartments with narration of each family's struggle. Visitors choose a family and take a 1- to 2-hour walk through their life. Take a virtual tour on the museum's website; Google the name of the museum and go to the home page.

The Trail of Tears is a 2,200-mile route over land and water that follows the exile of the Cherokee Indians who in 1838 were moved from their land in southern Appalachia and forced to walk to Indian Territory over 1,000 miles away, crossing the present-day states of Alabama, Arkansas, Georgia, Illinois, Kentucky, Missouri, North Carolina, Oklahoma, and Tennessee. A quarter to a half of their people died. Today, the National Park Service maintains the trail. An interactive map, maintained by the National Park Service on its website, tells stories of what happened at various places on the Trail.

The Brain and Empathy

Feeling empathy draws on many systems in the brain; it "transcend[s] those experiences directly available to the senses" (Feuerstein, Feuerstein, Falik, & Rand, 2006, p. 88). An FIE-Basic instrument that teaches 3- to 10-year-olds to read others' emotions lays the groundwork for empathy. The instrument builds the capacity to use information that comes secondhand, without having had an experience oneself.

To feel empathy, one must:

- be aware,
- find meaning,
- make comparisons,
- take another person's perspective,

- understand qualities of life such as freedom, individual rights, the common good, and other values.

Having empathy means representing the other in oneself to such an extent that one can consider it one's own experience and react accordingly.

Such experiences provide openings for mediators to engage children in dialogue, to talk about issues of deep importance—humans' consideration for one another, their hostility, or compassion. "Emotion and cognition," says Feuerstein, "play complementary roles in the feeling of empathy. In order to feel empathy, you must experience another's suffering. But you must also know what happened to the victim—a cognitive process—in order to identify with him." A characteristic of autism is an incapacity to feel what others feel; thus, children with autism may laugh when someone falls down or cries. Empathy-rousing experiences can be used to confront issues that, without sensitive mediation, are too often pushed aside—ridicule, bullying, tattling, sarcasm, verbal or physical abuse. These issues stand at the intersection between your image of yourself, other's attitude toward you, and their treatment of you.

Mediating Empathy

Exhibits that evoke empathy are powerful stimuli to help children interpret experiences critically:

- *Causation.* What caused (the Holocaust? King's assassination? waves of immigration? Native Americans' displacement?)
- *Values.* Was (name the event) fair? Why? Did anyone benefit? How? Why not? Was anyone hurt? How?
- *Reality.* Have you ever experienced prejudice? How did it make you feel? Did you ever express prejudice? How? Why?

Video, literature, museum exhibits, or one's own experiences evoke empathetic feelings. These feelings are fodder to stimulate discussion about values.

> Making children conscious of feelings builds empathy; making them conscious of brain functions builds cognition.

ACQUIRING NEW SKILLS

Adults take for granted the science projects, craft items, or art that children produce. They may *ooh* and *aah*, but few understand what has gone on in children's brains to result in these products. Here, we explain a craft activity and its relation to the brain.

Experience: Making a Chinese Emblem

The Chinese Dragon Boat Race is an annual festival on the Charles River near Harvard Yard in Cambridge, Massachusetts. It features Asian music, food, dance performances, and crafts-making designed by the Boston Children's Museum. At age 6, Lewin-Benham's grandson Sheppy loved the crafts. One required children to draw a design, trace it with a stylus to "emboss" thick gold foil, back the foil with cardboard, fold foil over the cardboard's edges, punch a hole, and insert a cord. Sheppy strung the cord with his design and colored beads—the result a handsome piece of jewelry. The experience mediated goal-seeking, goal-setting, goal-planning, and goal-achieving behaviors (Feuerstein, Rand, & Feuerstein, 2006).

The Brain and Skill

The craft required the brain to respond in varied ways that enlarge the cognitive repertoire and develop new hand skills. Children had to:

- focus and plan (input phase);
- work systematically (elaboration phase) to
  - ✓ select relevant behaviors
  - ✓ direct the hands to perform in highly articulated ways (elaboration phase);
- explain an intent clearly: "I want the hole in the corner, not the middle, so it doesn't spoil the design." (output phase).

Making something visually appealing satisfies the human desire for beauty. Becoming skilled builds self-confidence; having efforts appreciated fosters self-esteem. These feelings are important components of motivation. Motivation affects every cognitive act.

As you explore a museum, ask children what skills they would like to acquire: Would you like to paint like that? carve such a canoe? make dioramas? create electric sparks? Ask if children think it would be hard or easy. Ask how they would learn the skill. Ask what skills they possess, their friends or family members possess, what skills they admire. Mediate to bring skill—one's own and others'—to children's conscious attention (Feuerstein, Rand, & Feuerstein, 2006).

MASTERING VARIED MODALITIES

Most people know what the senses are; fewer know what modalities are. Senses are systems of specific, highly complex, special-purpose networks of neurons that connect humans with their environment. Sensory networks communicate seemingly instantly with other neuronal networks. Modalities are both the physical properties (light, sound, color, and so on) that trigger a sense to receive stimuli and the means that humans use to express themselves. There are, literally, thousands of receptive and expressive modalities. Some of the most common modalities are words, numbers, gestures, images, music, and symbols of every kind. Here, we explore connections between the senses and modalities and describe transformation—experiencing something in one modality and expressing it in another.

Using Hand/Vision Thinking

"Closed Boxes" is a common exhibit. Children put in their hand to identify an object (one object per box) by feeling, then describe what they have felt in words, pictures, or gestures. Feeling an object causes tactile (the feather is soft), haptic (tactile and movement combined—the golf ball is bumpy), and auditory stimulation (the bell rings) to trigger receptors in the brain. Describing the object—an expressive act—engages vocal, gestural, mark-making, or other modalities.

Vary the experience: Have children select from among several pictures (visual modality) the one that *precisely* represents the felt object. Selecting the picture requires the brain to translate a tactile experience to a visual representation.

Or, harder: Have children match what they felt to pictures that are each just a bit different from one another except for one picture that is an *exact* match. This is a more challenging cognitive task because children use their fingers to extract much more detailed information. As mediators observe children's responses to the "Closed Box," they can pinpoint deficiencies in receptive and expressive capacities.

Switching Modalities

Ask children to arrange the Montessori bells (13 movable bells, middle to high C), wood blocks, chimes, or any series of tones in a specific sequence (low to high, the major scale, the chord C-E-G). This is an auditory challenge. Translate the challenge into a visual modality by asking children to arrange the bells so they correspond to symbols. For example:

- A pattern of long lines and short lines (visual input) could be transformed to tones (auditory output) if long lines represented low tones and short lines represented high tones.
- Dots (visual input) toward the top of a page could represent high tones and dots at the bottom of a page could represent low tones—visual input to auditory output.

A teacher set out symbols—stars in a straight row, circles in a zigzag—and challenged children to "hop out" the pattern, transforming visual input to kinesthetic output. Another teacher had children use a different symbol for each part of speech (square for noun, circle for verb, and the like, a classic Montessori technique), transforming from a category of speech (an abstract concept) to a symbol, another abstraction. Such exercises challenge the brain's elaboration processes as children experience something one way but express the experience a different way. Each teacher talked with children about what brain functions they were using and why: You are using *auditory* cues to make a *spatial pattern*. Or, you are using *visual symbols* to *move your body* in particular directions. All these examples show children transforming information: receiving in one and expressing in a different modality—a high-level cognitive function.

"Reading" Modalities

When we transform letters into sounds (reading aloud) or spoken words into letters (writing), we use conventional signs (letters) as substitutes for words. Words represent real objects, experiences, or ideas but are themselves symbolic. In the following three descriptions, children must "read" increasingly abstract transformations (see Chapter 5).

Traces. Traces, the least abstract transformation, are close substitutes for real objects—for example, paw prints, shadows, Hansel and Gretel's trail of bread crumbs, the waft of a scent, an eagle's scream. Traces are relatively easy to read as, for example, stepping alongside paw prints, interpreting shadows' outline, recognizing Dad by his aftershave. Traces are expressed in visual, tactile, auditory, and myriad other modalities; they trigger different forms of sensory awareness.

Symbols. Symbols are more abstract substitutes for reality than traces because symbols are more personal systems. Recognizing symbols depends on mediation because many symbols are not universal. For example, national anthems symbolize a group's unity: Voices fervently sing the song; patriotic feelings surge but only in those who have been taught the music's meaning. Banners, called Rofur, carried by fearsome Samurai warriors in 16th- and 17th-century Japan, struck terror in their enemies' hearts. To us, they are merely images of trees, chrysanthemums, and other graceful natural forms because we have neither personal experience nor education about their meaning in their culture.

Abstract Symbols. Words, numerals, and similar conventions are the most abstract substitutes for reality. In themselves, they convey no meaning; therefore, it requires highly systematic mediation to learn them. Reading skills, for example, are taught over 3 to 6 years; playing musical instruments is taught over many years. Examples of abstract systems include:

- sign language (gestural),
- hobo code (pictorial),
- semaphore (visual and kinesthetic),
- Morse code (kinesthetic and auditory),
- icons and road signs (visual),
- Braille (kinesthetic),
- pig Latin (auditory).

Sign language is a natural system because it is created spontaneously and then modified meaningfully by those who use it. Language is so integral a part of being human that children who are born deaf, if left to their own devices, will invent a sign language. Signing uses the same syntactical forms as speech—plurals, past and future tense, spatial relations, conditionals (could, would, should). Linguists cite spontaneous signing as evidence that, barring congenital brain damage, the brain is prewired with linguistic forms. Although word order, prefixes, suffixes, and other grammatical forms are endlessly varied across cultures, every language, including sign language, enables its speakers to express negatives, conditionals, pretense, and many other kinds of cognitive/emotional thinking. In other words, linguists have found the same underlying structure in all language (Pinker, 1994).

Variations in languages, while enormous barriers between peoples, are merely different modalities in which the innate human capacity for language is expressed.

Music is a universal brain system that powerfully transmits feelings. Neurologist Oliver Sacks (2008) says:

> Musical fragments make their way to the thalamocortical systems that underlie consciousness and self, and there they are elaborated and clothed with meaning and feeling. . . . By the time such fragments reach consciousness, meaning and feeling have already been attached. (p. 88)

Humans generate feelings and understand information that is received and transmitted in innumerable ways. The ability to transform one modality to another is one of many remarkable brain functions.

The Brain and Modalities

The more modalities children learn, the more options their brains have at the input and output phases of a mental act. Also, the more abstract the modality, the further a learner moves from direct experience and the greater the cognitive challenge. Mastering the challenges of "cognitive distance" leads to advanced thinking, creativity, and the ability to innovate. Accumulating research shows which neuronal networks are involved when higher-level brain functions perceive in one modality, process in many, and express in one or several others.

Identifying objects by feeling (see "Closed Boxes" exhibit above) requires several simultaneous cognitive acts:

- hold in mind what you have felt,
- retrieve the name from your "mental dictionary,"
- express a tactile experience verbally.

Translating from one modality to another requires regulation and control of behavior as children gather data. Those who fail to identify the objects, to name them, or to match an object to a picture may look or feel quickly and carelessly, may not plan, may be impulsive or unsystematic. Failure can occur at the input, elaboration, or output phase of the task (see Chapter 6). Failure could result from children's being "modality-blind" (unable to take in information in a certain modality) or "dumb" (unable to express themselves in a certain modality). Other possible reasons for failure are enumerated in the list of cognitive functions (Feuerstein, Rand, & Feuerstein, 2006; see Appendix A).

With hundreds of billions of possible neuronal connections, the brain moves, virtually instantly, from a sensory experience to a global concept. The concepts we form make us unique. According to Nobel Prize–winning neurobiologist Gerald Edelman, consciousness means reusing neuronal networks; in a highly subjective process, the brain continually maps and remaps experiences that gradually build networks and layers of networks. In Edelman's words: "Every single brain is absolutely individual. It's very likely that [each person's] own brain is unique in the history of the universe" (2009, p. 1). The fact that the meaning of stimuli can be conveyed in a virtually unlimited number of modalities enables mediators to help hard-to-reach children. Here mediators combine their skill in observing children with the art of selection (Feuerstein, Rand, & Feuerstein, 2006).

> "The number of possible interconnections between [brain] cells *is greater than the number of atoms in the universe*" (Ornstein & Thompson, 1984, p. 21).

COLLABORATING

A primary emphasis of education is to teach youngsters the skills of sharing, taking turns, listening, and collaborating. Some museums intentionally design exhibits that, like using a seesaw or playing checkers, require collaboration.

Exhibit: Sound Mirrors

A common science center exhibit that requires collaboration consists of a pair of parabolic sound mirrors set opposite one other across a large space (see Figure 8.1). The sound "mirror" reflects sound waves, not light waves. No matter how softly one person whispers into a dish, the other person hears clearly. But, without a partner, the exhibit won't function. Some children figure out how to use the exhibit by imitating, others only through a mediator's explanation. Few, if any, read the labels, although some adults use labels to explain how the exhibit works or what scientific principle(s) make the effect possible.

> Imitation trumps labels in helping children understand what to do. But mediation is required to help children understand principles.

Exhibit: The Blond Baldy

A popular collaborative exhibit, created by The Exploratorium, is "Everyone Is You and Me." Two people sit facing through a two-way mirror that is lit on each side (see Figure 8.2). Lowering or raising the light level superimposes one person's face on the other: A fair-haired girl sees herself with a dark mustache and steel-rimmed glasses; an old-timer sees his bald pate replaced with luxuriant blond hair. The exhibit compels strangers to remain together fiddling with their appearance.

The bizarre experience wakes up the brain and makes children aware of changes as they acquire attributes that are markedly another's and see themselves as partly that other. Collaboration occurs spontaneously, but understanding the principles about light and vision that explain the phenomenon requires mediation. Many experiences offer more than one focus for mediation—here, collaboration, forming hypotheses, or a lesson on light and optics.

Figure 8.1. A child at one end of the long hall who whispers into the parabolic sound mirror can be heard by a friend at the other mirror. The exhibit depends on collaboration and, most often, someone to explain what to do.

Illustrations by Daniel Feuerstein

Figure 8.2. Taking on another person's physical characteristics and clothing is intriguing and requires collaboration. A mediator must explain how lights, mirrors, and the visual system interact to create the effect.

The Brain and Collaboration

Individuals' different skills make collaboration possible. One reads instructions; another interprets them. One deftly manipulates complicated devices. Another's strong memory keeps track of turns. One notices small effects that others miss. Another has the interpersonal skill to forestall or solve disputes. Children expand their skills by observing others and exercise their strengths by working with others.

Collaboration stimulates children to explain, share observations, engage in dialogue, combine strategies, exercise patience, and complete tasks. Explaining something to another person builds your own understanding. Ultimately, it is through talk focused on problem solving—particularly among children who approach tasks differently—that learning occurs. "All higher mental functions . . . are initially created through collaborative activity" (Kozulin, 1988; Wertsch, 1985b, 1991a, quoted in Berk & Winsler, 1995, p. 20).

Mediators can make collaborative behaviors explicit by talking to children about their different individual strengths. Feuerstein calls this "mediation of individuation and psychological differentiation" and "shared behavior" (Feuerstein, Rand, & Feuerstein, 2006, pp. 423–424). When adults make children aware of collaboration, they are mediating reciprocity, helping children understand both the process and benefit of consciously sharing what you know with another (Feuerstein, Rand, & Feuerstein, 2006). Neurologist Frank Wilson (1998) hypothesizes that collaborative activity was the force that brought about changes in the brain that eventually enabled speech to evolve.

> The solitary work of some classrooms eliminates the possibility for collaboration.

Parent/Child Collaboration

In studying how parents and children collaborate on science exhibits, researchers Crowley and Callanan (1998) found that children who used exhibits with their parents present used the exhibit as designed, stayed at the exhibit longer, and performed each kind of exploration repeatedly.

> Children without parents present . . . most often . . . moved on to another exhibit after less than one minute of engagement. . . . In interactions where parents explained, children were more than twice as likely to *talk* about what they were seeing while exploring the exhibit . . . [and] in almost every case where children explained, they did so in response to an adult explanation. (p. 15)

Typically, we think that children consider evidence and construct theories on their own (see Myths, Chapter 1). But Crowley and Callanan conclude that this does not square with the literature on how children develop scientific thinking:

> Our findings suggest that theories of the development of scientific thinking need to be reformulated to account for the *parents' central role as guide and interpreter.*

Our findings also suggest that museums interested in supporting children's scientific thinking must consider designing not just for an audience of children but for an audience of children and parents engaged in collaborative learning. (1998, p. 15, emphasis added)

These conclusions extend not just to scientific thinking in museums but to thinking about any subject matter in any setting. Mediation to encourage adult/child collaboration is essential if we want learning to be effective or want children to think more efficiently about increasingly complex matters. By encouraging children to collaborate, teachers can effectively mediate sharing behavior, reciprocity, perception of feelings, transmission of values, and many other thinking/feeling acts (Feuerstein, Rand, & Feuerstein, 2006).

COMPLEX THINKING ACTS

Cognition may become very complex because there are many acts involved in thinking: focusing attention, selecting a stimulus to pay attention to, remaining focused, analyzing a situation, defining a problem, considering an approach, finding a solution, and expressing results.

The Basis for Expertise

Cognition is complex because it requires (1) thinking about highly differentiated problems and (2) using many different thinking skills in any one task. Consider: packing a suitcase, choosing the setting on a microwave, finding the least congested roads, solving problems in physics class. Initially, each is a high-level challenge that, through repetition, eventually leads to expertise so that the task can be done easily.

Expertise is a combination of skills that have been habituated and a kind of meta-knowledge that the expert exhibits while performing. Brain scientists are hard-pressed to quantify expertise although many top labs research the topic. Consider chess masters' thinking that has been studied by, among others, the pioneering computer scientists William Chase and Herbert Simon. Chase and Simon (1973)

estimate[d] the size of a grandmaster chess player's repertoire of chess patterns . . . at about 50,000! "Not so unbelievable," they averred. This is roughly the vocabulary of an extremely literate English-speaker, and grandmaster level chess players are as literate as you can get in chess. (quoted in Perkins, 1995, p. 217)

Since then, the Chase/Simon estimate has been challenged, but it stands as an imposing testimony to the degree to which expert performance is memory dependent.

Continuing research suggests that visualization, thinking ahead, and neural mechanisms not yet understood may equally affect expertise (Chabris & Hearst, 2003).

David's mother realized that, at age 10, his handwriting was a stumbling block in his writing fluently but that he loved using the computer. She found a free touch-typing site with a program that follows a logical, step-by-step progression in series of exercises (http://www.typeonline.co.uk/lesson1.html). Each exercise gives immediate feedback about David's speed and accuracy so that he can, literally, watch the skill grow. The feedback motivated David to practice. Interestingly, the site is visually drab; there are no games, spacemen, aliens, or sounds—things adults assume must be present to hold children's attention. Hopefully, this link will be active for a long time because most of the programs we have tested miss the mark in motivating and holding a child's attention or in logical presentation of the subtasks to be mastered.

Expertise develops from the habituation of many different, separate skills that combine in the graceful, precise, and seemingly intuitive acts of the master athlete, surgeon, singer, architect, poet—or touch-typist. Setting children on a route toward expertise requires first nurturing an apparent interest or seeding an interest that arouses a child's passion. Next are the analyses of what cognitive functions comprise the skill, what stimuli will motivate the stick-to-itiveness required for mastery, and how to provide feedback so children can see their progress. The child's motivation will determine how aggressively he or she strives to acquire the skill, but motivation in turn is affected by the nature of the stimulus.

Thinking and Transfer

Cognition involves, among other factors, drawing on what an individual already knows to solve new problems. Cognitive psychologists call this transfer—learning something in one situation and applying it in different instances. Lewin-Benham's father told her to study Latin because its logical constructions would make her better at math. She recalls that learning Latin had no effect on math but enabled her to understand English grammar. Without knowing Latin's case endings, she would have found English grammar incomprehensible. Perkins (1995) says transfer can occur but needs "point-blank attention. In particular, the effective teaching of general thinking strategies demands plenty of work on . . . transfer with its emphasis on active, reflective connection making" (p. 227).

In Feuerstein's theory, transcendence, as an essential component of mediation, both develops a propensity to transfer and provides concrete experience in doing so. What transfers, says Feuerstein, are mental constructs—concepts, principles, strategies, vocabulary, rules. Recall the various factors that enabled Rachael, in Chapter 5, to acquire a new schemata. Or, why Sheppy (above) was able quickly to master—and appreciate—a new craft technique. Psychologist Lauren Resnik calls this "situated cognition," the idea that learning needs to be embedded in a context. When transfer occurs, we can assume that there has been effective mediation and a base of experience (schemata) from which a rule or "special purpose production system" (Perkins, 1995, p. 155) forms in the brain and is applied to different acts of thinking.

> Finding transcendent ideas is a way to generalize from one instance to others, or in other words, "transfer."

MUSEUMS' ABUNDANT EXPERIENCES

Museums provide far more kinds of experiences than schools, where domains are generally separate from one another, the modality of instruction is mostly verbal, and assessment is based mainly on written tests. Math is unlikely to be taught as part of learning to read; physics is generally taught only as science, independent of history or math. In contrast, museums mix domains, instruct in varied modalities, and make performance the basis for assessment.

You might, for example, encounter a physics exhibit organized on a historical timeline; see reenactments of the moment when revolutionary thinkers, such as Copernicus (1473–1543), have their startling insight; or manipulate models yourself to make the planets rotate and revolve. In school, you meet these ideas as words in books, lectures, algebraic equations, or physics problems. In museums, you use telescopes, see images from satellite flybys as you sit in the command module of a space vehicle, or manipulate computer simulations of complex ideas. The Museum of Science in Boston has simulations in which you genetically engineer food. In other words, you meet content in a context. Your understanding in school is judged by your written responses to test questions. In museums, your *performance* shows what you know—whether you manipulate models correctly, carry out experiments logically, ask questions that relate to what you see, or explain phenomena clearly.

When an exhibit grabs a child's attention, it provides an entry point for mediators to:

- explain or augment content,
- discuss related concepts,
- isolate deficient thought processes and build them beginning with concrete and moving to increasingly abstract experiences, and
- guide students to resources where they can find out more.

Museums' integrated subject matter and varied modalities level the playing field for students whose strong suits are not language or math. This does not mean the written modality is unnecessary. Just the opposite: Written, representational, essentially verbal modalities are the main medium of and help children move to higher-level thinking. If children cannot explain what they are thinking verbally, they will have difficulty elaborating. But verbal functions develop most readily when essential, lower-level brain functions have been engaged during children's early years, functions such as those discussed in Chapter 5—attention, imitation, spatial orientation, and movement.

Museums' many modalities enable teachers to observe children in new settings and thus see their capacities or deficiencies in a new light. With this added perspective, teachers are better equipped to plan what content to provide, strengths to build, or deficiencies to overcome. The goal is to equip children with the cognitive structures necessary to meet the challenges of an increasingly complex world.

SUMMARY: MEDIATING FOR COMPLEXITY

Whether in museum, classroom, or elsewhere, harnessing the brain depends on how experiences are mediated. As you move from museum or classroom into the less structured and stimulating outer world, the challenge is to apply the same ideas about stimuli, experience, and mediation in diverse places. The question—wherever you are—is how any direct experience can be mediated so that the brain embraces complexity, so it re-creates past experience, elaborates current experience, imagines future experience, and in the process makes connections, sees relationships, and applies principles.

Takeaways

1. Young children are naturally empathetic, a tendency that can be strengthened by a mediator's asking children to discuss their awareness of others' situation.
2. The more mediated experiences children have had, the easier it is for them to learn new skills or ideas that in some way relate to past experience.
3. Encouraging children to receive new information in varied modalities and to express themselves in different modalities expands the brain's capacities.
4. Collaboration stimulates children to show one another what they can do and thus reinforces skills and enhances feelings of competence.

CHAPTER 9

Blue Sky Partnerships

Do not be conformed to this word, but be transformed by your mind.

—Romans, 12:2

FEUERSTEIN'S IDEAS about mediation are expanded in this chapter with several ideas about how to develop or strengthen partnerships between schools and museums in order to further children's thinking and learning. The ideas fall in two categories: increasing the effectiveness of mediation and merging best features of museums and schools.

Ideas in this chapter expand a teaching repertoire from the Cognitive Map (Chapter 6), analysis of "thinking deficiencies" (see Chapter 6 and Appendix A), and mediation techniques (shown throughout the book) to include:

- soliloquy,
- mentoring, and
- unusual collaborations with museums.

Ideas in this chapter challenge museums to:

- provide props,
- collaborate with schools in creating museum-like exhibits, and
- adopt students as interns in diverse work settings.

Many museums run excellent and varied programs to apprentice students. Reaching more than the fortunate students who are selected would require new levels of school/museum collaboration, staffing commitments, and the belief that the benefits would be worth the investment.

BELIEFS ABOUT LEARNING

Some people use test scores as evidence of learning. Others use performance—babies' walking and talking, an improved golf swing. Feuerstein considers learning *growth in the efficiency and effectiveness with which the brain processes whatever challenges it faces*. Learning means that the brain changes so that we develop abilities such as using language precisely, sinking hook shots, launching rockets. In other words, learning is demonstrated growth in the ability to "mobilize" an expressive capacity or to solve challenges of increasing complexity.

133

What *Does* Learning Look Like?

Many believe only places that look like school are educational, that learning takes place mainly in classrooms with children at desks facing the teacher at front, that children learn when they are silent, still, or scared.

In reality, learning occurs when children are focused, active, and joyful. Learning also occurs when children are challenged, provided that challenges neither bore nor overwhelm. The popular phrase *in the zone* and the concept of *flow* (Csikszentmihalyi, 1990) describe the ideal state in which someone learns. Children's excitement and joy in museums do not match some people's mental image of learning. Yet, fun, excitement, laughter, and activity are all hallmarks of how learners behave and, more important, are powerful aides to learning. Yet, these behaviors typically occur out of school. John Falk and Lynn Dierking (2010), who write about learning in museums, find that nonschool resources account for the vast majority of America's science learning.

What Is Content?

Schools call content "curriculum;" playgrounds call it "recreation;" sports fields call it "practice." Museums call it "exhibit themes." Many content-rich environments have no label. Photographer Robert Capa, whose battlefront images revolutionized war photography and became icons of human emotion, used the city of Budapest as his learning ground. Before his teenage years, "He was intimate with every scrap of green space, every alley, every stop on the subway" (Marton, 2006, p. 53). Marton says of Michael Curtiz, director of the movie *Casablanca*: "Neither his parents nor his schools shaped Curtiz. It was Budapest" (2006, p. 16).

Compared with city streets, museum exhibits are highly formalized. Yet, exhibits rarely parallel the textbooks and curricula that many people believe are *the* checklists for what children should learn. Without considering either the content of school materials or what children actually learn from them, adults assume that, if materials are in classrooms, they are educational. But, for many children, a mediated experience in a museum may provide just the "takeaway" that makes sense of school learning. Rabbi Rafi Feuerstein (personal communication, April 20, 2010) said, "Through mediation a child learns a universal language that enables him to interact with content in many different contexts." In other words, mediation builds brain functions that underlie *all* thinking.

> Content, the "stuff" of thinking, is more than likely to be found out of school.

An Example: Math. The grocery store exhibit in children's museums may resemble the play grocery in preschools. However, on comparison, the museum exhibit probably has:

- scales that work—a precisely calibrated measurement device;
- a real cash register that displays values or prints an itemized list of purchases—forms of symbolic expression;

- realistic food—spurs comparison and categorization;
- variety of foods—heightens interest and offers novelty and complexity.

The exhibit lends itself to concrete early math experiences while the school grocery lends itself mainly to imitation. Imitation is important in learning. But, when a space is not well equipped, it limits what children can learn.

Consider that the well-equipped museum grocery store can be used to develop mathematical thinking skills when mediators encourage children to:

- count specific numbers of fruits, vegetables, or other foods;
- classify groceries into meats, dairy, baked goods;
- categorize items: beef, chicken, poultry, non-meat;
- learn to read a scale;
- assemble items in series: more or less heavy, numerous, colorful, aesthetic, healthful;
- make sets, like the set we eat at breakfast or dinner, the set we use to bake a cake;
- use one-to-one correspondence: We have four people in our family and each will eat one container of pudding. How many will we need?;
- learn to add money: Each jar costs $1; you have three jars; how many dollars will that cost?;
- learn the language of fractions: Buy half a loaf of bread, a quarter pound of butter;
- learn the language of arithmetic functions: three times as many apples;
- learn the language of containers: pint, quart, half gallon;
- learn the language of weight: ounce, pound.

Consider: Are there objects to manipulate so that children engage mental processes such as progressions or seriation? (See Chapter 6.) Are there different modalities so that children's receptive and expressive capacities grow? Is there variety so children can compare and establish a basis for precision in observing stimuli?

In a well-equipped "grocery," mediators can encourage children to organize items in numerous ways that draw on higher-level thinking skills. In addition to the mathematical example above, grocery items could be organized by what the body requires to be well nourished and maintain healthful weight; what processes food undergoes from source to table; the transportation required for the foods we eat; historical factors that determined what humans eat; geographical factors that influence different cultures' food.

In rich environments, opportunities for mediation abound and possibilities for connections are endless. Objects are the stimuli from which children construct concepts and, with mediation, expand, alter, or consolidate them. Caution: Worksheets—even with questions like those above—subvert mediation. Mediation is a two-way exchange between mediator and student(s) in which one's response influences the others. Filling in worksheets is not a responsive process.

Mediators observe for cues of what interests children. Of the features listed above, only some—perhaps only one—will interest a given child. Mediators' responses to individuals' interest(s) determine the content of the interaction. But mediators' interactions are determined by how well the environment is prepared.

Another Example: History. Most elementary schools teach children about their town's history, and most towns have historic houses, portraying bygone days or recalling famous residents. The school version of the history may be written in textbook-ese with limited vocabulary and politically correct "facts" that are sterile, devoid of conflict, and closed to interpretation. Historic houses capture imagination with real artifacts, demonstrations, and storytelling by staff who excel as "historic enactors," dressing and portraying noted historic persons or common residents of particular periods.

Consider the story of Thomas Jefferson's perpetual clock, installed in 1792 at his home, Monticello, in Charlottesville, Virginia:

> Jefferson designed the clock for a home in Philadelphia, and upon the arrival of weights for its installation at Monticello, it was discovered that the height of the Entrance Hall was shorter than the length of the ropes. Jefferson's solution? Allow the weights "to descend naked till they get to the floor where they enter a square hole and descend to the cellar floor. . . ." The holes were cut, the weights were hung, and the marker for Saturday may be found on the basement level of the house. (Monticello, 2011)

How exciting for children to realize that a great statesman/inventor/president made a mistake and to learn how he rectified it. Jefferson relied on content knowledge and know-how:

- representing time by marking segments on a rope
- using varied modalities: auditory, visual, and kinesthetic
- using spatial thinking to visualize what was below the Entrance Hall so he could predict where the weights would go
- thinking efficiently in the three phases of a mental act
- using cognitive operations, including
  - ✓ analysis of a difficult problem
  - ✓ analogous reasoning
  - ✓ transformation
- confronting complexity, evident in the numerous kinds of information required to solve the problem
- engaging in abstract and symbolic thinking: representing the passage of time (an abstract concept) with weights and rope (symbolic representation)
- working efficiently
- persevering.

Jefferson's success is apparent in the fact that the clock has worked accurately for over 200 years.

Mediators can:

- ask challenging questions: How could Jefferson predict where to cut holes in the floor?
- draw on the Cognitive Map (Chapter 6) as we have done above,
- encourage children to find examples of Jefferson's goal-seeking, goal-achieving, scheduling, and spatial orientation, thus connecting each example to an essential thinking skill,
- challenge students to re-create a similar clock or devise an original one.

> Content provides the "stuff" of which mental acts are made.

Content: The "Stuff" of Thinking. Few people aside from psychologists can identify the mental acts necessary to understand and solve problems. Teachers may not be skilled at analyzing how or what children are learning. Not knowing how to judge whether children are learning reinforces the belief that children only learn in school. As an analytic tool, the Cognitive Map can reveal the nature of the tasks in an experience. However, adults still must realize that:

- Deep engagement is evidence that children are learning. (Yet, we see deeply engaged children pulled away to see the next exhibit.)
- Repetition, which is essential for learning almost anything, occurs when children are deeply engaged. (Interruptions prevent children's repeating.)
- Variety makes repetition palatable.

Connections between the content of museum exhibits and school curricula may not be obvious. For example, certain modern paintings—Kenneth Noland, Josef Albers, Piet Mondrian—offer a curriculum in shape, color, repetition, ratio, proportion, and other math concepts that draw on geometry and symmetry. Search the web to find sites that connect art and mathematical properties.

In a lecture at the Capital Children's Museum mathematician, computer scientist, and epistemologist Seymour Papert said, "You cannot think without thinking about *something*." In other words, content is the "stuff" the brain uses to analyze, infer, deduce, synthesize, and perform any mental operation. The more content children know, the more they can think about. Lewin-Benham recalls:

> Shep, age 6, and I exited from the wrong stop on Boston's MTA. Ahead was a towering glass-clad skyscraper and reflected in the glass was a late 1800s brownstone church. To me, the sight was overwhelming. I exclaimed: "Sheppy! Look at this juxtaposition of old and new." To which Sheppy responded, "It's like the layers of old and new rock inside the earth."

Sheppy's comparison of old and new buildings to rock layers of different ages revealed the rich "stuff" in his brain. Museums are full of rich stuff. Systematic mediation stimulates children to use the "stuff" in the environment thoughtfully.

Mediators don't always know what children will take from rich experiences. Mathematician and museum educator Eddie Goldstein recalls his daughter

Star's experience at the Denver Museum of Nature and Science exhibit "RocketWorks." Over several visits, Star worked for hours to build and launch a paper rocket to "hit the moon," 100 feet away. Months later, in a class about the planets, Star learned that, at their thinnest, Saturn's rings are only 100 feet thick. She told Eddie: "Do you know how far 100 feet is? That's how far I shot that rocket!" For Star, the content of "RocketWorks" became a measurement device.

> Adults' responsibility is to ensure that content is rich enough to be worthy of the brain's enormous capacity to form relationships.

ADULT INTERVENTIONS

How adults intervene in children's experiences matters. Two useful techniques are soliloquy, a type of adult performance; and mentoring, a set of behaviors to guide adult/child interactions.

Soliloquy

Soliloquy means that adults talk as they do something, explaining each step, describing changes, pointing out reactions as they occur, laying bare their own thought processes so children can imitate, collaborate, or adapt them. This becomes possible when children hear adults' self-talk as adults approach an exhibit, puzzle out how it works, and ponder what it means. Soliloquy is an important recent development in Feuerstein's conceptual and instructional repertoire (Feuerstein, Falik, & Feuerstein, in press).

In soliloquy, adults articulate every thought, the clues to how they "get it," the "a-ha!" that finally leads to understanding. Adults' soliloquies reveal their thought processes. Children listen to them think and simultaneously watch their actions. Adults may be genuine—thinking through an exhibit for the first time, or may "act" the soliloquy as if it were the first time.

Example with Air Pressure. Imagine this running commentary as you introduce children to the Bernoulli effect (see Chapter 6). Adult: "Look, the ball is staying in that stream of air. I wonder if I push it down what it will do. Look! It bounces up to its original position! It feels as if the air is pushing the ball up. But! Wait a minute! What will happen if I tilt the airstream? Wow! The ball still stays in the airstream. So I guess it's not just air pushing the ball. Something more must be happening. What shall we try next? Look! Here's a basket of objects. Let's see what happens to a balloon. I predict it will behave like the ball."

Benefits. By using explicit words, adults ensure that children perceive salient aspects of an experience. Soliloquy shows children what it means to follow a process logically, use fully articulated language, and engage different thought processes to accomplish tasks. In the above example, children would see:

- precise movement,
- close observation,
- prediction,
- recall,
- descriptive use of language,
- perseverance,
- joy and amazement.

When adults make mistakes, they can assume an exploratory attitude, enabling children to see persistence. Through soliloquy, mediators can talk through mental acts such as focus, selection of stimuli, scheduling, positive anticipation, and imitation (Feuerstein, Rand, & Feuerstein, 2006). Soliloquy enables children to understand how to approach and master tasks. Hearing adults soliloquize can, potentially, dispose children to seek challenge.

Mentoring

Adults who mentor are good museum partners. Mentoring techniques differ from teaching techniques. Many teachers are great mentors.

Definition. Here are definitions of mentoring strategies that some teachers have adapted:

- coach or guide;
- focus attention on one child at a time;
- observe;
- follow an emerging sequence of activity;
- base comments on observations of children's behavior or notes of what they say.

These mentoring acts are characteristic of good mediation.

Mentoring in Museums. Ideally, children choose what interests them and do it for as long as interest lasts. Mentors are watchful participants who:

- assist at difficult places to enlarge children's cognitive repertoire;
- question to introduce strategies that help children think about what is going on;
- converse about the meaning of experiences to enlarge children's content knowledge or concepts;
- ensure that their intervention does not break children's concentration;
- share their own (the mentor's) ideas in order to encourage children to talk about what they (the children) are doing and thereby build expressive capacity;
- after leaving the museum, discuss the experience to impress it in memory by reflecting on it;
- recall the experience when children encounter something similar in order to engage children in transcendent thinking.

Mentors base their intervention on what children do. Sometimes the mentor leads, other times the child leads. The interchanges are like balancing on a seesaw, with each person dependent on and responsive to the other. Mentors maintain quiet enjoyment in children's activity.

Mentors become mediators when they:

- become conscious and aware of being *intentional in selecting a stimulus*; for example, recall in Chapter 2 Glenna's teacher's intention in choosing candy as a stimulus or Lewin-Benham's intention in choosing syllables as the stimulus in Tom's lessons;
- make children aware of their (the teacher's) intention so that children grasp not only the purpose but how purpose and stimulus relate and the possibility for transcending this particular experience.

Mentors' role is one of thoughtful collaboration, support, encouragement, and observation, all essential aspects of mediation.

MUSEUMS AS PARTNERS

Visitors may feel overwhelmed by museums. Buildings are imposing, their floor plans are complex, and their content is unfamiliar. Overcoming these barriers offers opportunities to mediate. Almost all museums use handouts. Those described below support mediation.

Parsed Floor Plans

These are one-page floor plans that suggest what to do with children of specific ages in specific amounts of time. Such plans break large exhibits into manageable units. The "Sound and Silence" exhibit hall at the Capital Children's Museum (CCM) was so large that any single area could occupy a visitor for over an hour. Parsed floor plans alert teachers beforehand to how much time they can expect to spend. This helps teachers decide where to go and how long to remain. With a time guide, teachers may more willingly allow children to pursue an activity until their interest wanes and thus build concentration. Children who concentrate learn to maintain focus, which is the *sine qua non* (without which nothing) of self-regulation, and therefore of learning.

Themed Maps

Themed maps tie experiences together by briefly describing exhibits in which ideas relate to one another. If ideas are not obvious, the maps make them explicit. Themed maps show connections among exhibits that look different or are located at opposite ends of a large building. Such maps set up a train of thought that might support the brain to see similarities, identify relationships, and formulate principles or rules. Themed maps highlight patterns, as in the following examples.

Pattern Seeking: Example 1. In the "City Room" exhibit at CCM was an old-fashioned, pre-electronic fire alarm box with the number 2638 in heavy raised metal on the cover (see Figure 9.1). The number was the basis for a system of gears notched in a specific pattern—*two* notches, space, *six* notches, space, *three* notches, space, *eight* notches, space. The exhibit also contained a fire station with a map showing numbered city blocks; one block was numbered *2638*. Thus, you could find the specific block where the fire alarm box in the exhibit was located.

When an alarm in the fire station sounded with the pattern *two* bells, pause, *six* bells, pause, *three* bells, pause, *eight* bells, pause, firefighters identified the box's location by matching the sound pattern to the number on the map, and thus knew where the fire was. Fully aware that people's lives depended on their skill, firefighters masterfully transformed auditory signals to symbolic modes in numerical and visual form, then transformed the symbolic representation to a spatial representation—a specific block on a map.

Firefighters' brains in the pre-electronic era contained a large amount of "stuff"—the location of virtually all the boxes in the city. They were motivated by knowing that they would save lives and preserve property. Something—probably mediation at a very young age—shapes the disposition and establishes the foundation for the skill sets of people who become firefighters—assuming responsibility, displaying empathy, collaborating to unusual extents, exhibiting spatial and kinesthetic thinking and bravery (Feuerstein, Rand, & Feuerstein, 2006).

Figure 9.1. The elaborate number pattern in the old-fashioned electromechanical fire alarm box alerted firemen visually, auditorily, and spatially.

Illustration by Daniel Feuerstein

Pattern Seeking: Example 2. In an exhibit called "Pattern and Shape" was a wall hanging of a complex maze. The solution was nearby on a card. Visitors could try out the maze with or without the card. Hanging and card were in different modes—symbolic (the card) and visual (the maze). Mastering the maze required changing symbolic/visual symbols into action (kinesthetic mode). The relation to the fire alarm is that it also showed a code in different modes—symbolic (the numerals), visual and kinesthetic (the gears' notches), auditory (the alarm).

Ten-year-olds, excited by codes, could take a "code tour," discovering codes they might overlook without the themed map. Such maps make children aware that information can be codified in diverse ways, each an example of a different modality. Themed tours show that similar principles underlie different experiences; thus, they offer teachers ideas for transcending—making relationships among differences.

Prompt Cards

Prompt cards offer guidance for using an exhibit, explain its purpose, provide questions to ask children, and make exhibits' meanings transparent.

Think of a natural history museum's exhibit of minerals. Its prompt card reads:

Intention: Comparing colors of minerals improves students' observational skills and engages them in techniques used by field geologists to identify rocks.

Activity: Notice how the minerals' colors differ.

How It Works: Ask children to choose a mineral from the tray near the exhibit case, examine it carefully, and try to match its color to a specimen in the case. Talk with children about each mineral they examine.

Questions: What colors do you see?

Do any minerals in the case have the same colors?

How does the specimen you chose look the same or different from those in the case?

Meaning: You said your specimen looks blue and purple and glisten-y. (Use words the children used.) See if you can find a picture of your mineral on the cards.

What might have formed your mineral's color?

What might have made it glisten?

Connections: Choose another mineral and compare its color.

How are the minerals the same?

How are they different?

How do minerals in the case compare to other minerals in the tray?

Help children use comparative behavior to notice differences in color, glisteny-ness, hardness, cleavage, inclusions, streaking, color, and other obvious features.

Transcendence: What else can you think of that glistens?

What do these colors make you think of?

How could you find out more about galena? fluorite? pyrite? quartz?

Different Mode: Can you draw galena (or another mineral)?

Prompt cards are a form of script, providing ways for teachers to encourage focus, convey meaning, and elicit comparative behavior. Prompt cards tell teachers what cognitive functions to use to engage higher-level thinking in experiences that otherwise might only be imitative. Prompt cards help mediators make children aware of the relationships in an ever-widening world (Feuerstein, Rand, & Feuerstein, 2006).

Summary: Props to Support Teachers

Museum/school partnerships are not new. Many museums help teachers prepare for or follow up on visits. Sometimes museum staff and teachers collaborate to find the overlaps between museum themes and school curricula. Museums provide kits for classrooms with experiments, trunks with artifacts, or boxes of themed materials from a museum's collection. Bringing the museum into schools adds awe and wonder to children's lives, especially those whose families are not museumgoers. Such efforts are creative, exemplary, and far too numerous to describe. Today, museums reach many teachers and parents via websites. Some offer high-quality interactive experiences. Others help teachers organize visits in advance or follow through after a visit.

"WHAT IF" IDEAS

A youth service corps, museums in schools, exhibits created by students—these and other ideas are envisioned here.

A Service Corps for the Brain

Our culture's widespread violence, lack of empathy, and mindless pastimes stem partly from some adolescents' not having a meaningful role in society. One way to provide adolescents with meaningful out-of-school activity could be to enlist them in museum service as an honor corps. Youth could be trained:

- as exhibit guides to help visitors locate specific exhibits;
- to converse with younger students about the meaning in exhibits;
- to help visitors listen, think about exhibits, and express ideas as youth, present in exhibits, demonstrate, ask leading questions ("Why do you think the pendulum always swings to the left?", "What do you think makes the car slow down?"), or respond to visitors' questions and comments;
- to be intentional in selecting stimuli to use for demonstrations; for example, if different objects are to be tested in a vacuum, selecting those objects first that are most familiar to visitors;
- to make younger children aware of stimuli's meaning by encouraging them to describe what they see and to use precise language (recall the teacher in the Introduction, who asked for increasingly precise answers);

- to add transcendent ideas to discussions or demonstrations of exhibits by offering visitors examples ("You can see something similar in Telephone Hall."), or asking questions ("What does this remind you of?" "Where could you find a similar reaction?").

Issues to be addressed in apprenticeship programs include, among others, recruiting/admission procedures, management within the museum clearly requiring a dedicated staff member, relations between the youth and others in a museum's volunteer or docent program, space considerations to give youth a place for their belongings, breaks, meetings, and socializing. We had two active youth programs at CCM, one for junior high schoolers, the other for college interns. The Exploratorium (science/arts museum, San Francisco) for decades has run a teenage "explainer" program. Because models already exist for youth involvement in museums, there is a body of information that could be gathered on management and related issues. Museums could provide youth with meaningful activity directed at service to others.

A Museum in Every School

Combining features of schools and museums could bring out the best of both: Museums would be challenged to relinquish their autonomy in choosing exhibit subject matter and schools would be challenged to relinquish their monopoly as places that educate. Howard Gardner (1992) has said:

> I think the challenge is to wed the genius of . . . museum(s) with the genius of the school and to bring museum-type thinking into schools and school types of problems and skills into museums. . . . If we are going to be able to use museums educationally, we can't afford to turn our back on the schools . . . [and] schools can[not] afford to close their minds to what goes on in museums. (pp. 4–5)

If there were a museum in every school:

- One room would be designed as an exhibit hall, larger than a typical classroom, extra-wide doorways, higher ceilings, many electrical outlets, track lighting, systems to hang panels or mount objects.
- Students and teachers would negotiate exhibit subject matter, conceive exhibits, and conduct the research.
- Students would perform important tasks:
    - ✓ staff exhibits;
    - ✓ design, fabricate, and prepare exhibits and spaces;
    - ✓ create written materials—signage, fact sheets, themed maps, prompt cards;
    - ✓ mediate, intervening to help others learn from the exhibit.

Museum staff learn tremendous amounts when they design exhibits. The work involves studying huge amounts of information, selecting interest-rousing topics, extricating salient facts. Students could learn to do this. Exhibits that change regularly would be catalysts for students to learn about diverse subjects. Creating exhibits would require students to hone reading skills, write well, and apply math in real applications. Students would be motivated to master skills not to pass tests but to create tangible outcomes because exhibit work requires goal-seeking, goal-setting, goal-planning, goal-achieving, scheduling, spatial orientation, sharing, and numerous other cognitive acts.

Student-Created Exhibits

On occasion at CCM school and museum merged. One example was an exhibit created by all 100 students at Options School, CCM's museum-based school for 7th-graders at risk of dropping out.

Personnel in D.C. Public Schools called Options School students their "100 worst." All came from homes beset by poverty and from crime-ridden neighborhoods. Inspired by Lettie Battle, a brilliant teacher and graduate of a Feuerstein training program, students each conceived a shrine to memorialize someone they knew who had been killed. Story line and content were determined by students. Some used objects, others poetry, prose, photos, or mixed media. Each exhibit included a photo and a brief description of the student/designer (except two who wanted to remain anonymous).

The project was challenging. Battle held the students to a standard of excellence so their exhibit would be on a par with the museum's other exhibits. The shrines were displayed near the main entrance. Visitors who studied them often left in tears. The students learned to transform memories and feelings into 3-D displays, to set and achieve goals, to schedule a complex task, and to solve the spatial challenge of working in a small space. All these processes are parameters for mediation.

Imagine if high school diplomas required all students to participate in creating a museum exhibit. Students would have to conduct research, synthesize it, "package" ideas, and present them for peer review. Students would be required to find original source material, analyze it, master building and display techniques, write pithy information, and collaborate among themselves. With museum staff, students would raise funds and pack, transport, install, and maintain the exhibit. In such work, each student's own strengths would be put to highest and best use. Museum-in-school offers endless opportunity to add meaning to youths' lives.

Again, the question of scale arises. The solution to involving more students must be local—programs developed collaboratively by museums and schools.

Apprenticeships

Apprenticeships, a cultural form as old as history, transmit from generation to generation the complex skills that are essential for a culture's survival. Yet, today, opportunities for apprenticeships are rare. Huge divides separate formal schooling and the workplace. Employers complain that graduates—high school, college, and beyond—are unprepared, that they lack the skills and disposition to work.

Situated Cognition. If students apprenticed in tasks that matched their intrinsic talents and interests to meaningful, challenging enterprise, they would enter employment ready to work. Leaders in today's science of teaching and learning advocate a return to apprenticeships as a way to provide authentic work experience (Gardner, 1991; Lave & Wenger, 1991; Resnick, 1991; Rogoff, 1991). "It is clear," says Resnick (1991),

> that much of human cognition is so varied and so sensitive to cultural context that we must . . . seek mechanisms by which people actively shape each other's knowledge and reasoning processes. . . . We seem to be in the midst of multiple efforts to merge the social and cognitive, treating them as essential aspects of one another. (pp. 2–3)

Benefits of Apprenticeships. Museums are ideally suited for apprenticeships. The scope of tasks museums require is wider than in most workplaces. Museums' mission is to educate. Staff members are creative, talented, motivated, and oriented to produce. Exhibits require fabrication in diverse media (e.g., wood, metal, plastic, fiber), skill in audio and video production, and computer savvy.

Museums need a limitless supply of exhibit guides, a task for students interested in psychology or education. Public relations and communication would suit students with linguistic and interpersonal skills. Conducting market surveys of visitor reactions, studying what visitors learn, or collecting data on potential donors would challenge students' logical reasoning and pattern-seeking skills.

Working in administrative functions—from office support to the highest executive levels—would involve students in varied projects and expose them to the complex problem solving required by real work. Maintenance of buildings and grounds, gift shops, and restaurants draw on diverse skills, including public service, inventory control, logistics, accounting, food preparation, display, and management.

If museums apprenticed students across such varied functions, youth would acquire workplace know-how. If museum staff were trained in mediation theory and techniques, they would make students aware of the different cognitive functions required by each task. In apprenticeship programs, museum staff would use most of the mediation techniques described in this book.

Building Public Understanding

The general public harbors misconceptions and conflicting information about what it means to learn. Imagine if moving images, with titles like "Look What I Just Learned!" could be harnessed to shape the public's ideas about learning. Images would show learning wherever it occurs. Narration would interpret what is happening *as it happens*, describing learning and mediation as they occur. First, we watch a situation with no learning, then we watch the same situation as someone *does* learn. Voice-over explains when and why someone *is* or *is not* learning. Lack of mediation and effective mediation are contrasted and explained.

Assume such images are played in public areas—stations, airports, lobbies, or wherever people wait; on television; at trade fairs and state fairs; in teacher education courses; in courses for expectant parents and counseling for new parents; and, of course, on the web. With repetition and saturation, we gradually change cultural beliefs about learning, showing that it *can* be joyous, that mediation *is* essential, and what effective mediation looks like. We show that tired or sugar-fed children *are* less likely to learn, that excessive absorption in mindless pastimes *does* kill motivation to persevere in tough subjects. Over time, we replace prevalent beliefs about learning with new images so the public grasps what learning is and how it occurs.

Commercial television changed U.S. behavior in a generation: If, in the 1950s, we had viewed the television of the 1990s, we might have banned the medium! Every aspect of today's TV—verbal, gestural, sexual—would have offended the sensibilities of an earlier generation. But, because the change took place gradually and the medium was pervasive—TVs always on everywhere—the images and behaviors portrayed on TV became the norm. We became what we beheld.

In the 1960s and 1970s, relentless, effective use of media campaigns made people wear seat belts. Two decades later, media so persuasively changed attitudes about smoking that many gave up the habit, many public places banned smoking, others isolated smokers, and such efforts continue.

Today's reality-based YouTube videos are a different model. Given that many children have cell phones with built-in video cameras, schools could create YouTube channels where students could upload videos about what they learned, how they learned it, and the role their brain played. Given today's social networking and images that "go viral," it is realistic to think about harnessing the power of the moving image to shape thinking in support of learning.

EMILY'S STORY: MOTHER AS MEDIATOR

The "City Room" exhibit was a CCM favorite—a city street with real objects, an actual fire engine, hydrant and hose, sliding brass pole in the Fire Station, sewer system under the street, manhole to enter, and more. In various places were uniforms of different city workers.

Lewin-Benham recalls:

> I observed a mother coaching her daughter to try on each uniform and act out the role of the worker. As she elicited what the child knew, listening closely to her daughter's descriptions, the mother filled in details or added new information. Her mediation was responsive to her daughter's actions; her questions stimulated the child to think. As the child finished wearing each uniform, the mother asked: "What do you think about *that*, Emily?"

The mailman's uniform remained to be tried on. Familiar with the routine, Emily anticipated her mother's question and, running to the uniform, exclaimed gleefully: "I see! You can be anything you want to be!" Effective mediation enabled a 5-year-old to transcend an exhibit experience by relating it to an observation about one's options in life.

SUMMARY: MUSEUMS AS LEARNING CENTERS

When adults share their observations and encourage children to focus, compare, seek patterns, draw inferences, and find rules, they are mediating and thereby fostering learning in museums. An ideal ratio of guide to visitor is one-to-one. Museums cannot provide this many staff or volunteers. But helping parents and teachers learn to be mediators would be a win/win situation and would merge the best features of museums and schools

Caution: Mediating means understanding the situations when mediation should *not* be used: If a child reaches for something hot or runs into a street, he needs to be stopped instantly and emphatically. If children are concentrating intently, seeking patterns, or solving problems spontaneously, they should not be interrupted. Mediation can come later. Certain situations in classrooms do not call for mediation: For example, teachers are, at times, pipelines for information; they need to convey huge amounts of information. Those are not times to mediate. Common sense is the guiding factor!

In the late 1970s, at a museum conference that offered visits to a number of museums, Lloyd Hezekiah, then director of the Brooklyn Children's Museum, the United States' oldest, welcomed visitors. During his welcome he called children's museums "palaces of learning." There is general agreement among cognitive scientists that to learn means to understand. Perkins (1995) agrees with Feuerstein that intelligence can be taught—indeed, must be (pp. 177–189). Feuerstein says we are made human by our capacity to learn and that, once we have acquired a passion for learning, it becomes boundless.

In this chapter, we have shown the museum as "learning palace," fostering the kind of active understanding that many psychologists consider the litmus for whether learning has in fact occurred.

Takeaways

1. Learning may look different from what we know as school.
2. Soliloquy and mentoring can be effective ways to mediate.
3. Museums can help teachers maximize visits' effect by providing parsed floor plans, themed maps, and prompt cards.
4. Novel ways to capitalize on museums' resources are to develop youth Service Corps, create museums in schools, offer apprenticeships, and saturate media with video that educates the public about what learning looks like.
5. The examples of mediation in museums are applicable to any situation in which adults intervene in children's experiences to help them learn.

CHAPTER 10

Enlarging the Cognitive Repertoire

Noble is the mind in search of meanings.

—Gates of Repentance, 1978

WHEN TEACHERS UNDERSTAND what factors influence thinking, they are more effective mediators. In this chapter, we examine five different experiences and show how to use each to influence thinking and learning capacities. The experiences are:

- incongruence,
- repetition,
- transformation,
- illusion,
- stereognostic experience (tactile/visual).

Each experience is based on different capacities and triggers different activity in the brain. We describe how to use each to stretch children's thinking.

INCONGRUENCE

Incongruence means something so incompatible with what is known that it shatters equilibrium and compels children to observe and seek answers. But noticing incongruence causes disequilibrium *only if* children:

- are familiar with what *typically* happens (see Chapters 1 and 7),
- have the *prerequisite knowledge* to understand the content,
- routinely use *thinking acts* such as comparing and analyzing.

When children *do* notice incongruity, it causes them to look, then look again at the startling effect.

Incongruent experiences create an enormous need for resolution; they drive children to observe more carefully, gather data more precisely, and find ways to confirm or deny what their senses tell them. Feuerstein believes that creating a state of disequilibrium is the situation *most* likely to change thinking—provided children can reestablish equilibrium.

These phenomena might cause disequilibrium:

- fire that doesn't burn things up, as in the Biblical story when Moses looked at the burning bush,
- water that doesn't boil away or evaporate,
- pendula that swing arhythmically and therefore look bizarre,
- clocks that keep absurd time,
- balls that roll uphill,
- water that flows backward into a faucet.

Still, children might not notice because these phenomena are science-based, as are pulleys (Chapter 1), Bernoulli's Principle (Chapters 6 and 9), and vacuums (Chapter 7)—all phenomena that fall outside most children's experience. Children feel disequilibrium only if what they see contradicts something they know. (Caution: What children "know" may contradict fact.)

Alerting Attention

Exhibits could create these illusions:

- objects falling *up*, not down;
- a globe that is hot at the poles, icy at the equator, with jagged oceans, smooth mountains, sandy forests, and tree-filled deserts;
- small mechanical figures performing familiar processes—chopping down trees, cooking meals—in the wrong order;
- a prism mirrored on the inside to create infinite images;
- topsy-turvy, Lilliputian, or lopsided worlds;
- Escher-like, Gaudi-esque, Dali-esque, Giacomettian, or Modigliani-like worlds. Great artists' techniques could be used to produce visual incongruence. Imagine walking through Monet's colors, frolicking in Seurat's pointillist paintings, or climbing the stairs in Escher's *Relativity*—all experiences counter to what we know.

Incongruent experiences rearrange reality and therefore grab attention. *However*, going beyond the "fun house"/Disney World level requires serious teaching:

- *time* to explore;
- *resources* in the form of materials with which to vary the experience, related models to explore, books, video, and computer simulations;
- presence of a *knowledgeable adult* to stimulate discussion, provide feedback, question, and in other ways mediate.

Having children's attention is the gateway to encouraging them to think. But once "inside the gate," solid teaching is necessary to develop the cognitive skills that build a foundation for analytic thinking. If cognitive dissonance focuses children's attention, mediation must then help children build the thinking processes necessary to reestablish equilibrium.

Callslip Request   10/16/2013 9:35:12 PM

Request date:10/15/2013 07:20 PM
Request ID: 42475
Call Number:370.152 F423
Item Barcode:

Author: Feuerstein, Reuven.
Title: What learning looks like : mediated lean
Enumeration:c.1Year:
Patron Name:WHEATON PUB LIB ILLINET
Patron Barcode:

Patron comment:

Request number:

Route to:
I-Share Library:

Library Pick Up Location:

Gathering Data

The challenge in causing disequilibrium is to ensure that experiences strike children as unexpected, that what they see is contradictory. Data gathering could cause children to notice incongruence if it required:

- observing closely,
- describing,
- defining the problem,
- making comparisons,
- categorizing.

The processes on which data gathering depends need to be isolated and taught individually. Doing so is time well spent because systematic and precise data gathering is essential to all problem solving. Without precise data and mastery of lower-level thinking acts, the brain cannot elaborate—induce, infer, deduce, summarize, conclude.

Learning from Incongruence

Consider the vacuum exhibit (Chapter 7). The typical airless tube is about 4 feet high; children push a button to make objects drop. Because most children know nothing about falling objects in a vacuum and because objects fall instantaneously, this common exhibit fails to elicit anything but button pushing.

Children might notice *if* . . . the tube were:

- decorated to attract attention;
- so tall that the object's fall *would* be noticeable;
- alongside a second tube *with* air so the effects of air-filled and airless tubes could be compared;
- designed so that children could remove or add air;
- wired so noise sounds when objects hit bottom.

Or, children might notice if:

- they first took part in experiments (presented by museum staff) that show what happens in a vacuum to a lit match, a marshmallow, boiling water, and other familiar objects;
- children could somehow stop the object in mid-fall;
- the exhibit were located among related exhibits;
- exhibits were organized to cause children to explore systematically.

It might arrest attention if:

- the tube contained dramatically unusual objects;
- objects could be explored by hand and closely examined;
- video:

✓ provided a model for children to imitate;
✓ showed what to expect, making effects readily apparent;
✓ explained why something happened;
- computer simulations enabled visitors to manipulate variables such as height of tube, shape and weight of objects, presence or absence of air.

Exploration must be related, repeated, varied, and mediated to lay a foundation to learn how things behave and to make phenomena—like air-filled and airless spaces, pendula, mechanical advantage, and other physical processes—familiar. Science exhibits can rouse interest, but it requires time and conscious effort to develop interest into understanding.

Brain Booster: To Learn Something

Purpose: Compel children to become engaged so they build content knowledge and learn by questioning, observing, comparing, and predicting.
To learn something, children must:

1. observe,
2. compare, and as a result
3. feel enough disequilibrium
4. to question and
5. seek new information
6. in order to reestablish equilibrium,
7. see the point
8. and learn.

Creating exhibits that spur these behaviors *in sequence* would be a breakthrough in exhibit design. It would shift museums' focus from the exhibits' content to their impact on thinking. The basis for such design would be how in the brain:

- attention systems are alerted;
- focus is directed to one particular stimulus;
- focus is maintained;
- sensory impressions impinge;
- all but relevant stimuli are blocked;
- sensory and motor neurons connect;
- motivation intersects with responses;
- inference, deduction, and other analytic brain functions occur;
- conclusions are expressed in one or more modalities.

Someday children may be able to watch their brain in action as they engage in an experience. Brain scans, reflecting diverse reactions, hold intriguing possibilities for feedback about the workings of children's own brains.

> To make children aware of incongruity, the first step is to make them conscious of the importance of observation.

REPETITION

Feuerstein proposes that there are two kinds of repetition:

1. Repeating in order to *consolidate routines* so they become automatic—for example, the techniques musicians and athletes acquire through practice.
2. Repeating in order to *recognize patterns* no matter how components vary. For example, a square may look like a diamond but remains a square if it maintains four right angles (constancy of the object in spite of changes in position).

Here, we explore these ideas.

Consolidating Routines

Repetition is essential to master new procedures, which means consolidating actions or information so that the brain remembers. Children often find repetition boring. Therefore, Feuerstein emphasizes, variety must be an integral part of repetition. Museums can be repetitive in ingenious ways because they have numerous techniques, talented designers, and interdisciplinary teams. Consider the role of repetition in the following examples.

Handwriting. Shaping letters elegantly requires years of practice that gradually enables the eye/hand to make refined movements. Two teaching practices exercise brain/eye/hand with repetitive but varied activities.

Montessori schools strengthen hand/eye movements in dozens of ways:

*   collections of intriguing bottles and boxes to open and close;
*   activities to wash or polish real objects;
*   buttons, snaps, buckles and other closures to manipulate;
*   Metal Insets, a pencil/paper stencil-like activity.

Reggio schools engage children by age 12 months in painting, using glue, crumpling, tearing and shaping paper, and exploring dozens of other materials that engage hand/eye and require sophisticated movements. In both Montessori and Reggio schools, activities' great variety maintains children's interest as they repeat the kinds of eye/hand movements that build the musculature necessary to write.

Driving. Students learn to drive by practicing on parking lots or back roads. The purpose is to crystallize the movements, responses, and judgment to steer, brake, or accelerate so that, as beginning drivers, they can navigate facilely and safely. In the 1970s, authorities in Cairo, Egypt, were so alarmed by Egyptians' driving, they established a "driving museum" to train children to handle cars and learn road rules.

Reacting Speedily. Consider this common exhibit that relies on repetition. Children press a button that releases an object and are challenged to catch the object before a buzzer sounds. Students can vary the object or the timing so that the experience is easier or harder. The activity trains eyes/muscles to respond reflexively and quickly.

Establishing Principles

Another aspect of repetition is recognizing something despite change in its position, color, or other aspects. Through repetition—seeing the object numerous times in different configurations—children can learn that objects retain defining features (preserve their constancy) despite changing appearances.

> Repetition involves selecting a dimension, a skill, or a principle that we want children to master, then repeating in diverse ways.

Shape. Show children a square, then rotate it a quarter turn. Most now say it is a diamond because they no longer see a right angle. A mediator could soliloquize and thereby mediate the cognitive operation of analysis: "Look at the corner; this is a right angle! Keep your eye on the angle as I rotate the square. Has the angle changed? No! Have the sides changed? No! What has changed? Ah! Only the orientation!" For children to understand that the square remains a square no matter how it is oriented, they may have to manipulate the square repeatedly, with mediation, until they grasp the rules that define a square and can use these rules to override perception. *Flexibility means holding on to a rule in spite of conflicting perceptual information.*

Some children may see the square as a triangle because they only look at the apex. This may indicate blurred perception or no object constancy.

Feuerstein says that only providing an introduction and one or two examples "runs away," giving no opportunity to consolidate a principle. A paradox—and a reason that transfer is so difficult to attain—is the need to maintain flexibility in something that becomes fixed. Repetition means systematically applying a principle to progressively new variations of an initial task or experience until children fix it well enough in mind to use the principle flexibly, that is, in increasingly new and varied tasks.

Arithmetic. Many children learning arithmetic never sufficiently master the principles to see that $4 + 2 = 6$ is a variation of:

$2 + ? = 6$
$2 + 4 = ?$
$? + 4 = 6$
$6 - ? = 2$
$6 - ? = 4$

It requires mediation and repetition for children to learn this principle. If they do, arithmetic can be a wonderland of interlocking and predictable patterns. Then the challenges, especially in the early grades, are:

- to work with enough precision to keep the pattern intact. For example, children with poor handwriting may not be able to read what they have written or spot number patterns because they place numbers carelessly.
- to work efficiently; children who work too fast may know the correct answer but write it incorrectly (46 not 64) and so destroy the pattern.

If children have tasted the excitement of spotting patterns, that experience can be used as a reminder to write with care, double check, and thereby maintain the pattern or find a new one—perhaps be the *first* to find a new pattern, a challenge that stimulates children to go beyond the immediate lesson or experience. Feuerstein calls this mediating for challenge (Feuerstein, Rand, & Feuerstein, 2006, p. 423). Repetition with variety—and mediation—help children recognize patterns, and thereby establish principles.

Repetition and Novelty

Repetition without novelty is boring. Novelty stimulates interest which keeps the brain's reticular activation system (RAS) alert (Chapter 5). Research shows that both the RAS and the mirror neurons (Chapter 5) seek novelty, and that mental systems require novelty to stay awake and be ready to function. Rote learning, the mainstay of school, lacks novelty and therefore creates a limited amount of mental activity. Being interested is the first step to learning anything. Lack of novelty shuts down the brain.

Learning from Repetition

Without repetition, the thing to be learned may remain merely an episode. It is not possible to form concepts, make abstractions, or generalize from a single experience. If children do not repeat enough, processes will not stick in memory, and therefore will not be available for the brain to use in forming new, more complex thinking. *To learn, children must see principles, rules, natural laws—whatever is being taught—in operation across diverse phenomena.* The more varied the examples of a concept, the more likely it is to appeal to children with differing interests and experiences and to stick in the brain. Children who learn through repetition to recognize the same principle in varied forms habituate the thought process of constancy.

Constancy with variation is seen throughout nature: Spiders spin webs; shellfish lack skeletons; birds lay eggs. Nature provides endless examples of structures that remain the same while the form changes. Bach's contrapuntal compositions show endless variation within a structure. Modern painters use canvas and paint (the structure) in innumerable forms. Throughout nature and human endeavor, we find repetition with variety.

Children can be challenged to make drawings based on constancy: One element remains the same and is repeated across two entirely different objects (see Figure 10.1). Analyzing what is constant—what repeats across varied instances—gives children a new way to look at the world.

Figure 10.1. Can you see what the child held constant to transform the leaf into the butterfly? Look closely at the middle strip of the leaf in the top sketch and mentally open the flaps. Note how on the bottom sketch the mid-section of the leaf has become the butterfly's body.

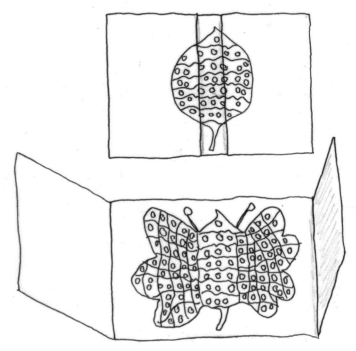

Illustration by Daniel Feuerstein

Brain Booster: Establish Relationships

Challenge: Establish a relationship. To help children learn to make relationships, repeat a principle as you increase the complexity. For example, find the relationships in this simple number series (mode: symbolic/numerical):

1	2	3
100	200	?

Or, find the relationships in the more challenging example in Figure 10.2 (mode: figural). Or, find the relationships in these words (mode: verbal/written):

Black	White	Gray
Go	Stop	Caution
Cold	Hot	?

Complexity is defined by how many different things have to be processed to solve a problem. The first example contains only one relationship—units to hundreds. The second example contains two relationships—shape and pattern. The third example contains three relationships with two extremes and a midpoint—gradations of gray, conditions of movement, and degrees of temperature.

Figure 10.2. Look at 10.2a. Determine how the top left figure transforms into the top
right figure. Then look at 10.2b. Determine which figure in 10.2b maintains the same
relationship as in the top pair of 10.2a.

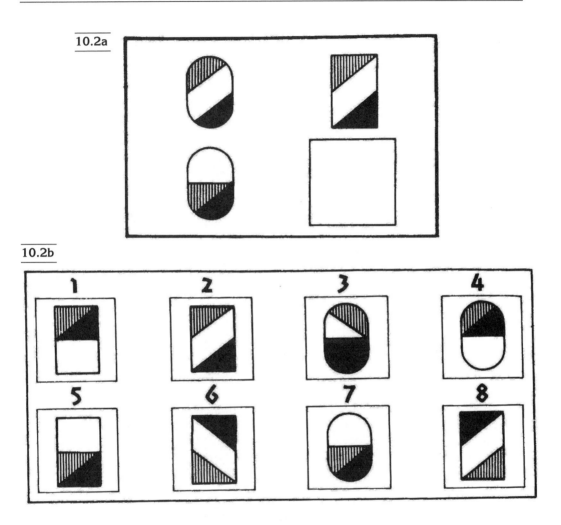

These examples began with a familiar relationship that contains little complexity and moved to less familiar, more complex relationships. The examples
were expressed in three different modalities—numerical, figural (see Figure 10.2),
and verbal. The same brain function—forming relationships—is used in exercises
that vary considerably in complexity and modality.

Making relationships requires focus, comparative behavior, short- and long-
term memory, and systematic exploration. Careful observation of children as they
form relationships reveals what cognitive functions they are using, what functions are deficient, and what aspects of the task must be explained or simplified.

In making these assessments, mediators analyze both the task (using the Cognitive Map) and children's performance.

TRANSFORMATION

> Relationships cannot be grasped through sensory perception. They are the product of a human mind.

Transformation means turning one thing into another. Examples abound in the physical, natural, and man-made worlds—match/fire, tree/table, water/steam, grain/bread, egg/chicken, gaseous cloud/star. (Challenge: Double the length of this list.) Metamorphosis, a form of transformation, is seen in the butterfly, ladybug, or housefly; in amphibians and crustaceans; in rock formations; in the vanish/transform/restore states of a magic act; in landscapes that change from wooded terrain to cloverleaf interchange; in Escher drawings; and in countless other examples.

We first describe transformation by discussing the zoetrope, then see how holding constants provides the basis for transformation, a high-level brain function.

Zoetrope Images

Zoetropes are cylindrical drums with parallel vertical slits set about two inches apart. Drums are constructed to spin rapidly when operated by a motor or turned by hand (see Figure 10.3). Zoetropes are popular exhibits in science, art, history, and technology museums and are used in some classrooms. The word comes from the Greek: *zoe*, meaning "life," and *trope*, meaning "to move toward."

Figure 10.3. Making zoetrope strips is a form of transformation: Children consider what to conserve and what to change in order to transform still lines into moving images.

How Zoetropes Work. Inside a drum is a strip of paper with a series of images representing action: a running animal, a clown tossing a ball, a flying bird. If you look through the slits as the zoetrope spins, the images appear to move. You can vary the experience by changing strips or drawing your own. Text explains what is going on. Illustrations show you how to draw zoetrope strips. Even something as simple as a dot or small line—if slightly different from frame to frame—appears to move.

History. Zoetropes played a role in the history of filmmaking. They began as popular parlor toys in the Victorian era. Books contained strips of decorative drawings to cut out and spin in zoetropes. Moving picture cameras and celluloid did not exist, so zoetropes satisfied humans' age-old desire to see lifelike movement. In our era, it is hard to conceive of not having moving images or to imagine the intense longing to see moving images of living creatures.

In the 1870s, Leland Stanford, the wealthy California governor who kept racehorses, decided to settle a centuries-old argument: When a horse gallops, are all four feet ever off the ground at the same time? Many illustrations pictured forelegs extended frontward, hind legs backward. Edward Muybridge, a prominent photographer, devised an experiment. Along Stanford's racetrack Muybridge positioned a row of cameras, tied a long string to each shutter, and stretched the strings across the race track. The horse's hooves tripped the strings, releasing each shutter in sequence. The captured images were fastened together and spun in a parlor zoetrope. There, for the first time, humans saw a moving image of a live animal—and settled the argument. If you have not seen Muybridge's famous horse photos animated, take a minute to find it on the web. It is well worth the time, especially considering that photography was in its infancy and moving pictures did not exist. You will see a historic event as you watch the horse photos come to life.

What the Brain Perceives. "The brain's inability to separate images that arrive too close to one another allows us to see a series of still images as a moving picture. . . . What holds for vision also holds for perception through the other senses; when two equally short spaced strokes tickle us, we feel them as one" (Pollack, 1999, p. 48). The brain, which is accustomed to seeing fluid movement, fills in the movements that are not on the zoetrope strip, making you believe you see motion.

Brain Booster: The Bizarre. Imagine arresting attention with zoetrope images that show bizarre movements—a clown tossing a ball up by flinging his arms *down*; or lines randomly placed so a movement is jerky. The more bizarre, the more likely the effect will be to hook children's interest. Using a zoetrope, or making and spinning their own strips, requires children to focus, select stimuli, schedule steps in a logical sequence, and set goals. These actions integrate higher-level thinking processes. Feuerstein says that such actions indicate children have modified their cognitive structure—or, in a word, learned.

Constants and Transformation

Transformation means changing one configuration into another but keeping the elements constant. For example, the sentence "Billy walks the dog" can be changed into "The dog is walked by Billy" without changing the meaning. Holding constants is the basis for symmetry, a universal principle that is significant because it reflects order in science, nature, and culture.

The mental activities necessary to understand transformations include:

- focusing on something;
- holding one or more elements constant;
- changing the other elements to create something new.

Transformations are seen in movement—common, such as walking, or unusual, such as crafting ceramics or performing Chinese acrobatics. Holding constants enables children to observe the transformation in a logically sequenced event. In the 1930s, researchers, looking for a cure for pneumonia, the major killer of the era, realized that understanding how pneumococci transformed was the key to conquering the virus. Their persistence in studying transformation led to the discovery of DNA (McCarty, 1985).

Children can be introduced to the principle of transformation. For example, imagine a set of templates with parts of a car: body first, chassis second, engine/transmission third, wheels fourth, windshields and windows fifth, seats sixth. Tracing each successive stencil retains the old as it adds new information. Holding constants in mind during a transformation makes assembly processes, scientific research, and the act of thinking possible.

Recognizing Constants. Constants are everywhere: The water initially was clear and transparent; now it is reddish. What happened? The water was solid ice; now it is fluid. What turned the ice into water? The water has boiled away. Where did it go? What changed? What does the first state have in common with the next state? the final state? Some children look, but are neither interested nor inclined to observe carefully or analyze what's happening.

To use constants to make transformations, it is important for children to:

- be aware of the stages,
- compare stages,
- spot differences,
- hold constants,
- search for causal relationships.

Each of these acts can be mediated.

> The ability to hold constants is a cognitive skill that is an essential part of many different thinking acts.

Making Transformations. Some children enjoy transforming pictures such as the one shown in Figure 10.1. Some enjoy tangrams (Chapter 5) in which they rearrange the same seven pieces into hundreds of different shapes. Or origami, an ancient Japanese art form, that uses square paper folded to form an endless variety of shapes. Whatever you create, the paper is always square. Folding paper airplanes and designing your own LEGO™ creations are other ways to transform materials that retain their identity through endless variation. Escher's drawings, in which one recognizable figure transforms into another, compel viewers to find constants. So, you stare at a fish turning into a bird, looking for the features that make each unique and those that are constant between them. Such activities require mental acts of comparison, constancy, and conservation.

Learning from Transformations

Children will wonder *why* something looks different as it is transformed *if* they are encouraged to think about the mental operations of holding constants and making transformations.

Content: Plasma. At extremely high temperatures, matter takes different states, turning from solid to liquid, gas, or plasma. Plasma is called the fourth state of matter; in plasma, molecules organize differently. Research on plasma is leading to "new manufacturing techniques, consumer products, the prospect of abundant energy, more efficient lighting, surface cleaning, waste removal, and many more applications" (General Atomics, 1994, p. 1). Using the Cognitive Map to analyze this information, children are unlikely to know about plasma, the content. Therefore, an adult must explain the content before talking with children about the transformation and constants.

Operations: Soap Films and Bubbles. When you dip a wire frame in soapy water, a soap film forms. The film creates the smallest surface area that spans the frame, usually called a minimal surface. When you blow on a soap film, your breath separates the film from the frame and the film forms a bubble. In theory, the shape of the bubble is always spherical—the least surface area that can contain the air. The operation—blowing, which must be done gently so the film does not break— transforms the two-dimensional film into a three-dimensional sphere. The principle is surface tension, a property of liquid that enables it to resist pressure (Miller, n.d.).

Providing *differently shaped* wire frames—circle, square, triangle, cube, or triangular prism—to dip into soap solution varies the experience. Using the frames in a sequence, children will observe different instances of surface tension and minimal surface. These principles are probably unfamiliar to most children. Help children learn the principles by:

- repeatedly using the words surface tension and minimal surface,
- systematically sequencing the experience by using the most common forms first,
- varying the forms to keep the experience novel,
- encouraging children to notice constants (the relation between film and frame), minimal surfaces, and surface tension.

Learning the principle of transformation requires children to:

- observe and gather data,
- determine the salient characteristics of objects (in this case shape and form),

- think analytically about what makes the soap film look different,
- make comparisons based on data they themselves gather about which characteristics change and which stay the same.

Each of these thinking acts requires gathering and manipulating data.

Operations: Popping a Balloon. Consider the mental operations describing the transformations that occur as you blow up and pop a balloon:

- *Gather data* about a balloon.
- *Determine* salient characteristics of the balloon's initial state.
- *Gather data* about the blown-up balloon; now it:
  - ✓ is roundish,
  - ✓ is firm to the touch,
  - ✓ can be batted back and forth.
- *Compare* the balloon's condition in its first state to its blown-up state.
- *Gather data* on the changes in the popped balloon; now it:
  - ✓ is small,
  - ✓ is limp,
  - ✓ immediately falls if batted.
- *Compare* the two sets of data.
- *Formulate causes* of the first transformation—filling the balloon with air— and of the second—the pinprick and consequent loss of air.
- *Analyze*: What is constant? The color, although it may be paler when blown up; the material, which is stretchy; the mouthpiece.
- *Repeat* the process with a helium-filled balloon, a Mylar balloon, larger or smaller balloons.
- *Analyze* what the balloons have in common and how they differ.

Seeking constants helps children understand that, despite changed appearances, an entity remains the same across a variety of conditions. The balloon is still a balloon; only its state has changed.

Cognitive functions employed in transformations include:

- comparing specific characteristics,
- establishing relationships,
- imagining hypothetical relationships,
- summarizing each time you compare or imagine a relationship,
- using logical evidence as you engage in a mental act. (Feuerstein, Feuerstein, Falik, & Rand, 2002, p. 142)

As they learn to gather data, make comparisons, and hold constants, children also learn to take more notice of transformations.

Brain Booster: Conserve Constancy

Ask children to analyze the transformation of the shapes in Figure 10.4; encourage them to use precise words to describe what they see.

Figure 10.4. This task differs from the task in Figure 10.2 in content and rule. The missing figure in this task is number 6. Describe the content and the rules that make your choice correct.

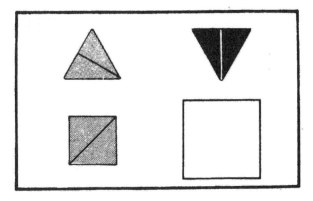

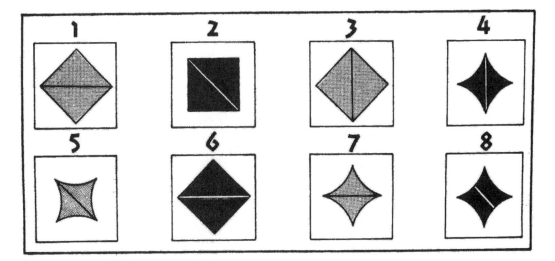

Top row:

- Content:
  - ✓ Left: triangle with line from angle in the lower right to opposite side transformed to . . .
  - ✓ Right: triangle with line from bottom angle to opposite side;
- Category: geometric shapes;
- Form: filled figures;
- Relationship:
  - ✓ Change:
- *Lightly shaded triangle* on the left transformed to *black triangle* on the right;
- Triangle on the left *rotated one turn* to the right;
  - ✓ Conservation: shape and line.

Bottom Row:

- Content:
  - ✓ Lightly shaded square on the left;
  - ✓ Line from top right to lower left;
- Category: geometric shape;
- Form: filled figure;
- Relationship: change and conservation.

Challenge: From examples 1 through 8 in Figure 10.4, choose the shape to fill the empty box.

Mediation in the form of questions helps children learn to form relationships:

- What is the same in the top examples? The content: Both are triangles.
- What is different in the top examples? The shading and the position.
- Which example in Figure 10.4 both conserves and changes the *square* in the same way as the triangles? In other words, which example completes the analogy correctly?

Although each of the four shapes *looks* different, the *relationships* among them are constant. The problem embodies variation and repetition and requires children to gather data, describe, compare, conserve, transform, and summarize. Mediators can make the experience effective by using terms such as *gather data, contrast, hold constant,* and others that describe brain functions. With repetition, children learn to manipulate the principles of change and conservation.

Some children, who readily solve problems like the one in Figure 10.4, cannot articulate what they are doing, how they arrive at solutions, or what the principles are. Other children do not know how to approach the problem. For the former, mediation helps children become conscious of their thought processes and able to articulate them. For the latter, mediation guides children through the essential and logical steps necessary to establish the relationships and eventually to derive the principles. Mediation helps all children become aware of what thought processes are required to solve increasingly harder analogies and to apply the principles of seeking constants.

> Teaching becomes mediation when it makes children aware of the mental processes they are using.

ILLUSION

Have children put a drinking straw in a transparent glass of water and observe the straw from the side: It appears bent. Ask them to cross their index and middle fingers, close their eyes, then rub their crossed finger tips on a table edge: It feels as if there are two edges. Have children look at the illusion that consists of parallel lines that appear to converge on a distant point. The power of illusions is so strong that you are forced to check and recheck what you see or feel.

Tickling Your Brain

Illusions challenge children to look closely, look again, and compare the differences between what they know and what their senses suggest. Consider the following examples.

Two Lines. A common visual illusion shows a vertical line meeting a horizontal line at the midpoint. Even when confirming the sameness by measuring carefully, invariably the vertical line appears longer!

Challenge children to draw the illusion in varied ways:

- Darken one line.
- Vary the lines' colors or thickness.
- Make one line dotted.
- Make one line segmented.
- Draw the vertical line off center.

To what extent, if any, do the variations affect children's perception of the vertical line? Illusions defy easy explanations.

The DeMoore Illusion. Two covered boxes are identical in every way except that one is noticeably taller. But, unbeknownst to children, the shorter box is considerably heavier. When children pick up both boxes simultaneously and declare which is heavier, invariably they say the big box! If children pick up the larger box (lighter weight) *after* the smaller, they tense and strain. Why? The children make a relationship between size and weight, and therefore do not expect that something smaller will be heavier. However, with young or low-functioning children, the experience is less pronounced because they do not connect size and weight and therefore do not expect that something larger will be heavier.

Counterintuitive information is startling. Based on visual perception, older children *expect* the big box to be heavier; therefore, they *over-prepare* to hoist. The preparation convinces the mind that it is hoisting a heavier object. Another way to think about the experience is to ask: How heavy must I make the big box so that it feels as heavy as the small one? See another counterintuitive illusion in Figure 10.5.

Figure 10.5. Cover the figure on the right. Look at squares A and B in the figure on the left. Describe how they are different. Now look at squares A and B in the figure on the right. Are they different?

Other Illusions. Illusions have the same fascination as facilely performed magic tricks, compelling children to pay attention. Classic illusions are the duck/rabbit, beautiful girl/old hag, vase/face, black-and-white blobs/cow. There are hundreds of examples and numerous websites with illusions, including some based on color or movement. Expect to spend some time because they are attention grabbers. On his website, leading neurologist V. S. Ramachandran explains the brain functions that give rise to several different kinds of illusions. The purpose of using illusions is not to teach children how perception works but to change children's state from boredom or apathy to interest or excitement. Illusions activate the brain functions of anticipation and comparison.

Learning from Illusions

Illusions fascinate because they present sensory enigmas that persist even once we know they are illusions! By providing bits of misinformation, illusions confuse systems in the brain that usually work well. Why illusions work and persist is complicated. Illusions result from how visual or kinesthetic and other brain/body systems interact. Some illusions are caused by "the brain's inability to separate perceptions that arrive too close to one another" (Pollack, 1999, p. 48). Illusion is a powerful modality that makes children highly focused, alert, and intent on solving the problem—states of attention that set the stage for learning.

> The incongruity between what one knows and what one sees makes children curious and triggers ingenious thinking.

Brain Booster: Look Again

Few people see through an illusion at first. But, once the brain "clicks in," images seem to flip back and forth like a blinking light. Then, as the brain becomes familiar with the particulars of each, people call up one or the other image at will, playing with a conundrum of vision processing. Because illusions command attention, they are excellent tools for mediation. Starting a mediated lesson by asking children to contemplate an illusion, puts them in an attentive and focused frame of mind.

The Feuerstein Instrumental Enrichment exercises systematically use different types of thinking in repetitive but varied and increasingly challenging ways to help children acquire specific brain functions. The instrument on illusions prepares children to accept others' views because they learn that what they see is not necessarily what you see. This instrument encourages children to see others' goals as legitimate and, as a result, to become less egocentric and less likely to consider their own view the only possible one. The capacity to listen to another person's interpretation is the hallmark of someone who is thoughtful.

STEREOGNOSTIC (HAND/VISION) EXPERIENCES

Stereognostic, also called *haptic* perception, means knowing through a sense of touch. "Almost all physical skill flows from the maturation of motor skills under the guidance of both visual and kinesthetic monitoring" (Wilson, 1998, p. 97). The combined use of visual and kinesthetic senses is called the *haptic sense*. Some websites offer fascinating demonstrations. At the time of the book's writing, a demonstration that could readily be duplicated in the classroom could be seen at http://www.roblesdelatorre.com/gabriel/vsdemof.htm. The haptic sense is frequently used, far more complex than once realized, and important in the field of virtual reality.

Finger/Eye Connection

When you handle and perceive an object visually, you extract information about it *simultaneously* in a visual and tactile process. You can deduce what the back of the object looks like even if you cannot see it. In contrast, nonvisual perception, also called tactile, haptic, or stereognostic—the kind of vision a blind person has—works differently: You identify an object merely by touch without seeing it. For children who are visually impaired to have a total and precise image of all an object's details, they must explore by using their finger or hand to *successively* touch the entire object—diameter, height, width, apertures, appendages.

It is impossible to experience simultaneous perception by exploring successively. Instead of seeing the entire object at once, you follow a *temporal* sequence: Touch, measure the size, take in the distance, figure out the contours—sequential movements in no particular order. Because the experience is successive, not simultaneous, the imagery—blind children's imagined world—is imprecise and haphazard. Recall how six blind men described an elephant (Saxe, 1881): The one who touched the tusk called the creature a spear; the one who touched the tail called the elephant a snake; the one who touched a leg called the elephant a tree, and on. The story is told in rhyme as a parable (Google "blind men and elephant") and some websites have clever illustrations.

Learning from Stereognostic Exploration

Motivated by blind students' poor descriptions of an airplane, Feuerstein and his colleagues developed FIE instruments for the blind in *nonvisual* modalities. One is a tactile instrument: Objects that have distinct shapes are reduced in size and represented in a raised double outline. Using two fingers, blind children thoroughly explore the contour by feeling the protuberant lines of plane, car, chair, apple, cup, and other common objects.

Another instrument uses 3-D outlines. Children are asked to recognize by touch or even draw something that is perceived tactilely. These instruments are also used with sighted children to encourage them to focus in a more systematic way than the visual modality does. They feel the lines while blindfolded, then identify what they felt by looking at several similar pictures, one exact, others with varying degrees of difference. Some differences are gross and therefore easy to perceive; the slighter the difference, the greater the challenge.

Remember: Sighted children usually explore *simultaneously in a visual mode*. With the above instruments, in order to recognize a 2-D representation of a 3-D object, sighted children must learn to explore *successively in a tactile mode*. The experience is an example of a representational mental act. If children explore by palming, mediators must show them how to use their "feeling fingers" (Chapter 6). The goal is for children to find the salient features—corners, contours, shape, and other details.

The tactile experience that is closest to seeing is to feel a three-dimensional object. Next closest is to feel a three-dimensional *outline*, which is a stereognostic experience. The least similar is to use conventional signs, such as Braille, that have nothing in common with the object they represent. Using Braille gives a blind person nothing with which to form an image—a representation—of what the Braille depicts. Because they provide an image, FIE exercises for blind children have been widely used.

Young sighted children enjoy the tactile/successive exercises, do quite well at them, and learn a new way to explore visually. These exercises help children with ADHD, children who act impulsively, and others who do not make precise observations but have sweeping perception, fleeting attention, and other focusing problems. Using their fingers to "look" at an object compels them to look successively. Thus, they collect information that they cannot perceive in any other way. Stereognostic exploration is an entirely different sensory experience—feeling detail by detail something that is normally perceived as a whole. The experience prepares children to make an investment, as it were, in what they are perceiving. The experience can be reinforced by having children recognize what they felt from among many different objects and, at a later time, draw it. When they explore precisely in a tactile mode, children whose visual system or attention functions are compromised can better grasp objects' features.

Brain Booster: Develop Hand Smarts

In "The Closed Boxes" exhibit (see Chapter 8), children can easily identify a feather with one hand, but not most other things. It is not possible to systematically explore an unfamiliar object with a single hand. It is better to provide boxes with two holes so children can explore with two hands, using one to feel and the other to check out the properties. This enables children to use some of the same clues as when they explore visually. Mediators can point out the transcendent benefits of exploring in different ways and thereby help children understand that some kinds of exploration yield more information than others. This is mediation for systematic exploration, visual imaging, and transforming from a tactile to a visual modality. Making children aware of the difference between stereognostic and simultaneous perception can make them more effective observers.

SUMMARY: CHALLENGING DESIGNS

Creating experiences that mediate is a challenge to lesson planners and exhibit designers. The five types of experiences described in this chapter show what impact specific effects have on different brain functions, how mediators can make children aware of what cognitive acts they are engaging and thus boost the brain's cognitive capacities. The principles emphasized in Chapters 6 through 10 are the raw materials of exhibits and other experiences that make children think.

Takeaways

1. Incongruence sets up conflicts in the mind. It makes it easy to grab children's attention because conflict is unsettling and motivates children to reconcile the conflict.
2. Repetition is essential to consolidate new procedures and to remember salient features of objects, patterns, and experiences.
3. Transformation requires the brain to maintain focus so that it holds an aspect of an object or an act constant while analyzing how other aspects change.
4. Illusions challenge the brain to check and double-check, then check again to determine why something one knows to be the case appears not to be.
5. Simultaneous exploration with hand or fingertips *and* eyes boosts the brain's ability to tease information from an object.

CHAPTER 11

Stretching the Brain
to Make Learning Happen

A change in anything instantly leads to a change in all things around it.

—John von Neumann (Macrae, 1992)

MUSEUM EXHIBITS have been used throughout this book as a vehicle to show mediation in action and to suggest many specific techniques that teachers can use to sharpen thinking. As stated in the Introduction, by showing examples of mediation in museums, we generalize mediation to any situation where teachers want students to develop thinking skills and, ultimately, become their own mediators. In many chapters examples of mediation are also shown in classrooms, where children spend the preponderance of their time.

The bridges between learning in museums and school are (1) the group of techniques that teachers can use to analyze the nature of a task, exhibit, or experience (Cognitive Map, Chapter 6), and (2) the list of functions that guide teachers to see which aspects of children's thinking may be underdeveloped, poorly developed, arrested, impaired, or seldom and inefficiently used (Chapter 6 and Appendix A). Most examples illustrate how stimuli are used to arrest children's attention and, once arrested, show children focusing and building new or underdeveloped cognitive functions.

Powerful stimuli abound in museums. Yet, despite the availability of powerful stimuli, some children do not learn as well or as easily as others. Why are there these differences? How can we turn exhibits into *mediating* exhibits? What makes *any* experience mediate? How can we help children become effective learners who *analyze their own thinking and pinpoint deficiencies themselves*? That is the ultimate goal of mediation.

Motivation and change from low-level to high-level thinking both play important roles in learning. In the first part of this chapter, we discuss various aspects of motivation. In the second part, we discuss how to go from low-level to high-level thinking with an emphasis on the important relation between movement and thinking.

MOTIVATION

Motivation, an essential brain function, directs emotional responses and integrates emotion and actions (Ratey, 2002, p. 247). Recall efficiency on the Cognitive

Map (Chapter 6). Efficiency is the ease with which students respond to the demands of a cognitive task. One way to think of motivation is as an indication of how students view their responses. Motivation is the determining factor in the eagerness, resistance, speed, accuracy, energy—or their lack—in children's performance.

Here, we discuss the inseparability of cognition and motivation, how to mediate motivation, and what the role of intentionality is in mediating motivation.

Motivation Redefined

As recently as the 1980s and as far back as Greek times, mind and body were considered separate entities, a view now discredited by neuroscientists, although still debated in the fields of philosophy and theology. Once considered its own entity, motivation is now understood as integral to all brain functions. Neurologist Antonio Damasio, in his book *Descartes' Error* (1994), showed conclusively that the brain's control of motivation is integral to anything someone does. Damasio describes the continual two-way traffic of neurons—brain to body and body to brain—that monitor, inform, control, and motivate all we do. He concludes:

> *feelings are just as cognitive as any other perceptual image*, and just as dependent on cerebral-cortex processing. . . . Feelings are first and foremost about the body. . . . [They] offer us a glimpse of what goes on in our flesh, as a momentary image of that flesh is juxtaposed to the images of other objects and situations; in so doing feelings modify our comprehensive notion of those other objects and situations . . . [and] give a *quality* of goodness or badness, of pleasure or pain. (Damasio, 1994, p. 159, emphases in original)

Feuerstein, considering the relation between cognition and motivation, adapted the Piaget metaphor that they are "two sides of a coin." Feuerstein calls the coin "transparent" to emphasize the strong interaction between these two major forces in life. Cognition and motivation are so much a part of every thinking act that they "interfere" with one another.

> Motivation is inseparable from cognition; it is an integral part of every cognitive act.

Mediating Motivation

The *cognitive* aspect of an act is intention: *what* we do and *how* we do something. The *affective* aspect of an act is motivation—*why* we do something. Effective mediation targets both the cognitive and affective aspects of thinking.

Recall the basic principle of mediation: The *intention* to mediate creates changes in the three partners of an interaction—stimuli, mediatee, and mediator. Intention, the most important aspect of mediation, is essential to its success. Particularly important is the mediator's informing a child of why he (the mediator) says or does what he does. That is, the mediator tells a child what his own intention is.

Mediating Cognition. When mediators intend to mediate cognitive function, they explain their intention to children. For example:

- When mediators intend to help children understand *why* they (mediators) choose particular stimuli, they explain: "I am using *blue* because I know it is your favorite color and hope it will keep your attention focused."
- When mediators intend to make children aware of *how* they intend to focus children's attention, they explain: "I have picked a *new* example so you won't become bored."
- When mediators intend to make children aware of how they (the mediators) *focus attention*, they explain: "I am calling your name *forcefully* to be sure I have your attention."
- When mediators intend to make children aware of their own (the child's) thinking processes, they explain:
    - ✓ "You used such relevant examples of a metaphor, it shows your brain builds good relationships among ideas." Or,
    - ✓ "You did that division problem in a flash; you must have a good model in your brain for how division works." Or,
    - ✓ "Your observation that a magnet and gravity have something in common shows that you can build relationships in your brain between two very different phenomena."

Letting children "in on the secret" of how adults think and how they themselves (the children) think helps children understand thinking processes.

Mediating Affect. Children's state of mind affects their motivation. The reason to change a child's state of mind is to make an unmotivated child motivated. (States of mind are also called *affect* and reflect the degree of alertness or desire to capture a happening and its meaning.) An effective technique is to emphasize the positive by making children aware of what they do well. Examples include:

- "Since you move so rapidly, please be the official 'passer out' of papers."
- "You have a natural sense of humor; I'll call on you when we need to break the tension in a difficult lesson."
- "Since you are good at paying attention to more than one thing at a time, please let us know if the snow is falling more heavily."

Mediators can change a state of mind by telling children in very specific terms what they do well and how their actions help others.

Interactions That Modify Cognition and Motivation. If children lack motivation, mediators can assess whether the cause is *cognitive*. If cognitive, mediators can use these techniques:

- explain content,
- demonstrate required mental operations,

- change the modality,
- simplify the task to make it less complex or abstract.

If mediators determine that the cause is *affective* (a reflection of students' motivation), they can modify children's feelings by:

- mirroring children's state then, gradually, changing their own affect as children imitate;
- using humor;
- singing;
- breaking into rhyme;
- drawing a picture;
- changing the subject;
- talking about something of interest to the student(s) before continuing the lesson.

> There are as many ways to motivate a child as there are creative, caring teachers.

Revealing a State of Mind

Today, the link between brain, body, and mind is called emotional intelligence. Some consider EQ more important than IQ. EQ is a hot topic (Goleman, 1995; LeDoux, 1998; Siegel, 2007). Csikszentmihalyi (1990) writes compellingly that to learn one must feel joy. The converse is true: Children who learn feel better about themselves.

Negative Feelings. Seldom do young children say what they are feeling. Ten-year-old Jimmy was an exception. He told his mother he was too nervous to go back to school on the first day because he was worried that his teacher would not like him. Jimmy's comment reveals that some children have deep fears about school. Unlike Jimmy, many children never voice what is on their mind.

Ten-year-old Joanne, the night before the first day of school, could not fall asleep. Five minutes after her bedtime ritual of story reading and prayer with her dad had finished, she called him to lie down with her. Twice he lay with her to comfort her. On her third call he remained until long after she was soundly asleep. Next morning, a torrent of words poured out of Joanne with crying, long sighs, and pauses to catch her breath: "I don't know if any of my old friends will be in my class or if I'll like my teacher or she'll like me . . ."

Children's brains are often swamped by feelings that they can neither express nor control. Mediators—and parents—have to read these feelings in subtle clues—children's posture, eyes, or silence. Sometimes an adult's verbalizing the feeling can change a child's state of mind. It may be easier to help a child change his affect than it is to help a child build the multiple analytic brain functions necessary to, for example, understand science phenomena, a process that requires replacing naïve/incorrect assumptions with several types of demanding cognitive functions.

Changing Negative Feelings. Have you ever watched an adult try to teach something to a child who is in a bad mood? Watch the following responses—first a parent's, then a school's.

Lewin-Benham recalls:

Around age 5, I asked my father for Bing Crosby's recording of "Wishing on a Star." I was bitterly disappointed when he brought comedian Jerry Colonna's version that, to my ear, mocked a song I loved. I broke into a full-blown pout. In response, my father chuckled: "C'mon, Annie, lemme see a smile," and smiled broadly. Against my will, I smiled and my mood changed.

Options School, briefly described in Chapter 9, was a dropout prevention program for 100 students referred by public school personnel as their "100 worst." Students would tell the teachers, "Don't drive me home after dark. That's when the shooting starts." If word spread that a student had received a death threat, faculty took it seriously, stopped teaching, and called an assembly of all students and teachers to discuss the threat and determine how to protect the student.

Students were 5 or 6 years behind academically, but after a year at Options, most caught up and graduated with their class. Why? When their fears were acknowledged, they gradually developed trust in the Options staff. With trust, their tough-guy/gal attitude faded, replaced by the desire to learn that is a basic human need. Cognitive processes can alleviate fear and anxiety.

> Motivation is the driving factor in anyone's learning anything.

Selecting Stimuli That Are Motivating

A pivotal factor in mediating is what stimuli to select as the focus of a lesson, intervention, or any other interaction. Mediators choose stimuli with the intention of making children aware of some specific meaning, thought process, or other cognitive factors salient to the experience at hand. Equally important is the selection of stimuli that impact a child's affect, and that will attract, intrigue, provoke thought, and thereby motivate children to become involved. Powerful stimuli make youngsters question what they are seeing, wonder what is happening, become alert, and *want* to search for answers. Such stimuli focus the brain's attention systems, keep them focused, and make children *aware*.

Here, we discuss the relationship between stimuli and awareness in the brain, the effect of stimuli on children's motivation, and how stimuli reflect mediators' intention.

Stimuli and the Brain. Director of Physiology and Neuroscience at New York University, often called a founding father of modern brain science, Rodolfo Llinas has conducted research on what happens in the brain when we are aware of something. His theory is that awareness and consciousness, which he calls "mindness," evolved into a nervous system in order to allow animals to move safely through the environment by predicting the outcome of each movement based on sensory data. Thus, he maintains, the capacity to predict is most likely the ultimate brain function and has a physiological basis in the electrical activity of neurons. Mind, he concludes, results from both the interactions between what we sense and the continuous oscillations—electrical pulses—generated in the brain (Llinas, 2001).

John Ratey, clinical professor of psychiatry at Harvard Medical School, explains that because neurons are always active, the brain is always in a ready state, "always tuned to the never-ending incoming stream of perceptions" (Ratey, 2002, p. 111). "Attention," says Ratey, "is much more than simply taking note of incoming stimuli. It involves a number of distinct processes, from filtering out perceptions, to balancing multiple perceptions, to attaching emotional significance to them" (2002, p. 114). Current research on the brain's attention systems by Posner, Michael Graziano, and many other neuroscientists is putting hard science behind theories of how the mind works proposed by Damasio, Edelman, Llinas and other brilliant researchers. Posner and his colleagues say: "Any training that truly engages the interest of the child and *motivates* the child can serve to help train attention" (Posner et al., 2008, p. 2, emphasis added).

How Stimuli Affect Children. For children to make precise use of many of the different functions within the brain's capacity, they must grasp the meaning of stimuli. Effective stimuli cause children to:

- gather relevant information: "Which spring is the right size to make this device work?"
- seek evidence: "Let me try it out."
- make comparisons: "I wonder if it would work better with a shorter spring?"
- look for relationships: "The shorter the spring, the faster the device shoots, but the longer the spring, the farther it goes."

These behaviors typify the high-level brain functions of children who are motivated to learn and therefore benefit from exhibits and classroom lessons.

You know stimuli have motivated children when you hear them:

- recall experiences accurately, and
- use what they learn to make other experiences meaningful.

In a history class, for example, effective stimuli that are motivating—interest-provoking and well presented—cause students to respond thoughtfully as these examples show:

- "Patrick Henry's cry, 'Give me liberty or give me death' was like John Paul Jones's rallying cry: 'I have not yet begun to fight.'" (analogy)
- "If Native Americans had not shown them how to plant, the settlers would have starved." (cause and effect)
- "Washington's crossing the Delaware was like Caesar's crossing the Rubicon: Neither could turn back! The die was cast." (analogy)
- "When Lincoln supplied Fort Sumter, the outbreak of war was assured." (deductive reasoning)

These and other high-level thinking processes are relevant for thinking about classroom lessons, museum exhibits, or any experience. We know children are motivated when they grasp meaning, transcend its immediacy, and bridge to other situations.

How Stimuli Reflect Intention. Selection of compelling stimuli reflects a mediator's intention. What is the evidence that mediators *intend* to modify stimulus, mediatee, and mediator?

In classrooms, we look at how environments are designed. Are there:

- challenging games, materials, and books?
- easy-to-move furniture?
- computers with thought-provoking software?

Or are there only textbooks?

Are lessons:

- given to full class *and* small groups *and* one-on-one?
- teacher-dominated or full of reciprocal conversation?
- reflective of children's interests?
- numerous and brief, or fewer in number and of greater depth?

In museums, we look at how an exhibit topic is developed:

- Is the meaning clear?
- What techniques convey meaning?
- How are visitors helped to understand the meaning?

Intentional designers and lesson planners consider:

- What are provocative questions? compelling facts? intriguing stories? What topics will stimulate intense dialogue? What will attract children by tapping into their personal interests?
- What must children see so that meaning is *conspicuous*?
- How many *different modalities* can illustrate the same meaning?
- Which modality/ies *best* represent a particular meaning?
- What are the roles of movement and imitation?
- What about the exhibit is rich?
- How can experiences *vary* and simultaneously repeat the principle?
- Where should exhibits be located (or how should lessons be structured) *in relation to one another* to make principles, laws, and rules apparent?
- What are the roles of collaboration and dialogue?

The design of exhibits and lessons reveals mediators' intentions and determines how motivated students will be to learn. The evidence that mediators' intentions have been realized is that children attend, become engaged, and learn.

SUMMARY: FOUR INTERRELATED FACTORS IN LEARNING

Think of the learning process as a tetrahedron, the three-dimensional figure with four equilateral triangles for sides that come to a point wherever three sides meet. One side represents who a child is cognitively and affectively. A second side represents the stimuli that affect the child. A third side represents the mediator who selects and shapes the stimuli. The fourth side represents many factors that influence what adults in the child's life believe about how to interact with children so that they learn. Within the prism is the child's "being" as the mix of factors impinges and shapes his or her cognitive/affective capacities. The forces are dynamic, affecting one another in powerful, unpredictable, and surprising ways. That is the mystery of human development that current sciences are beginning to quantify (see Figure 11.1).

MOVING FROM CONCRETE TO ABSTRACT THINKING

Concrete experiences enable children to perceive directly from reality. Young children acquire a large body of knowledge—naming objects (nouns), actions (verbs), qualities (adjectives)—from concrete experience. But moving to higher-level abstract thinking becomes increasingly important as children grow older. Abstract thinking means recognizing not just names or attributes but functions

Figure 11.1. Children are impacted by many things—their own mind and body, mediators, available stimuli, and how adults around them believe children learn.

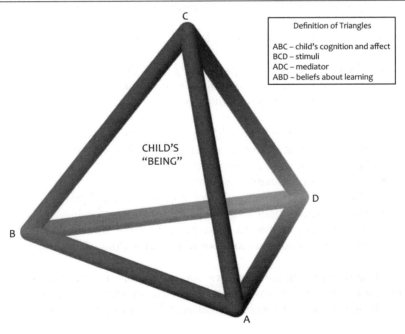

Definition of Triangles

ABC – child's cognition and affect
BCD – stimuli
ADC – mediator
ABD – beliefs about learning

CHILD'S "BEING"

and relationships that are produced by comparing stimuli, by classification, categorization, transitive relations, and syllogistic thinking, all higher-order mental operations. As thinking skills grow, children not only call a lead-based writing implement a "pencil" but can find one to use for their own purposes, eventually understand that writing represents someone's thoughts, and one day grapple with the meaning of the Grand Inquisitor's words in Fyodor Dostoevsky's novel *Crime and Punishment* or find meaning in the sketches of Leonardo da Vinci or Albrecht Dürer. (Google the names if you are unfamiliar with these works.)

As neuronal networks increase, the brain can make more abstract connections. Recall Merzenich's research (Chapter 2), now widely replicated, on how neuronal networks in the brain rewire, called neural plasticity. This trend resonates with Feuerstein's theory of structural cognitive modifiability and his observations of individuals' capacity to overcome deficiencies, regardless of cause, severity, or age.

Here, we discuss how mediators encourage abstract thinking, provide examples of the diverse ways in which humans have developed language systems that include concrete and abstract elements, and discuss implications of how to design lessons or exhibits that build from concrete to abstract.

Encouraging Abstract Thinking

Mediators help children become more abstract by encouraging them to *elaborate* their thinking:

- *Attend:* "Look! That doesn't make sense! Why?"
- *Question:* "What's happening here?"
- *Observe:* "What's the evidence? Show me the (piece, part, color, action, sound) that makes you say that."
- *Compare:* "How does this differ from the exhibit over there? (the slide we saw at the park? the pulleys we have at home?)"
- *Verbalize:* "Explain this in your *own* words."
- *Draw:* "Sketch what that means."
- *Analyze:* "Why is that colored red?" Or, "Why does the light shine *there*?" Or, "Why is it making *that* noise?" Or, "Diagram the relationships."
- *Transcend:* "What else we can find here that is similar?" Or, "Remember the exhibit with the (name something)?" Or, "What happened here that contradicts (name something)?"
- *Conclude:* "What's the main idea here?"
- *Summarize:* "Briefly, how did you figure this out?" Or, "Briefly, tell me what this means."

If children have difficulty using these higher brain functions, mediators can name them, model them, simplify them, break them into more basic thinking acts, and relate the process to something in a child's own experience.

> **Goal**—to find children's present capacity and stretch it by advancing them from concrete to increasingly abstract thinking.

Example: 5-Year-Olds and Picasso Paintings. You are taking 5-year-olds to an exhibit of Picasso's paintings. Simply say: "We are going to see an exhibit of paintings by a great artist. His name is Picasso." Start by looking at the paintings from Picasso's blue period; if children do not spontaneously comment, direct attention to one particular painting by pointing at it. Ask: "Does something in this painting look different?" Young children, who rarely censor their remarks, react strongly to things that differ from what they know. The blue people differ markedly! Children would be likely to comment: "But! They're all blue!" Or, "That's funny!"

Any relevant comment indicates that children are paying attention. Attention is the essential first step to learn anything. So, with attention focused, ask another question: "Why would an artist paint someone blue?" "Because," children might respond, "he painted it blue." Children's repetition of strong visual elements that directly reflect physical attributes shows that they are focused on a *concrete* aspect of the painting.

To move children to more abstract thinking, direct them: "Look carefully at the people's faces and hands. What do you notice?" If children say, "They're long," they are still concrete. So, using the children's words, ask a direct question about something more abstract: "How do you think the people with the long faces *feel*?" Or, "How would you feel if your face looked like that?" If children respond that the blue people feel sad, you have moved the children to a more abstract level; they are now thinking about something *representational*—a feeling the painting portrays. Or ask: "Do you think the people are blue? Or are the people normal color and the artist painted them blue?" This asks children to differentiate the painting's subject from the artist's representation. To move from concrete thinking, refocus children from *content* to *what the content represents*.

Example: Grasping a Science Principle. At the Denver Museum of Nature and Science, designers of the exhibit "Space Odyssey" analyzed what visitors must do to learn how objects—such as space shuttles—move in the frictionless environment of space. Children know that cars stop when you take your foot off the gas and, at some point, learn that a force called friction slows the car when the energy source (gasoline) is lessened (foot off the gas pedal). But, in frictionless space, shuttles keep flying forward even after the engines are turned off. To stop the shuttle, thrusters must be fired in the opposite direction.

To simulate space, the designers used air jets to create a frictionless table (like air hockey tables) and a concrete challenge: Park a model space shuttle. The exhibit includes:

- a written explanation with pictures of the effect of friction; it is titled "In Space There's Nothing to Slow You Down;"
- a start button;
- two joysticks to maneuver the model spaceship into its docking;
- a gauge that shows fuel running out, to act as a timer.

To meet the challenge, visitors must grasp the idea of how objects move in a frictionless environment.

If the exhibit rouses interest, a mediator can grab the concrete experience to help children build understanding. Moving from the concrete—manipulating the model—to the abstract—understanding the effect of frictionless space—requires building on many prerequisite understandings—about vehicles' movement, about friction, about movement in Earth's atmosphere, about movement in space, about operation of space shuttles, about what thrusters do, about the difficulties in docking a shuttle. The mediator must draw out what a child thinks is going on, pinpoint whether content or thinking functions are missing, provide the content, and/or teaching the thinking skill(s). But the first step is interest (the motivating factor).

Forms of Literacy: Concrete and Abstract

Different cultures' writing, speaking, and reading testify to humans' diverse higher-level thinking capacities. Consider the degree of concreteness or abstraction in each example that follows.

Writing and Speaking. Written and spoken languages vary greatly in how concrete or abstract they are:

- Egyptian hieroglyphs, a mix of stylized pictures (concrete) and phonetic and other symbolic representation;
- Chinese pictograms, a system with 10,000 characters that over millennia have morphed from actual pictures (wavy lines for a river, a stick with bristles on the end for a broom) to abstract signs;
- African click speech of the !Kung and other people of East Africa, distinctive clicking sounds to represent certain consonants (Connor, 2003) (symbolic). On the web, listen to Miriam Makeba sing "The Click Song";
- biblical Hebrew with no vowel markings (symbolic);
- Hawaiian with only 11 consonant sounds (symbolic);
- phonetic alphabets, such as English, that reduce the representation of all thought and speech to a small number of abstract symbols—a mere 26 in the English alphabet.

Varied as they are, all languages facilitate human thought, interaction, and learning.

Reading. Reading capacities enable different cultures to meet the need to nourish themselves, navigate, communicate, convey values and morals, and understand the lingo of a particular time and place. Consider:

- hunter/gatherer societies' ability to "read" vast numbers of edible plants and of animal tracks;
- Eskimos' ability to navigate in a blind white environment by reading wind, sky, snow, and stars;
- American Indian cultures' ability to use elaborate dances to present information ranging from hunting procedures to tribal hierarchies;

- South Seas people's agility in navigating vast stretches of ocean by reading sea, sun, stars, and horizon;
- complex myths, like the Gilgamesh tales from 2,700 B.C., that enable people to "read" about their own beginnings, history, relation to the supernatural, and morality;
- readers' ability to recognize letters whether they are oriented horizontally or vertically;
- 21st-century persons' ability to "read" the meaning in icons.

The varied reading capacities show huge variety in the ways concrete and abstract knowledge interact. Thinking requires a vast store of concrete information with which to form abstract concepts.

Implications: Exhibit Design and Lesson Planning

The extent to which exhibits or lessons build from concrete to abstract thinking is determined by:

- their organization,
- what variations they incorporate,
- how repetition is achieved.

Whether in museum or classroom, designers and lesson planners help children think by:

- defining the problem,
- providing concrete examples,
- repeating ideas,
- making comparisons,
- posing analogies,
- pointing out relationships.

These principles imply designing exhibits and lessons so that meaning is reiterated, thinking skills are stimulated through redundant exercises, and presentation modalities vary. The aim is for children to manipulate information systematically and repeatedly. The challenge is to keep the material novel so that children remain interested.

> The design of exhibits and the plan of lessons influence what children learn and how they think.

Implications: Mediating in Museums

Art museums cannot regroup masterpieces to benefit children, but museums can (and many do) pre-think exhibits from a particular perspective. Using Picasso paintings as an example, a museum prepared a simple page with small black-and-white copies of six Picasso paintings from his major periods—the blue period, the rose period, African-influenced, cubist, surrealistic, and neoclassic. The page provided handles for mediators by:

- stating the most obvious features;
- noting the painterly techniques;
- suggesting what the painting might represent (meaning);
- posing questions that lead children from concrete to abstract thinking;
- suggesting relationships with other paintings.

Teachers and museum educators could collaborate on the development of such aids.

The reasons to repeat and vary modalities are, first and foremost, to develop learners' readiness to be alert to the changes produced in what they experience. In other words, children must be conscious that they are comparing what is known to changes and variations, defining differences, solving problems by generalization, and transferring what they know to new situations. Repetition and variety:

- alert the brain;
- eliminate boredom;
- reach people with specific weaknesses, diverse interests, or dissimilar experience;
- challenge the brain with novel ways to receive and express thoughts;
- repeat because onetime experience will not crystallize into learned behaviors.

Cellular biologist and Nobel laureate Eric Kandel (2006) has described the processes through which learning and memory interact, explaining the role of repetition. In brief, the more often a neuronal network fires, the more ingrained the learning becomes.

> The art of mediation is to recognize where a child is and to select the exercise, exhibit, challenge, or experience to move the child to a higher level.

Summary: The Fertile Brain

The human brain is equipped with endless ways—modalities—to receive and express information. Varying modalities give children markedly different experiences with which to repeat the same principle. If children are weak in particular modalities—tone deaf, color-blind, unable to decode print—learning to think in other modalities can make a weakness less debilitating.

THE BRAIN AND LEARNING

What criteria can we extract from the theory of mediation so any environment becomes a mediating environment? To make exhibits—or any experiences—foster learning, we must ask: What kinds of thinking are demanded? What must a brain organize to meet those demands? Here, we show what learning looks like by analyzing children's responses in an exhibit based on movement and by observing children's reactions to an experience based on visualization.

What Learning Looks Like

The brain is considered the most complex thing in the universe. For a sense of the brain's complexity, consider what is involved in moving.

Movement. Movement is so basic to life, we take it for granted. Yet analyzing any mental act reveals its basis in movement. First, we need an idea (or stimulus) to compel us to act: We want to lift a stack of books onto a shelf. This goal, or any other, is set by "mental agents" (also called "executive functions" or "attention systems") of the brain.

> No matter how many agents we have in our minds, we each have exactly one body. Custody of each major part must be granted to a controller that selects a plan from the hubbub of competing agents. The eyes have to point at one object at a time; they can't fixate on the empty space halfway between two intersecting objects or wobble between them in a tug-of-war. The limbs must be choreographed to pull the body of objects along a path that attains the goal of just one of the mind's agents (Pinker, 1997, p. 144).

Even our intuitive knowledge of objects is based on movement: If you try to define something as basic as an object, the best definition is a "thing" which, if you move one part, the rest comes along (Pinker, 1994). Highly complex systems are located in the brain and throughout the nervous system to control attention, planning, locomotion, vision, the hand, and the hierarchy of executive functions that together enable us to get the stack of books onto the shelf, accomplish the tasks in a hands-on exhibit, or puzzle through the challenge in a minds-on exhibit.

Exhibit: Hitting a Moving Hole. Children could connect thinking and moving with this challenge: Roll a ball into a moving hole. Tell children who find the challenge frustrating: "Here's a rule—don't roll the ball to where the hole is *now*. Roll it to where the hole is *going to be*." The rule enables children to be reflective about how to adjust their movements.

When children master the challenge, add a variable:

- Change the *speed* at which the hole moves or *where* the hole moves. Modify the rule: "The hole is moving faster (or up, down, sideways, diagonally), so I'd better aim *there*."
- Wear glasses with filters or distorting lenses. Use perception to change behavior: "The filter is blue so I can't see the blue ball." "The hole looks farther away, so I'd better change my aim."
- Use balls of different weight, shape, or texture. "This ball is so heavy (light), I need to throw harder (gentler)."
- Give children control over when and how to change the variables. "It will be harder to hit the hole if the hole moves faster *and* diagonally."
- Solve the problem in a different modality by explaining the challenge in words.
- Draw a picture of the challenge.

A mediator could say, "Your brain is working hard to coordinate your eye (hand, sense of direction, balance, other movements)." If children hear such comments consistently, they become aware that the brain controls action.

Imagine: Electrodes connect you to one of the recent noninvasive technologies that show the brain in action. As a result, you can track your actions by watching different areas of your brain light up as regions become involved. Someday, techniques that are now used only in labs or tests will be used in exhibits and classrooms to enable students to see images of what their brain is doing (or not doing). Feedback could improve brain/body coordination; in some therapeutic situations, it already does.

Neurologist Frank Wilson (1998), in his seminal book *The Hand*, calls movement, of the hand in particular, a "basic imperative of human life" (p. 10). The understanding by Wilson and other neuroscientists of movement's role in thinking challenges us to rethink the immobility of classrooms and the inflexibility of one-right-answer testing. Mediators can incorporate movement in their interactions with children to engage thought processes that are essential to understand exhibits or complete lessons.

Visualization

Activity can be made complex by requiring a physical task to be done mentally, for example, visualizing a design. Consider this challenge in a concrete form, then in more abstract variations, and watch how thinking is stretched.

Challenge. Arrange a group of geometric shapes into this pattern: diagonally striped circle above vertically striped square to the left of a horizontally striped triangle and to the right of a reverse-diagonally striped ellipse. Try to draw the pattern from the above description before looking at Figure 11.2 on page 186.

The challenge is concrete if children refer to the pattern as they move geometric shapes that match the description of the pattern (concrete experience/figural content). The experience becomes abstract if the child draws a picture of the description with reference only to the words, not to the geometric shapes.

Complex Variations. Make the challenge more abstract by having children:

- Arrange the objects to correspond with a *verbal* description *without looking* at the pattern. To accomplish this, children must, at the input phase, understand content and concept; in all phases, use linguistic and symbolic modalities.
- *Remove a shape* at random and identify what is missing. To accomplish this, children must:
  - ✓ at the input phase, gather data and observe;
  - ✓ at the elaboration phase, use visual transfer and analysis of whole/part relationships;
  - ✓ at the output phase, consolidate thought processes, use recall, and engage an expressive modality (speak, write, draw, gesture, and so on).

- *Draw* a missing part. To accomplish this, children must:
  - ✓ at the input phase, gather data, focus, and recall;
  - ✓ at the elaboration phase, transpose from a visual or verbal mode to a graphic mode;
  - ✓ at the output phase, use a graphic modality.

Movement underlies each of the above challenges. To solve these challenges, Feuerstein says children must "carry an image in the mind's eye from one place to another without losing it on the way" (Feuerstein, Feuerstein, Falik, & Rand, 2002, p. 152).

The Brain and Visual Transport

Transporting a pattern mentally in order to compare it with another representation requires both internalization of an act (visualization or verbalization of the pattern) and switching modality. Consider what the brain must do in each of the above three complex variations:

1. Verbal description: Transform verbal input, which is *abstract*, to figural output, which is more *concrete* and in a different modality.
2. Recall missing piece: Transform *visual* input in a figural modality to *verbal* output, also in a figural modality.
3. Draw: Transform visual input in a *figural* modality to visual output in a *graphic* modality.

Challenging? Yes! Fun? Yes! Possible variations, mix of input and output modalities, and mental operations? Endless! Brain activity? Use of the numerous neuronal networks in which thinking and movement are integrated! To solve the challenge you must either actually move something or represent the movement in your brain.

Ratey (2002) says: "Mounting evidence shows that movement is crucial to every other brain function, including memory, emotion, language, and learning. . . . [O]ur 'higher' brain functions have evolved from movement and still depend on it" (p. 148). Feuerstein says: "Using movement as the basis for mental activity is more likely to make the brain function available for other kinds of direct and indirect experiences."

> Incorporate movement in diverse ways to stretch children's thinking.

SUMMARY: WHEN WE THINK AND LEARN

A relationship is a product of the human mind. It does not exist in reality. Making relationships is a powerful outcome of *all* mental operations and the foundation for increasingly complex mental acts. Linkages between acts occur as complex networks of neurons react to the stimuli in every experience and as those reactions in turn trigger other mental operations. The best evidence of children's mental

Figure 11.2. Challenge: Try to arrange the shapes as they are described in the text. Using actual shapes to match a pattern is a concrete exercise; using only words is abstract because words are abstract.

Illustration by Daniel Feuerstein

activity is what relationships they make. If you can analyze how children relate two things, you can infer what thinking processes children use or fail to use. Recall Brown and Burton's research on subtraction (Chapter 6).

Children learn when:

- Designers and lesson planners know which brain functions they want to engage: Are we asking children to compare? see causality? analyze? infer? educe? produce logical modifications? use transitive thinking? use seriation? (See examples of cognitive operations in Chapter 6.)
- Exhibits or lessons make children aware of their own thought processes (see, for examples, Introduction; Glenna in Chapter 2; scenarios in Chapters 3 and 4; Rachael and internal representations in Chapter 5; James in Chapter 6; Scriptorium, Durer/McNeill, and rethinking falling objects in Chapter 7; exhibits that evoke empathy in Chapter 8)
- Exhibits or lessons provide teachers with openings to make children *conscious* of their thought processes:

✓ "Nan, you figured that out by *repeating* the process again and again. Repetition is a great technique for learning anything! Good work!"

✓ "Derrick, you *compared* the effect of the pulleys with the effect of the levers! Comparison is an excellent way to see how two things are related! Good thinking!"

✓ "Chandra, you looked around to see who could work this exhibit, watched carefully while Glenn operated it, then *imitated* him precisely. Imitation is a good strategy. How smart of you to select someone competent to imitate."

✓ "William, when you said the whale nurses its young so it must be a mammal, you made a *deduction*. When you make a deduction, you use facts that you know to figure out facts you do not know! Clever job!"

The purpose is not to teach specific science, math, or cultural content (although children will indeed learn some), but to make children aware of how they are thinking and delighted at knowing what their brains are doing to solve problems.

Above all, the purpose of mediation is (1) to make children aware of the thought processes they are using to solve problems and (2) to enable them to select the mental act that will accomplish a task effectively. When children can explain their thinking processes, you have evidence that they have learned.

In the 1980s, the advent of children's museums caused science museums to redesign exhibits so that visitors could become involved beyond pushing buttons and caused other museums to bring carts with hands-on activities into galleries. These were major changes. It is time for another major change in the presentation of exhibits.

Today's challenge is to use research at the forefront of our understanding of how the brain works as the basis for the design of exhibits and also for lesson planning. Throughout this book are theories of how learning occurs, research that supports those theories, and examples of mental processes that are the foundation for thinking.

A theory-based, systematic approach to helping children learn to think will:

- gradually introduce each skill,
- require the brain to exercise the skill again and again by applying it to new and progressively more difficult variations of the initial task,
- make children conscious of the process.

With repeated use and strong mediation, the skill will become flexible enough to be adaptable to entirely new tasks that are less and less related to the skill as initially learned.

When children use skills flexibly, they will have learned how to think. They will have consolidated new mental skills that can solve varied problems. As we watch children use those skills, we will see evidence that the brain is engaged in significant mental acts that are creative, complex, original, competent, and joyful. In other words, we will see what learning looks like.

Takeaways

1. Intention—having a goal and making it known so children can adapt mediators' intent—is the most powerful tool adults can use to encourage children to think.
2. Feelings affect motivation. To motivate children who are in a bad mood, lack interest, or misbehave, do something to change their state of mind.
3. To make the most of an exhibit or lesson, determine the meaning, how it is organized, what modalities it incorporates, and what relationships can be made.
4. Above all, realize: When you notice children building relationships between an exhibit, a lesson, or an experience and something they have experienced in the past or can imagine in the future, you are seeing what learning looks like.

CHAPTER 12

After Words

Happy are they . . . who get understanding.

—Proverbs, 3:13

WE HAVE SEEN MUSEUM VISITS go right and go wrong, and we have seen exhibits that are better or worse at spurring learning. The most important point in this chapter is the value of joy, humor, and fun in museum exhibits or any learning experiences. Joy revs up the brain, humor enlivens experiences, and fun motivates children to repeat, search for answers, and value the process of learning.

This chapter contains practical advice—a blend of checklist, ideas, and design guide—to help teachers focus a visit to a museum, park, landmark, or other out-of-classroom experience, support their understanding of design, and consolidate ideas about using exhibits to boost thinking and learning.

FOR TEACHERS

"Teachable" moments occur before, during, and after experiences. Here are ideas about how to make the most of each.

Before You Visit

The results of grocery shopping depend on the preparation: Did you make a list? Peruse what is already in your cupboards? Review your recipe? If not, you may return with more of the juice you have aplenty, but without a make-or-break ingredient for your recipe. If you live far from the store, lack of planning can ruin a dinner.

So it is with any outing or task. Each of the following bits of planning will encourage children to learn. Most examples are couched in terms of museum visits, but ideas are applicable to many classroom lessons or any field trip.

> Anticipation is a powerful force in arousing children's curiosity.

Museums' Contents. If this is a first visit, check the website for information about offerings, daily events, specific times, virtual tours, or suggested itineraries. If the website lacks information, call. If you know the museum well, recall what your children did on recent visits. Are there areas where they wanted to stay longer than time allowed? Are there areas that reflect children's interests or something they are reading about? The more matches between children's interests and what they will see, the more they are likely to learn.

Selection. The museum is huge, with enough to see over several days, but you have only 4 hours. The larger the museum, the more children benefit from selecting in advance what they want to see. Develop a list of options with your children. Then, honor their choices! Engaging children in a selection process gives them a sense of agency, the confidence that they can choose well, and the knowledge that you trust their judgment. These are empowering feelings; they build self-confidence and strengthen children's interest in what they have selected.

> Selection is part of the brain's attention systems; the more you exercise the process of selection, the more you refine the brain's ability to attend and focus.

Pre-Thinking. Several 7-year-old boys want to see the airplanes. Draw out what they have in mind: Does a particular kind of plane interest them? What do they want to know about the helicopter? What do they already know about (whatever they have mentioned)? Write down what interests them as entry points for the visit.

At school, involve children in a search for the information they want—books, the library, the web. The more information children have, the more questions it will spur. Converse with your class in a 90/10 ratio: Children talk 90% of the time; adult talks 10%. In other words, listen! It is the best way to determine children's knowledge and interests. When children have mental hooks—ideas, or schemata, like Rachel and the globe (Chapter 5)—they integrate experiences in a neural network.

Plan. Using the information you have gathered and your conversations with the children, plan with the class what you will see and how much time you will spend at different locations. Discuss the fact that a plan is a guideline, not a straitjacket, and that you can deviate from the plan if you become deeply involved. If parents are accompanying you, consider breaking into small groups— two to five children with one adult. If interests diverge greatly, children will benefit far more from pursuing their own interests in a small group than from staying together. Later, groups can share by reporting their experiences to the whole class.

A plan consists of a list of what you will see and an approximate time for each. Planning helps children understand that they may not be able to stay as long as they would like, provides practice in budgeting time, and familiarizes children with divisions of minutes, half hour, and longer time spans. Don't forget time for logistics—stowing coats, getting oriented, bathroom and water breaks, and eating snack or lunch.

> Planning and scheduling are high-level brain functions.

On the Way

Turn off electronic devices so you can converse about what you are looking forward to. A portable mike improves communication on a bus.

Establishing a Mind-Set. The day has arrived; you're on your way. Your children are excited because they will see what they have asked to see. Ask if they remember what they want to see, what they said was of interest, and what their questions were. Some children recall every detail of what they want to find out; others forget everything they have said. Both are normal responses. Use your notes to remind children who have forgotten and to prompt them on questions they want answered. Repetition is essential to fix something in memory. When you ask children to recall and prompt them, you are engaging children in repetitive behavior and thus increasing the likelihood that they will remember.

Anticipating. Ask children about details of the drive: Do they recall specific streets? highways? landmarks? Ask them to describe the museum building. Some children have a different place in mind from the one you are visiting. If they refer to the tall building with the glass tower, remind them that that is the science museum, but today you are going to the art museum. Describe a feature of the architecture—the color of the brick or stone, a detail of the entryway, a piece of identifying sculpture. The Metropolitan Museum of Art (Manhattan) has wide stairs leading to three front doors, each set under an enormous arch. The Hirshhorn Museum (Washington, D.C.) is circular. The Art Institute (Chicago) is flanked by two immense bronze lions with a green patina. The Don Harrington Discovery Center (Amarillo; see Figure 12.1) has huge spotlights that cast beams of light visible from miles away at night. Dramatic buildings make a huge impression on children. Talking about the special features of a place alerts children. Some children know you are approaching, know you have arrived, or spot particular features. These children are using visual/spatial brain networks. Anticipation causes children to gather information from different centers in the brain and connect it.

Visiting any great museum is as much about the aura of the place as what you will see. The Carnegie Museum of Science (Pittsburgh) is situated on the Ohio River with incredible vistas of river traffic from floor-to-ceiling windows, as intriguing as any exhibit. The San Diego Museum of Man is set in an 1,100-acre park, housed beneath a huge ornate dome and 200-foot-tall tower visible for miles. The 20-acre Israel Museum complex (Jerusalem) is set on a hill overlooking the city's white stone buildings. On your way, discuss whatever is special about the site.

> Looking for details engages the brain's capacity to recall and focus, acts that are essential for all learning.

Arrival

Arrival is a big moment in any experience. You've fought the traffic and found parking, or managed to get seats on the Metro and identify the closest exit.

Figure 12.1. Part of museums' allure is that they convey a strong sense of place and announce themselves in diverse ways. At the Don Harrington Discovery Center in Amarillo, huge beams of light, visible from miles away at night, identify the museum's location.

Photo by Chip Lindsay

You've walked along bustling city streets or through an expansive park. Perhaps you are spatially challenged, so can relax when, finally, you find the entry. Stop and savor it. Architects put great thought into entryways. Ask children why they think the building looks like it does, how they know they are at the entrance, what features they notice. Spark their interest in how the thoughts in their brains reflect what the architect who designed all those details might have thought. If the architect is famous, like Frank Gehry or I. M. Pei, the children can research them on the Internet.

Entries mark passages in time and space. Time changes from the hassle of getting there to concentration on sensations. Spaces enclose shafts of sunlight, glimpses of sky, or long corridors. Dead ends prompt children to spot exits. Chambers echo. Marble stair rails feel cold. Smells from cleaning supplies and crowds overwhelm the brain. Objects are unusual—gigantic, frightening, magnificent, ancient. Materials are rare or precious. Savor these impressions, talk about them, describe them to one another.

> Sensory experience is the dominant part of memory; making perceptions explicit reinforces children's memory.

Orienting to Time. Sensory experiences happen in time frames. Sights may be mere glimpses or lingering scenes. Objects change as you walk around them, paintings as you pass by. The brain quickly tires of odor, so you shortly cease to notice the sweet aroma that attracts or the sour smell that offends. Touch is the only sense in which receptors that communicate with the brain are in direct contact with an object. Touch stimulates lengthy exploration—notice how some children run their hands along any available surface. Grab these times to make children aware of how their senses alert the brain. Suggest that they describe these impressions and identify the part of the body responsible. The more children are aware of what causes their responses, the more likely they will be to use their senses as a way to direct their attention. For children 7, 8, or older, suggest timing their sensations to make children conscious of different lengths of time.

Budgeting time is difficult. When children eagerly anticipate a visit, and if it meets expectations, children will resist leaving. If you have planned your time in advance, after savoring the arrival, gather the children, review your plan, possibly break into groups, briefly recall how much time you allowed for each part of the experience, and check a clock to remind you of departure time. Timing is a critical aspect in all human behavior. Being conscious of time and its role in activities sharpens the brain's awareness.

Orienting to Space. Maps are intrinsically interesting to some and baffling to others. From age 2 or 3, children can be shown where they are on a floor plan and the route to where they are going. If they are made aware of icons, even very young children can recognize stairwells, elevators, water fountains, and restrooms.

At the Ruben Fleet Science Center in San Diego with a group of five children, the 10-year-old found a floor plan and studied it. Immediately, the three 6-year-olds and the 4-year-old each took a floor plan. The 10-year-old's frequent references to the plan showed the younger children what to do. Without older children, teachers can model how to use floor plans.

Museums are large. Exhibit layouts may seem obtuse because large exhibitions must accommodate to fixed walls, ceilings, and corridors. The East Wing of the National Gallery of Art, in Washington, D.C., is an extreme example (see Figure 12.2). Sited on a small, irregular plot of land, the building, designed by I. M. Pei, is made up of more than a dozen interlocking triangular prisms. Some of the spaces are soaring. Others are so small that exhibitions may begin on the second floor, continue on the third, and conclude on the first. For children, the space is like a giant three-dimensional puzzle. Look at other blueprints of this complex building on the web. Children savor complexity.

If you are unsure how to read maps and floor plans, so much the better. When adults genuinely struggle to understand, children imitate both the *process* (cognition) and a positive *attitude* (motivation) toward learning new things. Spatial orientation, which children learn from using floor plans, can be transferred to reading other floor plans, maps, and drawing their own maps. Following a floor plan makes children conscious of where they are in relation to the space they are in.

> Spatial orientation is a foundational brain skill and the basis for many higher-level thinking processes.

Figure 12.2. Architect I. M. Pei had the challenge of building a major museum to conform to a small, triangular plot of land. Can you see the actual building from looking at the plan? How many triangles can you find?

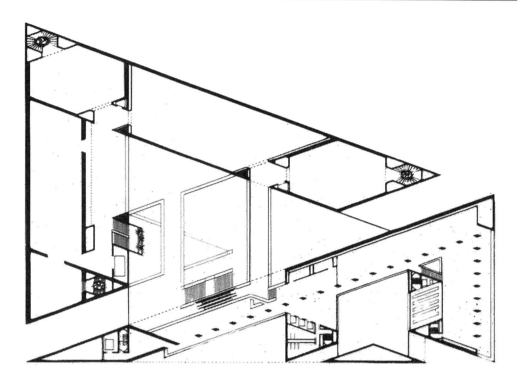

Reprinted by permission of Pei Cobb Freed & Partners

Summary: Preparations

There are as many ways to prepare as there are places to go. The point is to make some preparation and thus alert the brain's attention systems, focus on concepts, plan, and feel motivated to make the visit.

QUESTIONS TO ASK OF EXHIBITS

Artists' success is determined by critics' reactions, exhibits' success by visitors' reactions, and teachers' success by children's responses to their questions.

What Are the Handles for Learning?

Exhibit content spans all areas of human thought. This is evident as you consider different ways to challenge children to think in an art, a science, or a history museum.

Art Exhibit

The Museum of Great Art has recently opened an exhibit of works by Edgar Degas. The curator of impressionist art conceived the exhibit 8 years earlier; it required considerable vision, scholarship, research, persuasion, security assurances, fund-raising, and collaboration to make the idea a reality. It is a comprehensive show from Degas's early to late works. Some think of Degas as a painter of ballet dancers and racehorses. In fact, he painted landscapes, historical scenes, intimate interiors, nudes, theatergoers and performers, and numerous portraits. Some of his portraits are explicitly about moods, with titles like "Sulking" or "Melancholy"; they show isolation, austerity, modesty, shyness, and a range of other emotions.

What are the handles in an exhibit? The title sometimes gives a clue, but this show was titled merely "Degas." In retrospectives that follow an artist's life chronologically, you can talk with children about how old an artist was when he did certain things or encourage them to look for patterns or changes across the artist's life in technique or subject. Lacking those handles, here are some ideas for the Degas show.

Overview. Challenge children to establish a structure by asking them to determine how works are organized. The Degas show was organized by subject—what the artist painted. In two galleries were all the dancers, in several galleries the portraits, and so on. Chronology was ignored and paintings were grouped by subtheme—dancers at rehearsals, solos, chorus, pre- or post-performance. Portraits were grouped by individuals, families, the artist's family, self-portraits.

> Establishing a structure provides ways for children to compare, organize, and analyze what they see.

Details. Focus children's interest by challenging them to find specific things. Ask younger children about the subject of the paintings, such questions as:

- Which dancer is performing the most difficult steps?
- What do you think the dancing teacher is saying?
- Which dancer seems the most beautiful to you? Why?

Or, in the portrait galleries:

- There is a lady with a wide red border on her dress. Whisper to me when you have found her. Keep it a secret until others find her.
- Degas painted a family's pet. Try to find it and remember where it is so you can show it to us before we leave.

With older children, ask:

- How many different shades of red has Degas used? Remember and we'll take a "red tour" before we leave.

- Artists may arrange objects in their paintings in a triangle. Did Degas do this? If so, remember where, and show us before we leave.
- Degas captured his subjects' feelings. What different feelings can you find? Remember them and we'll take a "feelings" tour once everyone has looked.

Ask older students to carry small notebooks in which to record answers:

- Some artists use perspective to make a scene realistic. Where does Degas use perspective?
- Degas painted his subjects' hands with great finesse. What do the hands in his paintings suggest?
- Can you find two paintings in which the source of the light is completely different?

Ask children of any age: Comparing all the portraits (or dancers, landscapes, and so on), which two are the most different? Why? Allow time to hear children's perspective, emotions, ideas.

Key Points:

1. Art exhibits require children to search for meaning.
2. Comparison, an underlying brain function, can be well exercised by finding similarities or differences among paintings.
3. Artists' techniques can be used as a way to engage thinking and feeling.
4. The emotion in great art speaks to people of all ages. When children look for emotion, it builds awareness of others' feelings, which in turn builds empathy.

Science Exhibit

Sure crowd-pleasers, motion machines are endlessly fascinating. They consist of (usually) a metal frame, frequently rectangular. Inside are runways along which balls move at different pitches and through diverse drops. Some machines are powered by electricity; in a few, children themselves can drop a ball at different entries. The one in the Museum of Science (Boston), centered in a wide spiral stairway, rises two full stories. Some children spend over an hour watching balls move along pathways (see Chapter 5). If your class has parent-led groups, children who want to remain at the exhibit can do so. Suggest that parents use questions (see below).

The fascination of the rollways is that the balls

- go through loop-de-loops;
- speed over roller coasters;
- whirl in a vortex;
- bounce on trampolines;

- activate varied switches or gates, some Y-shaped, others paddle-like, that direct the balls on different paths;
- sound chimes, xylophones, or other noisemakers;
- swing pendula;
- back up in ball catchers until their weight makes them fall.

The machines are complex, with no limit to the variations. Most use collector tracks, banked curves, drops, speed routes, or traps to accelerate or slow the balls. Rollways exhibit many different physics principles. Children's fascination can be channeled by challenging them to think about cause and effect.

Focus younger children's attention by asking:

- How many balls do you see?
- What color are the balls?

With their attention focused, ask questions that require analytic thinking:

- What happens to the balls?
- Why do you think the red ball (stops, falls, collects—whatever verbs children use)?

Ask older children:

- What forces make the balls move?
- Name and count the forces that act on the balls.
- If you want balls to move really fast, where would you place them? Why?
- If you want balls to slow down, where would you place them? Why?

Or, focus on a particular ball:

- How would you describe where the red ball is and where the blue ball is?
- How is the position likely to change before the ball hits bottom?
- What sources of energy make the ball move?
- What forces slow the ball down?

The website for a construction set called "Chaos Tower" has a wealth of information to encourage children to think about rollway exhibits. Rollway exhibits require children to be precise, use evidence logically, and apply physics principles of how moving objects behave.

> Thinking precisely, logically, and using physics principles are high-level brain functions.

On the Way Home . . . or Later

Children may be exhausted after an outing. The enormity of the place, the huge number of stimuli, and interactions with others are tiring, especially if children have not had a healthful snack. It may be best not to review but to nap or to listen to Debussy or Brahms.

If children themselves ask questions, discuss them. If you don't know the answers, ask how we can find out. Be sure to do so. If children don't say anything, at a later time ask:

- What do you remember about our trip?
- What was your favorite part?
- What would you like to find out about (whatever children mention)?
- How could we find out?
- If we went again, what would you want to do?

Key Points:

1. To consolidate information the brain requires digestion time.
2. Discussing experiences helps to consolidate and fix them in memory.

SUMMARY: PREPARE, QUESTION, DISCUSS

Pre-visit preparation arouses expectations. If preparation is frequent, repetitive, and short, children can establish a network of information with handles that alert them to the meaning in an experience. Their involvement in planning gives them ownership of the experience that will increase their readiness to learn. Questions focus attention. Discussion consolidates information so that it becomes a permanent part of children's thinking.

UNDERSTANDING EXHIBIT DESIGN

Designing exhibits is exhilarating and exhausting. When teachers know how exhibits are designed, they can make use of design principles to help children learn by enticing them to ask and helping them formulate questions. Here, we analyze design.

Intention

As the Cheshire Cat knew, if you don't know where you're going, any road will get you there. "Knowing where you're going" is another way to say that you have a clear idea of what you want an exhibit to do. The clearer the idea, the more likely children are to learn. Clarifying questions follow.

Why Produce This Exhibit? Reasons vary. Museums with large collections feel obligated to rotate what they display. Museums may have a master exhibit plan. Topics that resonate with a museum's mission may be hot (a new dinosaur or other scientific find, a political happening, the death of a personage of local importance). Donors may hinge gifts on the production of a particular exhibit. Curators may finally convince donors to fund a long-desired exhibit. Grant funds may be available in particular areas of scholarship. The marketing department may convince others that exhibits on particular subjects will increase visitorship. Your school system may have requested particular topics. (School admission fees represent an important part of museums' income: Don't hesitate to ask for exhibits that support your curriculum.) Reasons museums produce exhibits are diverse and complex. Availability of funds is more common than admitted. Understanding why a museum undertakes an exhibit may provide insight about how it is presented, what to emphasize, what to omit, and what the exhibit relates to.

Who Will Benefit? Knowing what audience the exhibit was designed for clarifies issues. Is it for children alone or children and adults? If children alone, what ages? Is it for the general public or scholars? Must the audience be familiar with the topic? Or, will a technical exhibit offer enough information that the uninitiated can grasp the meaning? Teachers can ask such questions of museum staff before planning a visit.

A renowned museum in a major city had a collection of cultural objects that were displayed along with native song, dance, food, storytelling, and festivals. After many successful years, different management took over, built a striking building—a showcase for artifacts, put the objects in magnificent cases, and discontinued cultural programming. Despite having moved to a prominent location, the museum received far fewer visitors, visitors stayed for shorter periods, and children found the museum boring. It now had great appeal for other museum curators, for students of the culture, and for visitors who use museums for the pleasure of looking at objects. But it had become a different institution. Understanding the audience that an exhibit is designed to attract can determine what to visit and how to focus the trip.

What Is the Exhibit's Meaning? This important question may generate different answers from those who create the exhibit and those who run the exhibit once built. Directors negotiate the mission of the museum and the cost. Fundraisers have donors' perspective in mind. Marketing directors want to reach the largest possible audience. Curators want to be true to the meaning they have chosen to emphasize. Educators want to expand visitors' knowledge. Designers have particular constraints in mind: Exhibits must fit specific spaces, achieve a certain look, cover certain concepts. Audiences (visitors—*you*) have their own expectations. Some museums hold focus groups to solicit teachers' opinions before or as they build an exhibit. Find out if your museum does; if not, ask if they would consider doing so. Remember, your admission fees matter to the museum. Melding all the perspectives requires leadership to bring about collaboration, honor differing viewpoints, forge consensus, and listen to audiences. Without such leadership, the meaning of an exhibit may be muddled.

What Are the Transcendent Ideas? We've talked a lot about transcendence. Here, we raise it as a main question in considering exhibits. Transcendence means making a mental bridge (or bridges) from the meaning in an exhibit to other meanings that relate to it. These can be other exhibits, other experiences children have had, or ideas triggered by the exhibit. So, the "Degas" exhibit (above) may bring to mind something as close to the topic as a ballet that children once viewed or as distant as an uncle whose name is Edgar. Ball rollways may bring to mind a theme park roller coaster or pitching a baseball. Adults' facility in recognizing transcendent ideas and encouraging children to make connections expands children's understanding of exhibits' meaning.

> Transcendent ideas are powerful handles to develop children's ability to make relationships and generalize them to other situations.

Modalities

Designers can chose from visual, auditory, graphic, 3-D, hands-on experiences, and more. Each offers a range of sensations that alert the brain in different ways. Teachers' skill lies in arousing interest without overwhelming the brain. Too little stimulation and the brain fails to take notice; too much and the brain is overloaded and turns off.

Humans have the intrinsic capacity to receive and send information in many different modalities, but often use only a fraction of that capacity. By presenting exhibits in many different modalities, museums can stretch the human capacity to "read" in greatly varied ways. Teachers can help children spot as many modalities as possible in exhibits and then determine which modalities are most likely to engage specific children.

Repetitive Elements

Repeating content, processes, movements, or anything else is essential to make an impact on the brain. Onetime experiences rarely leave a trace. Unless there is repetition, one experience may as well not have happened.

Repetition is *the* most important way to impress something so the brain habituates it and in the future can use the skill, process, information, or principle. Find examples of repetition within a single exhibit or in a cluster of exhibits.

> Encourage children to find repetitive ideas in different exhibits.

Variation

Repetition without variation is boring. Boring things put the brain to sleep. To stay alert, the brain requires novelty. With their vast number of techniques, museums need never be boring.

> Find the novel aspects of exhibits that will keep children alert.

Movement

The brain is wired to pay attention to movement. Noticing movement, however slight, was a survival skill that protected our species during eons of evolution. If movement is intrinsic to an exhibit (as with the rollways exhibit above and other exhibits described throughout the book), call the movement to children's attention.

If an exhibit has no obvious movement, create ways for children to move as they examine the exhibit: What changes if you view it head on, from the left, from the right? Are those changes important? Why? If you were standing in the exhibit looking out, what would you see that is the same or different, that contradicts the exhibit's meaning? that supports the meaning?

> Incorporating movement in an exhibit keeps the brain alert.

Organization

How an exhibit is organized can determine what ideas children see. Consider exhibits that contain the same idea and are grouped together. Such organization enables you to lead children from the most concrete to increasingly abstract experiences; the progression helps children more readily grasp concepts. If exhibits are not so organized, consider imposing such organization by the order in which you see exhibits and how you encourage children to build relationships among them.

> The brain builds abstractions from concrete knowledge.

Feedback

Feedback is information about how someone has performed. Blinking lights, sounding buzzers, or a voice saying, "Ahem!" draw attention to missed cues or off-the-mark responses. If exhibits have no feedback devices, look for ways to give feedback to children's responses. What in the exhibit provides evidence? lacks evidence? contains important ideas? relates to children's ideas?

> If the brain has crystallized patterns of thinking that are "hasty, narrow, fuzzy, or sprawling" (Perkins, 1995, p. 153), it requires point-blank attention to change the pattern.

SUMMARY: BRINGING LEARNING HOME

Museums' potential to impact learning is often misunderstood or unrealized. But museums can powerfully affect thinking and help children learn. The secret lies in structuring adult/child interactions that provoke children to question and help them formulate questions. Then, when they answer, congratulating them for asking thought-provoking questions. How teachers use museums, how museum staff conceive an exhibit, and how museums support visitors make all the difference.

After visiting, children may say, "This reminds me of . . .", and mention something they gleaned. Or children may ask, "Do you remember that . . .", and refer to something they saw. Such remarks indicate that something in the experience is bubbling around in the brain. Children learn when teachers:

- recognize children's remarks as evidence that the brain is elaborating,
- follow children's ideas with conversation,
- involve children in a search for answers.

Different factors draw visitors to museums. Some adults, who understand that museums stimulate thinking and learning, visit frequently, explore at children's pace, and mediate beautifully. Some children naturally concentrate or have had mediation that has prepared them to observe and question. Some children are so startled by effects that they question and ponder. Others crystallize experience (Rachael, Chapter 5), thereby turning an instance into a globally useful concept. Feuerstein says, "Mediation can overcome seemingly intractable barriers to learning—length of time the condition has been present, its cause, or severity." Mediators tackle thinking deficiencies a step at a time using many stimuli.

Museum objects, dioramas, or novel experiences grab attention, enlarge perspective, and instill mental images that will be lifelong sources of wonder, pleasure, or understanding. Mediation evokes children's thoughtful acts and leads them to consolidate their thinking. Children who focus, question, and build relationships show us what learning looks like.

Takeaways

1. Preparation focuses the brain.
2. Finding the handles in exhibits means recognizing how to connect exhibit ideas with what children know.
3. Understanding design principles provides insight into how to use exhibits.
4. Knowing how to learn from museum exhibits is a paradigm for how to structure any learning experience.

List of Deficient Cognitive Functions

(Adapted from Appendix B in
Feuerstein, Rand, & Feuerstein, 2006, pp. 427–429)

Familiarity with deficiencies in cognitive function enables mediators to pinpoint the source of an individual's difficulties.

Deficient Cognitive Functions at the Input Phase of a Mental Act

1. Blurred and sweeping perception.
2. Unplanned, impulsive, and unsystematic exploratory behavior.
3. Lack of or impaired receptive verbal tools that affect discrimination (e.g., objects, events, and relationships are not appropriately labeled).
4. Lack of or impaired spatial orientation and lack of stable systems of reference (cannot see space from a personal vantage point—left, right; cannot see space as an absolute universal system—east, west).
5. Lack of or impaired temporal concepts (cannot understand time as either an object or a dimension; does not see time as a measurable, stable interval or as a flow from past to present to future).
6. Lack of or impaired conservation of constancies (e.g., size, shape, quality, color, orientation) across variations in one or more dimensions.
7. Lack of or deficient need for precision and accuracy in data gathering.
8. Lack of capacity to consider two or more sources of information at once. This is reflected in dealing with data in a piecemeal fashion rather than as a unit of organized facts.

Deficient Cognitive Functions at the Elaboration Phase of a Mental Act

1. Inadequate perception of the existence of a problem and its definition.
2. Inability to select relevant, as opposed to irrelevant, cues in defining a problem.
3. Lack of spontaneous comparative behavior or the limitation of its application to a restricted need system (cannot compare things effectively).
4. Narrowness of the mental field (lacks meaning, concepts, or cannot put something in a context).
5. Episodic grasp of reality (does not seek or project relationships, or group, organize, or summarize stimuli).

6. Lack of need for education (drawing on given facts) or establishment of relationships.
7. Lack of need for, and/or exercise of, summative behavior.
8. Lack of or impaired need for pursuing logical evidence.
9. Lack of or impaired inferential hypothetical ("if . . . then") thinking.
10. Lack of or impaired strategies for hypothesis testing.
11. Lack of or impaired planning behavior.
12. Lack of or impaired interiorization (cannot internalize an instruction, object, or experience). Example: Cannot make moral judgments such as recognizing the meaning, value, or ethics of thoughts or actions.
13. Non-elaboration of certain cognitive categories because the verbal concepts are not part of the individual's verbal inventory on a receptive level, or because they are not mobilized at the expressive level.

Deficient Cognitive Functions at the Output Phase of a Mental Act

1. Egocentric communication modalities (sees no need to express meaning clearly or to provide evidence).
2. Difficulties in projecting virtual relationships; that is, cannot restructure relationships between objects and events from one type of relationship to another. In other words, a child might recognize that a square is made up of four sides but not be able to pick out a square when it is tilted, patterned, or divided by diagonal or horizontal lines.
3. Blocking. Students resist: "I can't." "It's too hard." "I don't know how."
4. Trial-and-error responses.
5. Lack of or impaired verbal or other tools for communicating adequately elaborated responses.
6. Lack of or impaired need for precision and accuracy in the communication of one's responses.
7. Deficiency of visual transport; that is, cannot hold an image "in the mind's eye" during a task that requires matching, comparing, completing a figure, or in other ways using visual memory.
8. Impulsive, random, unplanned behavior.

Children with Learning Challenges: Notes for Parents and Exhibit Designers

PARENTS

To mediate effectively, adults—parents and educators—must believe that children can learn even if they appear to have cognitive challenges that would make learning more difficult. Teachers and museum staff can show parents how to go the extra mile. In fact, parents of children with cognitive, emotional, movement, social, or other challenges may need support from a teacher, guidance counselor, or psychologist specializing in learning to:

- make them aware of the need for mediation;
- show them their potential to mediate;
- teach them how to translate what they know about their child's nature, strengths, and weaknesses into techniques that help children learn;
- guide them in how to help children with homework assignments, with the kinds of informal parent/child teaching that occurs spontaneously, or with techniques for learning from museum exhibits;
- clarify the meaning in lessons or exhibits;
- model how to explore with purpose so children can imitate;
- express satisfaction with their children's performance;
- interact with their children with enthusiasm, joy, and optimism.

Teachers and museum staff can go out of their way to increase parent/child interaction by encouraging parents with:

- *Body language*—affirmative nods, eye contact, smiles of approval.
- *Praise*—"Great job, Mom!"
- *Observation*—"Look at how hard your daughter's trying!" Or, "Your son just attempted something really challenging."
- *Appreciation*—"*You* helped your child master that."

These seemingly small actions are potent forces to motivate parents and can change the way parents see their children.

EXHIBITS

If the strong stimuli of an exhibit fail to rouse a child, impacts must be greatly increased with effects shockingly different from the expected. What if:

- a sidewalk moves backward,
- a lion whinnies like a horse,
- a ball rolls sideways on an incline,
- a "fire" is cold to the touch,
- a small rubber-looking ball is heavy as lead?

Museums can make such things happen—metaphorically, an "Inside-out, Back-side-front Surprise Effect Exhibit." Such exhibits intensify drama, cause children to attend, to question, or to suppose "why." Mediators can encourage parents to use children's responses to help them find absurdities, seek causes, and discuss *why* something seems absurd.

References

Aebli, H. (1970). Piaget and beyond. *Interchange, 1*(1), 12–24. Available from www.springer-link.com/content/f150457258v81544

Allen, S. (1997). Sociocultural theory in museums: Insights and suggestions. *Journal of Museum Education, 22*(2/3, Part 1), 8–9. Washington, DC: Museum Education Roundtable.

Beaino, G., Khoshnood, B., Kaminski, M., Marret, S., Pierrat, V., Vieux, R., Thiriez, G., Martis, J., Roze, J., Alberge, C., Larroque, B., Breart, G., & Ancep, P. (2011). Predictors of the risk of cognitive deficiency in very preterm infants: The EPIPAGE prospective cohort. *Acta Paediatrica, 100*(9), 370–378.

Ben-Hur, M. (2008). Feuerstein's instrumental enrichment: Evidence of effectiveness. Available at www.iriinc.us/PDF/FIE_Effectiveness_Report_(2002).pdf

Berk, L. E., & Winsler, A. (1995). *Scaffolding children's learning: Vygotsky and early childhood education.* Washington, DC: National Association for the Education of Young Children.

Blake, W. (1803). Auguries of innocence. *The Pickering manuscript.* Available at http://www.britannica com/bps/additionalcontent/17/17429/The-Pickering-Manuscript

Blakeslee, S. (2006). Cells that read minds. *The New York Times, Science.* Available at http://www.nytimes.com/2006/01/10/science/10mirr.html?_r=1&oref=slogin

Brown, J. S., & Burton, R. R. (1978). Diagnostic models for procedural bugs in basic mathematical skills. *Cognitive Science, 2*, 71–192.

Chabris, D. F., & Hearst, E. S. (2003). Visualization, pattern recognition, and forward search: Effects of playing speed and sight of position on grandmaster chess errors. *Cognitive Science, 27*, 637–648.

Chaucer, G. (1387–1400). *The Canterbury tales.* Available at http: //www.librarius.com/

Collins, W. (1998). *The moonstone.* New York: Oxford University Press. (Original work published 1874)

Collinson, S. (2002). Philosopher of the month: Kenneth Craik. *The Philosophers' Magazine* (J. Stangroom, Ed.). Available at http://www.philosophers.co.uk/cafe/phil_sep2002.htm

Connor, S. (2003, March 18). African click language "holds key to origins of earliest human speech." *The Independent.* Available at http://www.independent.co.uk/news/science/african-click-language-holds-key-to-origins-of-earliest-human-speech-591505.html

Crowley, K., & Callanan, M. (1998). Describing and supporting collaborative scientific thinking in parent-child interactions. *Journal of Museum Education, 23*(1), 12–17.

Csikszentmihalyi, M. (2010). Foreword. In A. Lewin-Benham, *Infants and toddlers at work: Using Reggio-inspired materials to support brain development* (pp. ix–x). New York: Teachers College Press.

Csikszentmihalyi, M. (1990). *Flow: The psychology of optimal experience.* New York: Harper-Collins.

Damasio, A. (1994). *Descartes' error.* New York: G. P. Putnam's Sons.

Edelman, G. (2009, January 16). What makes you uniquely you? *Discover Magazine*, pp. 1–3. Available at http://discovermagazine.com/2009/feb/16-what-makes-you-uniquely-you

European Science Foundation. (2008). What do mirror neurons mean? In G. Origgi (Ed.), *Interdisciplines.* Paris: Author. Available at http://www.interdisciplines.org/mirror

Evan-Moor Publishing. (2010). *Water, composition of.* Available at http://www.bookrags.com/research/water-composition-of-wsd/

Falk, J. H., & Dierking, L. D. (2010). The 95% solution. *American Scientist, 98,* 486–493.

Feldman, D. E., & Brecht, M. (2005, November). Map plasticity in somatosensory cortex, *Science, 310*(5749), 810–815. Available at http://www.sciencemag.org/cgi/content/abstract/310/5749/810

Feuerstein, F., Falik, L., & Feuerstein, R. S. (in press). *Mediated soliloquy: Theory, concept and a monograph series.* Jerusalem: International Center for the Enhancement of Learning Potential (ICELP) Press.

Feuerstein, R., Falik, L., & Feuerstein, R. S. (2006). *Definitions of essential concepts & terms.* Jerusalem: ICELP Press.

Feuerstein, R., & Feuerstein, R. S. (2003). *Feuerstein instrumental enrichment—Basic.* Jerusalem: ICELP Press.

Feuerstein, R., Feuerstein, R. S., & Falik, L. (2009). *Feuerstein instrumental enrichment—Basic: User's guide.* Jerusalem: ICELP Press.

Feuerstein, R. S., Feuerstein, R., & Falik, L. (2004). *User's guide to the theory and practice of the Feuerstein instrumental enrichment program—BASIC.* Jerusalem: ICELP Press.

Feuerstein, R., Feuerstein, R. S., Falik, L., & Rand, Y. (2006). *The Feuerstein instrumental enrichment program: Part I and Part II.* Jerusalem: ICELP Press.

Feuerstein, R., Feuerstein, R. S., Falik, L., & Rand, Y. (2002). *The dynamic assessment of cognitive modifiability.* Jerusalem: ICELP Press.

Feuerstein, R., Rand, Y., & Feuerstein, R. S. (2006). *You love me! Don't accept me as I am.* Jerusalem: ICELP Press.

Gallese, V., Fadiga, L., Fogassi, L., & Rizzolatti, G. (1996). Action recognition in the premotor cortex. *Brain 119,* 593–609. Available at http://www.unipr.it/arpa/mirror/english/staff/rizzolat.htm

Gardner, H. (1992). On psychology and youth museums: Toward an education for understanding. *Hand to Hand, 6,* 3. Association of Youth Museums, Memphis, TN.

Gardner, H. (1991). *The unschooled mind.* New York: Basic Books.

Gardner, H. (1985). *The mind's new science: A history of the cognitive revolution.* New York: Basic Books.

Gardner, H. (1983). *Frames of mind: The theory of multiple intelligences.* New York: Basic Books.

Gates of repentance: The new union prayer book for the days of awe. (1978). New York: Central Conference of American Rabbis.

Gazzaniga, M. (2008). Arts and cognition: Findings hint at relationships. In M. Gazzaniga, C. Asbury, & B. Rich (Eds.), *Learning, arts, and the brain: The Dana Consortium report on arts and cognition* (pp. v–viii). New York: Dana Press.

Gelman, R., & Au, T. (1996). Cognitive and perceptual development. In E. Carterette & M. Friedman (Eds.), *Handbook of perception and cognition XIII* (2nd ed., pp. 3–48). San Diego: Academic Press.

Gelman, R., Brenneman, K., MacDonald, G., & Roman, M. (2009). *Preschool pathways to science: Facilitating scientific ways of thinking, doing, and understanding.* Baltimore: Brookes.

Gelman, R., & Schatz, M. (1977). Appropriate speech adjustments: The operation of conversational constraints on talk to two-year-olds. In M. Lewis & L. Rosenblum (Eds.), *Interaction, conversation and the development of language.* New York: Wiley.

General Atomics. (1994). Perspectives on plasma. Available at http://www.plasmas.org/what-are-plasmas.htm

Gleitman, H. (1987). *Basic psychology.* New York: W. W. Norton.

Goleman, D. (1995). *Emotional intelligence: Why it can matter more than IQ.* New York: Bantam Books.

Goleman, D. (1985). *Vital lies, simple truths: The psychology of self-deception.* New York: Simon & Schuster.

Greenspan, S. I., & Shanker, S. G. (2004). *The first idea: How symbols, language, and intelligence evolved from our primate ancestors to modern humans.* Cambridge, MA: Da Capo Press.

Hall, E. (1970). A conversation with Jean Piaget and Barbel Inhelder. Available at http://www.abrae.com.br/entrevistas/entr_pia.htm

Hawkins, D. (1965). Messing about in science. Watertown, MA: Educational Services Incorporated. Reprinted from *Science and Children*, 2(5), 1–5.

Kandel, E. (2006). *In search of memory: The emergence of a new science of mind.* New York: Norton.

Kant, I. (1991). *Critique of pure reason* (V. Politis, Trans.). London: Dent. Available at http://sharp.bu.edu/~slehar/quotes/kant.html. (Original work published 1781)

Kozulin, A. (2006). Integration of culturally different students in mainstream classes. *Transylvanian Journal of Psychology, 2*(1, special issue), 99–105. Cluj, Romania: Transylvanian Journal in cooperation with EU Inclues Project.

Kozulin, A. (1988). *Thought and language.* Cambridge, MA: MIT Press.

Kozulin, A., Lebeer, J., Madella-Noja, A., Gonzalez, F., Jeffrey, I., Rosenthal, N., & Koslowsky, M. (2009, December 1). Cognitive modifiability of children with developmental disabilities: A multicenter study using Feuerstein's Instrumental Enrichment-Basic program. *Research in developmental disabilities,* doi: 10.1016/j.ridd,2009.12.001.

Kozulin, A., & Rand, B. (Eds.). (2000). *Experience of mediated learning: An impact of Feuerstein's theory in education and psychology.* Elmsford, NY: Pergamon.

Kupperberg, P. (2005). *Hubble and the big bang.* New York: Rosen Publishing Group.

Lamb, C. (1913). Mrs. Battle's opining on whist. *The essays of Elia.* London: J. M. Dent. (Original work published 1823)

Lave, J., & Wenger, E. (1991). *Situated learning: Legitimate peripheral participation.* New York: Cambridge University Press.

LeDoux, J. (1998). *The emotional brain: The mysterious underpinning of emotional life.* New York: Simon & Schuster.

Lewin, A. W. (1990). A response to Rochel Gelman's AYM keynote address: Cognitive development goes to the museum. *Hand to Hand*, 4(4), 2. Memphis, TN: Association of Youth Museums.

Lewin-Benham, A. (2008). *Powerful children: Understanding how to think and learn using the Reggio approach.* New York: Teachers College Press.

Lewin-Benham, A. (2006). *Possible schools: The Reggio approach to urban education.* New York: Teachers College Press.

Llinas, R. R. (2001). *I of the vortex: From neurons to self*. Cambridge, MA: MIT Press.

Macrae, N. (1992). *John von Neumann: The scientific genius who pioneered the modern computer, game theory, nuclear deterrence, and much more*. New York: Pantheon Books.

Malaguzzi, L. (1991). *The very little ones of silent pictures*. Reggio Emilia, Italy: Municipal Infant/Toddler Center.

Marton, K. (2006). *The great escape: Nine Jews who fled Hitler and changed the world*. New York: Simon & Schuster.

McCarty, M. (1985). *The transforming principle: Discovering that genes are made of DNA*. New York: W. W. Norton.

Merzenich, M. (2004). Michael Merzenich on rewiring the brain. Available at http://www.ted. com/index.php/talks/michael_merzenich_on_the_elastic_brain.html

Miller, J. S. (n.d.). Physics, soap bubbles, pt. 2. Available at http://www.truveo.com/search?query=surfacetensioninsoapbubbles&flv=1#surface%20tension%20in%20soap%20bubbles%20

Monticello. (2011). Available at http://explorer.monticello.org/text/index.php?id=106&type=4

Neville, H., Anderson, A., Bagdade, O., Bell, T., Currin, J., Fanning, J., Klein, S., Lauinger, B., Pakulak, E., Paulsen, D., Sabourin, L., Stevens, C., Sundborg, S., & Yamada, Y. (2008). Effects of music training on brain and cognitive development in under-privileged 3- to 5-year-old children: Preliminary results. In M. Gazzaniga, C. Asbury, & B. Rich (Eds.), *Learning, arts, and the brain: The Dana Consortium report on arts and cognition* (pp. 105–116). New York: Dana Press.

Omer, D. (1991). *The Teheran operation: The rescue of Jewish children from the Nazis*. Washington, DC: B'nai B'rith.

Ornstein, R., & Thompson, R. (1984). *The amazing brain*. Boston: Houghton Mifflin.

Orr, E. W. (1987). *Twice as less: Black English and the performance of black students in mathematics and science*. New York: Norton.

Perkins, D. (1992). *Smart schools*. New York: Free Press.

Perkins, D. (1995). *Outsmarting IQ*. New York: Free Press.

Piaget, J. (1973). *The child and reality: Problems of genetic psychology* (A. Rosin, trans.). New York: Grossman.

Pinker, S. (1997). *How the mind works*. New York: Norton.

Pinker, S. (1994). *The language instinct: How the mind creates language*. New York: William Morrow.

Pollack, R. (1999). *The missing moment: How the unconscious shapes modern science*. New York: Houghton Mifflin.

Posner, M., Rothbart, M., Sheese, B., & Kieras, J. (2008). How arts training influences cognition. In M. Gazzaniga, C. Asbury, & B. Rich (Eds.), *Learning, arts and the brain* (pp. 1–10). New York: Dana Press.

Postman, N. (1985). *Amusing ourselves to death: Public discourse in the age of show business*. New York: Penguin Books.

Presseisen, B., & Kozulin, A. (1994). Mediated learning: The contributions of Vygotsky and Feuerstein in theory and practice. In M. Ben-Hur (Ed.), *On Feuerstein's instrumental enrichment: A collection* (Section 1, pp. 51–81). Palantine, IL: IRI/Skylight.

Ratey, J. (2002). *A user's guide to the brain: Perception, attention, and the four theaters of the brain*. New York: Random House.

Resnick, L. B. (1991). Shared cognition: Thinking as social practice. In L. B. Resnick, J. M. Levine, & S. D. Teasley (Eds.), *Perspectives on socially shared cognition* (pp. 1–20). Washington, DC: American Psychological Association.

Rogoff, B. (1991). *Apprenticeship in thinking: Cognitive development in social context*. New York: Oxford University Press.

Sacks, O. (2008). *Musicophilia: Tales of music and the brain*. New York: Vintage Books.

Salas, N., Assael, C., Huepe, D., Pirez, T., Gonzalez, F., Morales, A., Arevado, R., & Espinoza, C. (2010). Application of IE-Basic program to promote cognitive and affective development in preschoolers: A Chilean study. *Journal of Cognitive Education and Psychology*, 9(3), 285–297.

Saxe, J. G. (1881). *The poems of John Godfrey Saxe* (Highgate Edition). Boston: Houghton Mifflin.

Schauble, L., Leinhardt, G., & Martin, L. (1997). A framework for organizing a cumulative research agenda in informal learning contexts. *Journal of Museum Education*, 22(2/3, Part 1).

Shavelson, R. J. (2003). Biographical memoirs. *Proceedings of the American philosophical society*, 147(4), 380–385.

Shreeve, J. (2004). *The genome war: How Craig Venter tried to capture the code of life and save the world*. New York: Ballantine Books.

Siegel, D. J. (2007). *The mindful brain: Reflection and attunement in the cultivation of well-being*. New York: W. W. Norton.

Spelke, E., & Kinzler, K. (2007). Core knowledge. *Developmental Science, 10*(1), 89–96. Available at http://www.wjh. harvard.edu/~lds/pdfs/SpelkeKinzler07.pdf

Stone, R. E. (n.d.). Defining authenticity. *Works of art: Met objectives*. Available at http://www.metmuseum.org/Works_of_Art/objects_conservation/fall_2002/define.asp

Tennyson, A. L. (1849). In memoriam A.H.H. Available at http://www.online-literature.com/tennyson/718/

Thompson, S. (n.d.). Science projects for kids: Bernoulli's theorem [video series]. Available at http://www.ehow.com/videos-on_4644_science-projects-kids_-bernoulli_s-theorem.html

Turismo. intoscana. it. (n.d.). Benvenuto Cellini, Perseus with the Head of Medusa. Available at http://www.turismo.intoscana.it/intoscana2/export/TurismoRTen/sito-TurismoRTen/Contenuti/Elementi-interesse/Monumenti/visualizza_asset.html_549916293. html

University of Minnesota, School of Physics and Astronomy. (n.d.). Available at http://www.physics.umn.edu/outreach/pforce/circus/Bernoulli.html

Vygotsky, L. S. (2007). *Mind in society: The development of higher psychological processes* (M. Cole, V. John-Steiner, S. Scribner, & E. Souberman, Eds.). Cambridge. MA: Harvard University Press. (Original works published 1930–1935)

Wilson, F. (1998). *The hand: How its use shapes the brain, human language, and culture*. New York: Pantheon.

Yeats, W. B. (1946). Long-legged fly. *A little treasury of modern poetry*. New York: Charles Scribner's Sons. (Original work published 1938–1939)

Index

ADHD (Attention Deficit Hyperactivity
   Disorder), 3, 37, 74, 101, 168
Aebli, Hans, 28
Albers, Josef, 137
Allen, Sue, 20
Attention, 26–27, 30, 38, 64, 72–74, 76–77, 83,
   84, 98, 100, 115, 122, 159, 170, 172, 174–
   175, 179, 183, 193, 194, 197
   exhibits that arrest, 150, 151–152
   and illusion, 150, 166
   and media, 40
   and museums, 11, 36, 37, 66, 72, 85, 103, 106,
      108, 131, 151, 152, 159, 193, 194, 197
   "train" the brain, 10, 22, 58, 74, 85, 116, 154,
      175
Authorized Training Centers, xii, 37, 58, 64
Autism, 3, 27

Blind, 167–168
Blurred perception, 72, 73, 154
Borodin, Alexander, 28
Brain. *See also* Cognition; Relationships;
   Transformations
   as a dynamic system, 29
   mental operations, 160, 161, 162, 164, 169
   "mindness," 175
   and novelty, 77, 78, 82, 107, 109, 135, 155,
      200
   plasticity, 27, 45, 178
   responses to exhibits, 152
   reticular activating system (RAS), 77, 155
Brown, John Seely, 90
Burton, R. R., 90

Callanan, Maureen, 20, 128–129
Cellini, Benvenuto, 110–111

Chase, William, 129
Cognition, 10, 11, 16, 22, 35, 64, 65, 69, 71–86,
   129, 149–169. *See also* Deficient cognitive
   functions; Relationships
   and chess, 129
   and complexity, 21, 29, 40–41, 82, 91, 93,
      129, 132, 156
   and empathy, 120–121
   and expertise, 129
   in FIE, 44–45, 52–53, 54–55
   and flexibility, 154
   and forming relationships, 156–158
   and illusion, 164–166
   and incongruence, 149–152, 166
   and media, 102
   and mediation, 28, 30, 32, 36, 42, 172–173
   and motivation, 26, 51, 171–172
   in museums, 103–111, 118–132, 145
   and novelty, 155, 181
   and repetition, 153–155
   and skill acquisition, 121–122
   and stereognostic experience, 166–168
   and transfer, 130
   and transformation, 91–92, 158–164
Cognitive dissonance, 66, 111–112, 114
Cognitive map, 87–94, 94–96, 102, 112–114,
   136, 171
   and complexity, 92–93, 94, 96, 109, 132,
      156–157
   elaboration, 178
   and stages of a mental act, 113–114, 203–204
   in use, 92–93, 95–96, 112–114, 151–152
Collaboration, 61–62, 63, 113, 126–129
   parent/child, 128–129
   school/museum, 133–146, 182
Comer, James, 69–70

Compare/comparison, 2, 11, 13, 21, 23, 24, 52,
    71, 94, 107
  and empathy, 120
  examples in use, 14, 16, 34–35, 41, 78–79, 91,
      108, 113, 137, 162, 196
  and exhibits, 104, 134–135, 142, 186
  and mediation, 105, 106, 114, 148, 149, 151,
      160, 164, 165, 181, 187, 195
  and mental acts, 152, 157, 161, 175, 178, 185,
      203, 204
  and object conservation, 97
  and redundancy, 109
  to reverse blurred perception, 73–74, 75
  at stages of mental act, 90–113
Complexity. *See also* Cognition
  in brain systems, 72
  in content, 14, 18, 20
  examples of in learning activities, 31, 61–62,
      65, 79, 80–82
  and exhibits, 113–114, 134–136, 193
  and imitation, 79
  and mediation, 29, 58, 63
  and movement, 84, 183–184
  and repetition, 155–158
  and spatial orientation, 84
  and transcendence, 40–41
  and understanding, 19, 21, 35
  and using FIE instruments, 45, 48
Cronbach, L. J., xv
Crowley, Kevin, 20, 128–129
Csikszentmihalyi, Mihaly, 77, 78

Dali, Salvador, 11
Damasio, Antonio, 171
Da Vinci, Leonardo, 178
Deficient cognitive functions, 1, 2–3, 14, 83, 97–
    98, 102, 125, 133, 203–204. *See also* ADHD,
    Blurred perception; Down syndrome
  and advice for parents and museum guides,
      205–206
  and attention, 74
  and movement, 75
  and spatial orientation, 74–75
Degas, Edgar, 195–196, 199
Dostoevesky, Fyodor, 178
Down syndrome, 3, 31
Durer, Albrecht, 108, 178
Dynamic assessment, 6–7

Edelman, Gerald, 125–126
Emotional intelligence, 173
Empathy, 32, 63, 66–68, 80, 118–121, 132, 141,
    143, 186, 196
Escher, M. C., 150, 158, 160

Feuerstein, Reuven
  and Andre Rey, 6
  and Capital Children's Museum, 5
  early work in Israel, 6–7
  early years in Romania, 5–6, 31
  and Holocaust, xiii, 6, 32, 59, 119
  and imitation, 78
  mediating with intention, 26–27
  personal motivation, 31, 59
  and Piaget, xiii, 27–28
Feuerstein Instrumental Enrichment–Basic
  and empathy, 120
  lesson, 53–55
  overview, 51–53
Feuerstein Instrumental Enrichment–
    Standard, 44–51, 58
  lesson, 45–51
  overview, 44–45

Galileo, Galelei, 13
Gardner, Howard, 19–20, 61, 82, 89
  and multiple intelligences, 114–116
Gehry, Frank, 192
Gelman, Rochel, 19
Greenberg, Katherine, 78

Haptic perception, 100, 123, 166
Hawkins, David, 9–10, 25
Hezekiah, Lloyd, 148
Holocaust exhibit (Remember the Children/
    Daniel's Story), 7, 66–68, 118–120
  mediation in, 69
Hugo, Victor, 111

Imitation, 72–74, 78, 79, 193
Incongruence. *See* Cognition
Intention, 1, 2, 3, 9, 21, 27, 29, 33, 37, 38–39,
    40, 43, 45, 47, 58, 59, 60, 61, 63–65, 74,
    91, 108, 117, 140, 171, 172, 176. *See also*
    Mediation
  and affect, 84, 171
  and cognition, 171

and exhibits, 10, 13, 120, 126, 142, 143, 176
and modes, 39, 200
and stimuli, 34–36, 66, 68, 116, 140, 174,
    198–200

Kandel, Eric, 182
Kishon, Ephriam, 30
Kozulin, Alex, 28

Lavoisier, Antoine-Laurent, 22
Learning, 72–74, 152. *See also* Cognition;
    Deficient cognitive functions; Modalities;
    Motivation; Movement; Museums and
    exhibits; Relationships; Repetition;
    Representation; Spatial Orientation;
    Transformations
    essential cognitive acts, 71–86, 118–132,
        149–169
    graphic representation of, 177
    in museums, 9–25, 103–117, 189–202,
        205–206
    myths about, 21–25
    when children learn, 24, 185, 186, 187, 189,
        202
Leinhardt, Gaea, 20
Llinas, Rodolfo, 174–176

Malaguzzi, Loris, 79
Martin, Laura, 20
McNeill, James Abbot, 108
Meaning, 39–40, 63, 64, 65
Mediated Learning Theory, 26–43
Mediation, 11, 26–43. *See also* Cognitive map;
    Intention
    adults' role in, 10, 11–12, 21, 74
    of affect or emotion, 26, 68, 121, 132, 145,
        172–174, 188
    and Cognitive map, 87, 112, 158
    essential aspects, 4, 36, 38–41, 58
    in FIE-Basic, 51–55
    in FIE-Standard, 45–51, 55–57
    learning cycle, 13
    and meaning, 39–40
    mediatee, 33, 34, 37, 38, 39, 43, 171, 176
    motivation, 26, 173
    in museums, 12, 17–18, 76, 127, 131, 135–
        138, 143, 147, 181
    stimuli, 15, 34, 36–37, 39, 59, 174–176

techniques, 58, 59, 65, 88, 98, 106, 109, 111,
    114, 116, 123, 126, 128, 139, 168, 171,
    172, 178–180, 184
three partners, 33–38, 43, 171
Mediator, 33–36, 59–70
    effective, 16, 35, 36, 38, 94, 105, 149–169, 188,
        202, 203–204
    environment as, 32
    giving FIE lessons, 44–58
    mother as, 32, 40–41, 117
    and soliloquy, 133, 138–139, 154
    students as their own, 8, 85, 169, 170
Mentoring, 132, 139–140
Merzenich, Michael, 29, 178
Metacognition, xiii, 36, 85, 98
Mirror neurons, 79–80, 100, 155
Modalities, 89–92, 98, 99, 103, 108, 113, 116–
    117, 122–126, 176, 181, 182, 184
    and cognition, 152, 157
    and intention, 39
    in museums, 3, 15, 82, 111, 131, 135, 200
Mondrian, Piet, 137
Monet, Claude, 11
Montessori, Maria
    bells, 123
    techniques, 98–101, 123, 153
Motivation, 32, 41, 171–172, 173–174, 193
    and children's interest, 61–62
    and exhibits, 180
    and intention, 19, 111, 171
Motor neurons, 85, 152
Movement
    and attention, 83, 84
    and coordination, 63, 74, 153
    and drawing, 83–84
    and exhibit design, 76, 176, 181–182
    in exhibits, 80–82, 83, 201
    and haptic perception, 100, 123
    and left/right awareness, 57, 75
    and mediation, 184
    and mental acts, 71, 75–76, 84, 93, 131, 182,
        183, 184, 185, 200
    and Multiple Intelligences, 114–115
    overcoming deficiencies in, 75–76, 205
    and repetition, 103, 104
    and sequencing, 53, 167
    and spatial awareness, 53, 85
    and transformation, 160

Multiple Intelligences, 114–116
Museums and exhibits. *See also* Attention;
    Brain; Compare/comparison;
    Complexity; Intention; Movement;
    Motivation; Relationships; Scenarios;
    Spatial orientation
  asking thoughtful questions, 195–196, 197,
    198
  design of, 76, 103, 104, 141–142, 148, 181,
    186, 200–201
  identifying features, 191
  issues in design, 198–200
  joyful learning, 189, 202
  and learning, 11, 12, 185–187, 191
  museum/school bridges, 133–148, 170
  orienting in, 193
  planning visits, 189–202, 198

Newton, Isaac, 13
Noland, Kenneth, 137

Organization of Dots (FIE-S), 44–51

Pattern, 20, 46, 47, 48, 79, 106, 108, 109, 112,
    123, 129, 140, 141–142, 146, 153, 154–156,
    163, 184, 185–186, 195, 201. *See also*
    Relationships
Pei, I. M., 192, 193–194
Perkins, David, 9, 21, 51, 72, 78, 82, 85, 112,
    129, 130, 148, 201
Piaget, Jean,
  and Aebli, Hans, 8
  and fixed intelligence, 27
  stages of, 27, 92
Picasso, Pablo, 179, 181
Pinker, Steven, 183
Posner, Michael, 10–11, 175
Postman, Neil, 40

Ratey, John, 15, 84, 175, 185
Reggio Emilia, 61, 64, 79, 153
Relationships, 2, 9, 12, 24, 52, 55, 85, 91, 114,
    117, 138, 165, 185, 186. *See also* Cognition;
    Pattern
  and abstract thinking, 94, 177–178
  in exhibits, 14, 17–18, 23, 138, 140, 142, 143,
    156–158, 201, 202

and deficient cognitive function, 203–204
and mediation, 29, 47, 58, 148, 164, 172, 175,
    181, 182, 186
and numbers, 90, 93, 141, 154–155, 156
and prepositions, 53–55, 82
and spatial thinking, 53–55, 83
and stages of a mental act, 184
and thinking process, 107
and time, 75–76
and transcendence, 60, 63, 132, 188, 200
and transformations, 159–164
Repetition
  and learning, 12, 67, 76–77, 104, 114, 117,
    137, 149, 153–155, 164, 166, 169, 179,
    182, 187, 191, 198, 200
  and blurred perception/ADHD, 73, 74
  and boredom, 77
  and brain rewiring, 45, 72, 77, 129. *See also*
    Merzenich, Michael
  and exhibit design, 76, 103, 104, 181
  and finding constants, 155–158
  and mediation, 105
  and variety or novelty, 53, 68, 103–104, 105,
    155, 200
Representation
  in Braille, 168
  of feelings, 179
Resnick, Lauren, 130, 146
Rizzolatti, Giacomo, 79

Sacks, Oliver, 125
Scenarios
  and adults' mistakes, 17, 18, 19
  animals' jaws, 14
  animation, 16–17
  ball and moving hole, 183–184
  Bernoulli effect, 94–96, 138, 150
  birthday gifts, 61–63
  clay horses and riders, 63–65
  climbing structures, 82
  closed boxes, 123, 125, 168
  comparing minerals, 142
  Cuisenaire rods, 23–24
  Degas exhibit, 195–196, 199
  docking a space shuttle, 179
  electromagnetic system, 20
  everyone is you and me, 126–127

falling objects, 112–114, 151–152
Glenna's stimulus, 33–36
grocery store, 19, 134–136
handwriting, 130
height of giraffe, 10
Holocaust exhibit, 66–69, 118–121
imitation, 78–79
Jefferson clock, 136
kitchen exhibit, 79
lioness and the kits. 117
making a Chinese emblem, 121–122
mechanical advantage, 15–16
mediating disposition, 41–42
momentum, 14
motion machines, 196–197
National Civil Rights Museum, 120
New York Tenement Museum, 120
non-phonetic reading, 92–93
pendula, 9–10
Picasso paintings, 179
popping a balloon, 162
Rachel and the globe, 71
rollways, 80–81
semaphore, 17–18
soap films, 161–162
sound mirrors, 126, 127
Star and "Rocket Works," 137–138
strobe theater, 22
syllables for Tom, 36–37
tangrams, 82
three states of water, 22
Trail of Tears, 120
vacuum, 112–113
zoetrope, 158–159
Schauble, Leona, 20
Schemata, 20, 71, 72, 76–77, 78, 83, 130, 190
Sign language, 124–125
Simon, Herbert, 129
Skill acquisition, 62–63
Sociocultural theory, 28
and situated cognition, 146

Soliloquy, 138–139
Spatial orientation, 74–75, 193
in exhibits, 80, 82, 107, 116, 123
in FIE-B, 53–55
in FIE-S, 55–57
and higher-level thinking, 82, 83, 136–137, 141, 145, 191, 193
and lower-level thinking, 72, 74–75, 131, 176, 193
in metaphor, 83
and movement, 84, 184
and movement deficiency, 75
and prepositions, 82, 86
in science, 83
in signing, 124
and stages of a mental act, 90
and thinking deficiencies, 203
Structural Cognitive Modifiability, xi, 27, 29, 30, 42, 178
Symbols, 123–124

Topol, 30
Transcendence, 40–41, 64, 65
Transformations, 82, 90, 133, 156–158, 162–164. *See also* Brain; Cognition; Relationships
and brain functions, 91–92, 111, 136
defined, 63, 158, 159
in FIE instruments, 45
and representation, 63, 122–125, 141, 168, 185
and transcendence, 59
and zoetropes, 158–159

Van Gogh, Vincent, 11
Venter, Craig, 92
Visual challenge, 184–185, 186
Visual/kinesthetic experience, 166–168
Vygotsky, Lev, 28, 78

Wilson, Frank, 184

About the Authors

Reuven Feuerstein, trained by Carl Jung, Jean Piaget, Andre Rey, and social psychologist Otto Kleinberg, received his Ph.D. from the Sorbonne (1970) in Developmental Psychology. His training and experience define him as a cognitive, theoretical, and clinical psychologist. Educators, parents, and psychologists worldwide have sought him to see children, youth, and adults whose functioning is compromised either genetically or through life circumstances or whose treatment has been abandoned as hopeless.

Feuerstein formed his ideas about mediation in the 1940s and 1950s, which led to his first theory, Structural Cognitive Modifiability (SCM), the idea that human intelligence is an open system that can be modified. This led in the 1960s to three applied systems: the Learning Potential Assessment Device, the Mediated Learning Experience (MLE), and Shaping Modifying Environments (SME), and also to the Feuerstein Instrumental Enrichment programs.

Feuerstein chairs the International Center for the Enhancement of Learning Potential (ICELP) that he founded in 1993. Since the end of World War II, when he was made director of Psychological Services for Youth Aliyah, Feuerstein has helped thousands of people overcome every conceivable barrier to achieve their potential. Today the ICELP, now called The Feuerstein Center, is directed by Feuerstein's son Rabbi Rafael Feuerstein

Feuerstein has published prolifically. His extensive contributions have been recognized in top prizes received in Israel, France, Canada, the United States, Spain, Chile, Italy, Czechoslovakia, and Romania. Most recently he was nominated for the Nobel Peace Prize.

Ann Lewin-Benham, educator and author, graduated from Bryn Mawr College. In the mid-1970s in an economically depressed area of Washington, D.C., she established an early children's museum that later grew into a major institution. As president/CEO for 20 years, she led an able staff in the design of innovative exhibits and many teacher education initiatives.

Lewin-Benham established three schools at the museum—an early computer-based individualized instruction center for out-of-work, out-of-school youth; an early charter school that became the public school system's safety net for junior high students on the verge of dropping out; and the Model Early Learning Center (MELC) for Head Start eligible families, which was the only school outside Reggio accredited by leaders of the world-renowned Reggio Emilia (Italy) Infant/Toddler Centers and Preschools.

Recently Lewin-Benham has written four books, all published by Teachers College Press: *Possible Schools* (2006) and *Powerful Children* (2008) on the MELC; *Infants and Toddlers at Work* (2010) on the intersection of early brain development and use of Reggio-inspired materials, and *Twelve Best Practices for Early Education* (2011) with new thinking on such topics as discipline, curriculum, assessment, and cognitive development.

Daniel Feuerstein, who created the drawings featured in this book, is an Israeli artist and illustrator, committee member of the Israeli Illustrators Organization, and member of the Society of Children's Book Writers and Illustrators (SCBWI). Daniel illustrates children's books, book covers, and educational tools. His works have been shown in several exhibitions. Daniel is also a practitioner of Theta-Healing and Reiki, conflict management mediator, and teacher.